WHEREON TO STAND:
THE ACTS OF THE APOSTLES
AND OURSELVES

Daniel Berrigan, S.J.

FORTKAMP PUBLISHING COMPANY
BALTIMORE, MARYLAND

ISBN: 1-879175-08-8

Library of Congress Catalogue Card Number: 91-072078

Laser typography by: Elizabeth McHale
                         Williamsburg, Massachusetts

FORTKAMP PUBLISHING COMPANY
202 Edgevale Road
Baltimore, Maryland 21210
1-800-43-PEACE
1-800-437-3223

Also by Daniel Berrigan, S.J.

PROSE

THE BRIDE; ESSAY IN THE CHURCH

THE BOW IN THE CLOUDS

CONSEQUENCES; TRUTH AND LOVE, LOVE AT THE END

THEY CALL US DEAD MEN

NIGHT FLIGHT TO HANOI

NO BARS TO MANHOOD

THE DARK NIGHT OF RESISTANCE

AMERICA IS HARD TO FIND

THE GEOGRAPHY OF FAITH (with Robert Coles)

ABSURD CONVICTIONS, MODEST HOPES (with Lee Lockwood)

JESUS CHRIST

LIGHTS ON IN THE HOUSE OF THE DEAD

THE RAFT IS NOT THE SHORE (with Thich Nhat Hanh)

A BOOK OF PARABLES

UNCOMMON PRAYER; A BOOK OF PSALMS

BESIDE THE SEA OF GLASS; THE SONG OF THE LAMB

THE WORDS OUR SAVIOR TAUGHT US

THE DISCIPLINE OF THE MOUNTAIN

WE DIE BEFORE WE LIVE

PORTRAITS; OF THOSE I LOVE

TEN COMMANDMENTS FOR THE LONG HAUL

THE NIGHTMARE OF GOD

STEADFASTNESS OF THE SAINTS

THE MISSION
TO LIVE IN PEACE; AUTOBIOGRAPHY
A BERRIGAN READER
STATIONS (with Margaret Parker)
SORROW BUILT A BRIDGE

POETRY
TIME WITHOUT NUMBER
ENCOUNTERS
THE WORLD FOR WEDDING RING
NO ONE WALKS WATERS
FALSE GODS, REAL MEN
TRIAL POEMS (with Tom Lewis)
PRISON POEMS
SELECTED & NEW POEMS
MAY ALL CREATURES LIVE
BLOCK ISLAND
IN THE COMPANY OF JESUS
JUBILEE

DRAMA
THE TRIAL OF THE CATONSVILLE NINE

In Memory of the Acts of:

Celina Ramos
Elba Julia Ramos
Ignacio Martin Baro, S.J.
Ignacio Ellacuria, S.J.
Juan Ramon Moreno Pardo, S.J.
Segundo Montes Mozo, S.J.
Amando Lopez Quintana, S.J.
Joaquin Lopez y Lopez, S.J.

ACKNOWLEDGEMENTS

The text of the Acts of the Apostles is reprinted in the Appendix with the permission of Oxford University Press.

Thank you to brother Jesuits Dave Toolan for his foreword and Bill McNichols for the cover art.

The manuscript was read with great care by George Hanst, the best proofreader in Rodgers Forge.

Special thanks to a special lady, Sally Kearsley, without whose encouragement and generosity this book could not have been published.

CONTENTS

FOREWORD

David S. Toolan, S.J.
Associate Editor, *America*

Whenever I think of biblical commentaries, I recall the story of
the young Karl Barth, a pastor in a small Swiss village,
preparing his sermon for the following Sunday. Inevitably, he
would turn to the commentaries—and, alas, come away frustrated and almost in despair at how little he was helped by the
vast erudition of the professors. That frustration was what drove
Barth to write his own famous commentary on the Epistle to the
Romans—in which one can still hear St. Paul's language ring
out like thunder and lightning. Karl Barth knew that his job was
simply to point, like an Ischenheim altarpiece, to the Word of
God.

What should a good biblical commentary do for us? I am not
sure I know the answer to that question. What I do know is that
all too many commentaries miss the essential point. They give
us lots of lexical and archaeological information, stuff our heads
with historical and sociological background detail—all very interesting and illuminating up to a point. But then they let us
down. It's not just that historical criticism tends to convince us
that we need a Ph.D. to understand the Scripture. Or that the text
we are meant to resonate with often disappears into the murky
fog of the remote past. It's that almost nowhere do we get the
sense that the object of all this antiquarian learning might be the
Word of God—either crashing down on a dazed Moses at Sinai,

or whispering a breeze, a "still small voice," into the inner ear of an Elijah. Certainly nothing to knock you off the horse you rode in on. If this is all there is to it, one wants to ask, why are the smallest details of the geography of an obscure little country on the eastern shores of the Mediterranean—a country never successful at empire—so impressed on Western brain circuitry that they virtually map our imaginative world? Reading most biblical commentaries, you'd never guess. Reading Daniel Berrigan, you will.

My brother Daniel has been meditating, acting on and giving courses on *Acts* for some thirty years now. My sense is that, like some latter-day Ezekiel, he has swallowed the scroll (Ez. 2:9-3:3). The text of *Acts* is now written on the inside of his DNA cells—which gives him a certain kind of insider's authority to guide us in apprehending what is going on in this book.

. . .

Traditionally ascribed to Luke, the writer of the third Gospel, *Acts* is a story of a great new birth, the birth of a community of faith and hope out of the wreckage of execution and death. Promise is seized from the jaws of defeat—a promise that unleashes immense historical forces from the most unlikely quarters. *Acts* is thus simultaneously a story about deadly politics above and spiritual awakenings below, at the bottom of the imperial pyramid. It is a story of moving the immovable.

When I ask myself what I would expect of a commentary on this book, as opposed to any other book of the New Testament, it has to be something like this: that I would want the author to incite my imagination from its usual torpor, to attune my soul, in other words, to one of those rare moments in history when uniform clock time is undergoing radical metamorphosis. As Luke tells it, history is actually changing faces before his eyes—and if he is to properly convey the transformation, the breakthrough disjunction between the old era and the new, he has to tell the story episodically. Like the Gospel narratives, *Acts* relates a series of discontinuous epiphanies. The old immobility of a master-slave dialectic which had held the world captive for millennia is cracking open and something genuinely unprecedented in earthly affairs is in the process of surfacing—*ex nihilo.*

Now there is something about Daniel Berrigan's poetic style, particularly the frequent breaks between his reflections on given passages in *Acts,* that matches and reinforces the rhythmic beat of Luke. It brings us close and evokes these freak events, these new beginnings that Luke portrays in such vivid but disjunctive style. We see and taste the impact on a succession of random individuals—fear-ridden, ordinary people like ourselves—of something that is hardly ever named, a power that vanishes the moment we try to corner it. And yet the impact, the transformation worked on this odd assortment of undistinguished people, seemingly chosen capriciously, is undeniable. For them, it means a startling series of first days—the Spirit hovering over the chaos and breathing forth new air into their dust.

Even at the time, no, especially at that time, this was big news—though of course not carried in diplomatic pouches or on Roman rumor mills. None of the big league pundits of the time caught what was blowing in the wind. Let me explain.

The published writers of ancient Greece and Rome knew different. From Thucydides down to Tacitus and Petronius, they knew, or thought they knew, that the order of society was as fixed as the geological plates of earth. To chronicle events was to record the comings and goings of an elite class, the guardians of a repetitious, go-nowhere cycle—the great Wheel of Fortune (or Fate). Not unlike the editors of the *New York Times* and our

TV anchors, classical writers belonged to that guardian class themselves, and consequently looked down, from a lofty aristocratic post in the social hierarchy, upon the common people, observing their impotent approval or tumultuous disapproval of the imperial games that the blue-bloods decided upon. And so the world turned. In no case were the common people a worthy subject for literary treatment. It was unthinkable for a Tacitus that someone like a Palestinian fisherman, a Samaritan, an adulteress or a no-account rabbi could assume a world-historical role. Simply out of the question. Utterly preposterous. At best, a lower-order upstart of this kind would be treated—in any major history, drama, or work of fiction—as a minor episode of farce or rude comedy. Something to draw derision.

In such a context, it is clear, the Gospels, the Acts of the Apostles and much of the Pauline Epistles represent a social and literary revolution. For they do choose to make what is happening among the common people the major subject of their discourse. (In this respect, they are the progenitors of the modern novel—which never would have happened if the classics of Greece and Rome had remained normative.) For instance, in singling out a Peter and making of him a tragic, heroic figure— his force derived precisely from his very weakness—the New Testament writings announce little else than the overturn of all the assumptions of the classical world.

Why, asked Erich Auerbach, does the story of Peter's betrayal "arouse in us the most serious and most significant sympathy?"

> Because [he answers] it portrays something which neither the poets nor the historians of antiquity ever set out to portray: the birth of a spiritual movement in the depths of the common people, from within the everyday occurrences of contemporary life, which thus assumes an

importance it could never have assumed in antique literature. What we witness is the awakening of "a new heart
and a new spirit." All this applies not only to Peter's
denial but also to every other occurrence which is related
in the New Testament. Every one of them is concerned
with the same question, the same conflict with which every human being is basically confronted and which
therefore remains infinite and eternally pending. It sets
man's whole world astir.... It is only by virtue of the
most general relation, that is, by virtue of the fact and
passion, that we experience "fear and pity." But Peter and
the other characters of the New Testament are caught in a
universal movement of the depths which at first remains
almost entirely below the surface and only very
gradually—the Acts of the Apostles show the beginnings
of this development—emerges into the foreground of
history, but which even now, from the beginning, lays
claim to being limitless and the direct concern of
everybody, and which absorbs all merely personal
conflicts into itself. What we see here is a world which on
the one hand is entirely real, average, identifiable as to
place, time, and circumstances, but which on the other
hand is shaken in its very foundations, is transforming
and renewing itself before our eyes. (*Mimesis,* p. 42-43)

Daniel Berrigan allows me to feel the foundations shaking,
and more, to be caught by the nameless energy that is transforming a Peter, a Stephen, a Paul into what they had never dreamed
of being—agents of historical change. He enables me to see that
their story is mine. This, I say, is what an effective biblical
commentary should do.

•   •   •

A successful biblical commentary, it is safe to say, ought to be a kind of hearing aid—something we turn to when we have gone a little deaf or have lost the ear for the Bible's music. It should not get in our way, overwhelm us with erudition, much less substitute for the Sound and Energy we are meant to connect with through the Scripture. The highest compliment I can pay Daniel Berrigan's commentary on *Acts* is that he stands aside, doesn't get in the way, lets the music of the text come to life, play on my strings and brass. Like Karl Barth, he points me in the right direction.

Luke's Gospel and its sequel, the Acts of the Apostles, are unfinished, open-ended books, he tells me. This is my story, our story, a kind of "family album" as Berrigan describes it, that the evangelist Luke has set down for our sake—"Where we come from, and from whom; the price of our birth." Luke surrounds us with a "noble ancestry," the labor and testings of great spirits who stand with us, from whom we can beg and borrow, and whom we can draw into our own life stories as we stumble about, cope, make do, even (on occasion) burst into song. Wonders of wonders, these forebears of ours require our acts, our choices, to complete their primal scenes, their opening bars of music.

A good commentary should get us into the act. And this one does. Like any good poet, Daniel of the Lion's Den collapses the linear time of chronological calendars. That is, he closes the gap between Peter and Paul's story "back then" and our story in the present tense. It is one and the same story—and an effective commentary should bring that home to us, as this one does.

To be sure, collapsing time can be disturbing. And from almost the first page, this story is. What form, we are asked, do our locked doors take? What prison have we built for ourselves off within—so that we won't hear the clamor of the undocumented, the disappeared, the forgotten refugees of this world? So that the rush of wind, the tongues of fire, and that voice stopped up in our throats no longer reach us?

Without softening them, Berrigan puts to us these hard questions. But in so doing he is no mere gloomy existentialist disrupting our complacency. Nor does he make the mistake of the humorless theologian who thinks that making us miserable is the proper prelude to Gospel truth. No, this is a story in which locked doors fly open, chains unravel, fire descends—and common people, as if intoxicated, cross barriers by speaking in languages they have no prior warrant to know. Their God is a trickster—and clearly the new story they have to tell, against all expectation, is (in Dante's sense) a *commedia*. The scribes of dull scholarship and humorless theology forget this, and have done more to replace the living spirit with the dead letter than the Holy Office of the Inquisition.

Berrigan does not forget. And so he does not neglect that other demand of an effective biblical commentary: that it should not be so deadly serious that we forget the great well of humor that irrigates this story. All his reflections, Berrigan tells us, hinge upon a single supposition, really a wonderful comedic image: "shrouds are not a permanent Christian costume."

Sackcloth and ashes are temporary, a passing phase. In the new era to which the Acts of the Apostles bear witness, dead men walk. Rivers clap their hands, mountains leap like young ewes. This is another world, festival country. The ancestors with whom we stand were sure of it. And not in the sense of pie in the sky, but sure of "another world" that had suddenly intersected with their own, breaking it open, giving new breath and movement to all that is here and now stuck and immovable.

. . .

Foreword

All we actually see in the text of *Acts* are the dramatic effects, I said, the impact upon a seemingly random group of ordinary people, and the unleashing through them of historical
forces that remain with us till this day. These characters are
somehow pulled out of themselves and their routine places in
society to become, in spite of themselves, world-movers. Those
who lord it over them are involved in institutional maintenance;
the world-movers of the New Way are not. Why? Because the
Spirit blows where it will—and they bend to that creative wind.

Which brings me back to brother Daniel's rhythmic beat,
that staccato style that, as I remarked above, echoes the rhythm
of the Gospels and Luke's *Acts*. There is something essential in
this stylistic maneuver that we can easily overlook. And perhaps
the best way to highlight its significance is to recall the passage
in John's Gospel (Jn. 3:3) where Jesus tells the furtive Nicode-
mus that those born of the Spirit are like the wind, in that no one
can say whence it comes or where it goes. This raises a serious
question for any writer who would present the life of a Jesus, or
that of the apostles Peter or Paul—individuals obviously Spirit-
born. How does one convey such a thing—the discontinuity of
these lives with the run-of-the-mill, the undefinable whence and
whereto of their free spirits?

Certain literary styles can be ruled out as subverting what
these free spirits have to tell us. The continuous prose of a biog-
raphy such as would be suitable for someone who didn't break
ranks with normal cultural conventions might make us comfort-
able, but it would not be the truth. It would simply confirm us in
our usual orbit. On the other hand, a series of utterly weird ap-
paritions by some disembodied phantom would be even worse
distortion. This tactic would simply send us into loose orbit—
out of radio contact with earth (the gnostic option, as it were).
So what's the solution? The Gospel writers hit upon one, more
or less satisfactory, with the invention of the "pericope"—a

short unit, usually marked by a paragraph in the standard texts, that describes an inspirited Jesus or one of the apostles appearing in a certain context that leads up to some crucial act, say a healing, or to a crucial saying such as a parable or moral pronouncement. The New Testament is built up, discontinuously, of such kernel-units—which is precisely what gives it that staccato beat that constantly evokes the living voice of the oral storyteller.

But something more important than the oral resonance is also evoked. I mean that every pending background that looms over any foreground detail in Scripture—the mystery in the midst of ordinary events, whose presence and creative movement we may be able to sense without being able to name. What I am saying is that Daniel Berrigan's staccato units of interpretation, the breaks in his pages—the empty spaces there—leave room for THAT. And evoke THAT—the inexpressible, numinous WHENCE and WHERETO of our life's breath.

So pay attention to the blank spaces in this commentary— the spaces in between the lines, spaces in which to breathe in a nameless fullness. And pay heed to its fragmentary, unfinished mood. You never get the claustrophobic feeling that Berrigan has settled matters, come up with a definitive formula that will enable his reader to stop thinking, imagining, praying, and acting on insight. Instead, each unit of interpretation serves as an incisive but provisional probe, pushing as far as the limited clues of image and language will go. Then—pause, the break in the line—to let go...and then begin again, as if empty-handed, from nothing. As we do in rising to meet each new day, indeed, as we do with every breath we take. What Berrigan's commentary gives us, then, is a broken field of fresh breaths, each passage honoring the mystery of the Spirit that blows where it will and finally cannot be put under constraint.

The rhythm here, the very arrangement of the page, I am saying, is important. It attunes us to await good news breaking from where we least expect it. The method is one of trust. We upstarts and no-accounts are drawn into an open, unfinished book, one that invites our acts, our stories, to complete themselves—to begin again, now.

Lent, 1991

PROLOGUE

Whereon to Stand:
The Acts of the Apostles and Ourselves

These reflections rest on a supposition best set down at the outset. It goes something like this: shrouds are not a permanent Christian costume.

According to the Gospel of Luke, Jesus did not wear a shroud for long. The dead Man walked abroad shortly after his execution. We reach a final page of Luke's Gospel, then surprisingly, other pages open. We shortly turn a first page of the book of *Acts*.

The beat goes on; *Acts* too never closes. While time lasts, the book remains unfinished. Life, hope, communities newly born invade the pages. Ourselves.

"Our acts" include the great events, choices, persons of our lifetime, all those we draw on for a breath of life itself, beg and borrow from, emulate, beckon into our personal history—the lives of saints and heroes. They stand with us day and night; through them we manage, cope, stumble about, made do, even, from time to time, raise our eyes and see the world anew, celebrate and break into song.

Make of it what we will, smudge its pages, excerpt, underscore, scrawl our notes in the margins, the book of noble ancestry is our own. Luke has set it down for our sake: the images, stories, homilies, struggles unparalleled, the small chance in the beginning of a truth that in time grows mighty, the cost, the labors, the testing of great spirits, and the vaunting of small minds. A family album; the family of faith. Where we come from, and from whom; the price of our birth.

So, as we dare hope, we too will leave a worthy legacy, our lives, useful, attractive, available to the unborn.

. . .

Were we on the contrary to close the book of *Acts*, we would imply something drastic about ourselves: that holiness and heroism had somehow been pre-empted by ancestors, but in our time had fled the earth. To leave the story open, unfinished, awaiting our acts and choices, on the other hand, is a sign of trust. Holiness and heroism, the faith that moves mountains and overcomes death, these are among us, within us; for God is God, and the world, and our poor selves, are charged with God's grandeur.

Another way of putting the matter: we are not to make of the book of *Acts* such an object of veneration (one might even venture, of superstition) that we take small account of this ongoing story, how God continues to write large the lives and deaths of our saints today. The great acts, momentous acts of hope against hope, of love against hatred!

A study of *Acts* is like a trail through a bloodstained thicket. We follow the clues, horrified and yet strangely uplifted, the footprints, the way of the holy, the violated blood of our sisters and brothers. The guide book and the trail, and we in search of meaning. These "acts" of today, these choices, the astonishing vitality of the church of the south, the violent deaths of the famous and the anonymous. How bloodstained is our lifetime; what a column of witnesses leads us on, living lives we are also called to; the glory and infamy, the pain and hope!

.   .   .

Then—we think of others, of those outside the pale. The throwaway lives, the anonymous poor, the multitudes commonly considered of no worth, unproductive, treated as such, tossed aside, lost on the frantic winds of change. The treatment, the contempt, are a disaster for all concerned. In the eyes of those so dealt with, a sense takes root: we are worth nothing, we count for nothing.

As for those who teach or preach or remain silent and so consent to the devaluing of others—we must speak of a crime, a sin. Many teachers so act with regard to the young. The crime is also committed against prisoners, the terminally ill, women in the church. Certain people might as well not have lived!

In a cultural sense, such contempt is a specious but valuable tool of control, control, be it insisted, not only of the poor. In their regard, let it be known, there is contempt through political instruments of hate, through neglect of education, housing, medical care: those most in need are simply thrust outside. Let them survive or die; it is simple as that. Let the daily struggle for existence consume all energies, ambitions, horizons. They will not then become thoughtful or critical of the system that destroys them.

So goes the reasoning, lethal, in the circles that formulate it, beyond appeal. And as for the middle and professional class, let political inertia flourish. Narrow the scope of concern to one's immediate prospering. Multiply distraction and appetite. And as far as more venturesome spirits are concerned, let the suggestion take hold: "Everything has been tried, nothing works by way of protest or resistance. What can I do?" The shrug says every-thing.

. . .

The book of *Acts* contradicts such ethical laissez-faire with all sternness, with the force of parable and example and miracle. Its pages throb like a living heart. Large questions are wrestled with: questions of property, betrayal and chicanery, fear, deso-lation of spirit, the prospering and falling away of community and marriage, radiant fidelity under duress. We see heroes and scoundrels, martyrs and executioners.

When the early community pauses for worship, it is as though a candle flares in a close place. Those faces, those hopes, those names invoked! The symbols on the table, bread and wine, are fresh across the centuries. They might have been of our own winepress and ovens, laid for our hunger, so dearly familiar they are.

Or we are told by Luke of public events that swirl around and within the community. Again a start of recognition: jailing and capital punishment, loneliness and violent death. We meet peerless heroes, names, honored, as well as the anonymous, all persevering in prayer, in public and personal endurance.

The rhythms of the story Luke tells are strikingly, even shockingly vivid. The Christians are no strangers to violence; it surrounds them, invades them, lays claim to them. Indeed we recognize a familiar pattern: the faith must survive a world of seemingly irresistible malice and might.

What to do, how cope? Gun against gun, gun against no gun? Today we are in great need of instruction; the questions hover on the bloody air of our lifetime.

.   .   .

A community of—no guns. This puts the matter baldly, inelegantly, for the sake of the Days of the Gun Multiplied. The women and men of the "Way" commended by Luke were graced with a far different resource than that of violence. Of the Gift of No Guns, a Gift they held close (and offered their world), the empire, surcharged with its pharaonic horses and warriors and chariots, could know precisely nothing. But the empire learned something now and again of the new Power, the Power of nonviolent love, from a defendant it haled in court. Still, the empire could only deride.

.   .   .

The Gift that literally disarmed the faithful is the Spirit of Jesus, a continuing pentecost in the midst of the gathered community. Thus it is put in classical form. We are told early on in *Acts* that the Spirit, the nonviolent Spirit of God, is given a few for the sake of many. For the sake of the world, despite all guns and gunsights.

And the sign? An event literally unimaginable, unattainable. A sign is given the world—resurrection; the Man who had been, so to speak, gunned down, walks.

Thus a null-and-void notice is laid against the tomb. Death itself is sentenced to death.

This setback offered death, the denial to death of the last word as to the meaning of human destiny, is by no means to be considered an event once occurring and then done with. The truth of the matter is—as the community *boldly* (a favorite word of Luke's) announces and bears witness to—the "good news" keeps invading personal and political and economic life, turning everything around. Everything stable and organized and set in place.

. . .

That news touches us here and now. Touches us "stable and organized and set in place"; or so we are described; and so we are persuaded to describe ourselves, with a certain self-satisfaction. Alas for us, so at mercy of hidden and overt persuaders, so disposed of, so condemned, so violated in our humanity, so wheeled and dealed and lied to and cheated of our political voice and defrauded by economic sharks, by gunmen in high places. So tossed about in mind, so rocked off balance by winds of public violence! In so sorrowful a plight we stand, that the dry bones of Ezekiel could not have greater need of a resurrecting word.

. . .

The people once heard that word, according to Luke. The rising of Jesus signaled the fall of the powers. The event reduced Roman might to the height and breadth of Lilliput. That might had seemed invincible; it was vindicated on a thousand battlefields. And at home, fear of consequence had magnified and inflated the imperium beyond all good sense; emperors and their cronies grew great exhaling a sour wind of fear. They could slay at random, at whim; and they did so in devastating incursions.

And all neatly within the law. Murder was legal, it was laudable, it was a winner. The Romans made high art of the game of winners and losers. The game played on, the outcome looked (to the winners) like a final platonic form. Rome and no equal, sempiternally.

This was literally a fearful situation; it drove women and men mad.

There were few choices: one must, as the price of citizenship, be content playing a vicious role, and sere; executioner or victim, killer or corpse. Or at the least, complicity, silence.

.   .   .

Who might break through this hideous impasse, declare another way? Could there be another way? It was beyond imagining; emperors could not imagine it, nor their seers. There existed in fact a very old tradition: the impasse of the powerful, it was called. Prophets told of it, again and again. The impasse of killing and cruelty. The impasse of implacable law. Perhaps, above all, the impasse of a future that offered nothing different, no breakthrough. The futility of it, the rise and fall of it. The wearying turn of the world's wheel, the victims bound there.

.   .   .

Then a breakthrough. Once and for all. The story of an unknown (and then known) One. At first a mere shift of rumor, so it was said, set in motion by a defeated crew of malcontents. Then, unaccountably, a wildfire combusting, racing; healings, confrontations, "boldness." The story held, the believers multiplied, emboldened, even as the imperial vise tightened. The empire, dead in its main parts, spiritually insolvent, heard with terror in its bones the story of a risen One, of a Spirit breathing, making of all flesh the dough of its insuperable leaven.

Thus arose, along with the risen God, something new in the world, unheard of: a confession of political responsibility. The wretched of the earth, responsible? In time, in the Spirit, yes. It becomes the pith and heart of the story; the awakening of the wretched, their literacy and passion, their outcry in the teeth of imperial winds. *Kyrios* Jesus lives! Freedom now!

· · ·

The story of *Acts* opens; we find the disciples, so recently discomfited, scattered, gathered in a remote room, silent and withdrawn, waiting. Come, Holy Spirit! They are helpless, awed, ridden with failure, bewildered in the face of death.

To them, unworthy, tried and found wanting, comes the majestic word, the summons.

The Spirit came to them. And from the upper room they went, into streets and public places, into turmoil and crowds and the lurking presence of the law. Their resource, an inwardness, a disposition toward prayer, self-understanding, solitude. And a word burning on their tongues.

In a time that seems wondrously foreshortened, we find certain among them "sent" to the utmost reaches of the world. They shake the public fabric with a sovereign word of justice and peace. And for so speaking, so insisting, they pay up in condign punishment.

· · ·

From the start, the new faith is presented in *Acts* as a drama in the course of which moral instruction plays only a minor part. This seems worth nothing. The force, the drawing power of the tradition are evoked in the telling of the ancestral stories, again and again, whether to Jew or Gentile, believer or pagan, by accused defendant before implacable official. The stories are the message; and all the stories, finally, are one.

It is a Jewish story, all said. There is a constant drawing of water from a literally bottomless wellspring of tradition. If Jesus is messiah, if He is drawn from the loins of Abraham, why then—something must follow; there is here the irrefutable logic of history.

And yet and yet—alas. The "something" never follows. The line of nature and grace is severed. Jew and Christian, never the twain are one. We have in *Acts* the material, raw and blood-ridden, of a tragedy that haunts the world to this day.

.   .   .

Still, something magnificent is achieved. A "way" they name it, noncommittal, colorless, a code even. The way to be followed, in life and death, in sacrament and prayer, in contention and community. The way takes hold.

It implies so much more than an ethic! "The way," if it is to prevail (even to survive), must include symbols that grant both access to and reverential distance from the Unspeakable, the Mystery. We name these symbols sacraments (perhaps not to our advantage, we catalogue and number them). Of these, the breaking of bread, the cup outpoured stand closest to ourselves. Also induction by water; and the tender anointing of the ill.

.   .   .

For the rest, there is the world, its principalities and emperors, its intellectuals and entrepreneurs, its nameless poor, all to be evangelized, welcomed, endured.

The outcome of all this, they (and we) will see. They have seen, so shall we. But for now, the book, and one another. Whereon to stand.

ONE

The Lord, departing, promises
that his spirit will abide with them.
They return to Jerusalem,
dejected but hopeful.

ACTS 1: 1–5*

We read and ponder this beginning. Our beginnings, we are told. What to make of it all? It seems we have no experience of such events, nothing to connect with. What we read seems altogether in the realm of the unimaginable.

Yet, here and elsewhere in *Acts*, faith is being named; inklings, hints, metaphors. In the matter of "all that Jesus did and taught from the beginning", the stories are there, available to believers, to the world. The stories, alas, are quite possibly as neglected as, say, their American translation in matters of nonviolent witness.

We see how, in the culture, in the church, the noblest traditions are invariably endangered; they can be so easily veiled or even wiped from the slate. The history of the saints, of sacramental understanding, of the exercise of authority as *diaconia*, service—in sharp contrast with that of the grand inquisitors of a given culture.

---

*Similar references throughout the text refer to *Acts*. For handy reference, the complete text of *Acts* is given in the Appendix.

. . .

There is also the matter of showing himself after his death and giving "ample proof that he was alive." A sticking point. Everything in the culture, everything in experience is against such *tekmeris,* "proofs". Everything assures, proves, takes for granted that death has the last word.

More, and worse; death, rather than life, is revered, even worshiped. Metaphors of death abound. The living, who according to *Acts* are the evidence of the living God, even children and the unborn, are despised, exploited, aborted, experimented on, put to the door.

. . .

In Central America and elsewhere, two themes of *Acts* come vividly to life before our horrified eyes. Bloody day after day, ample proof is offered that "He is alive", and equally ample proof is offered that such witness is inadmissible, indeed mortally dangerous.

The themes are almost unbearably dramatic; the *duellum mirandum,* the awesome conflict continues between the power of resurrection and the power of death in the world. Thus the faith becomes a brutally simple matter: a combat with the powers.

The early believers shortly learn this through the *epaggelian* of the Father, the "message, the messenger sent ahead." The Spirit bears a harsh word; the word is perennially unwelcome: the world will seek to dispose of you.

. . .

Are we to conclude that by implication, "other spirits" also lay claim to us? less holy spirits, or unholy? Everything in mature experience leads us to sorrowful agreement. From psychology to politics, we note the claim. It is perennial, unrelenting, generational. Nowhere, at no time more terrible than in our own era of darkness. Nuclear extinction is the ultimate claim on us of the spirits.

The view is in accord with Scriptures, beyond doubt. Jesus, Paul, the evangelists, are attentive to these "other spirits", rebuke, refuse their shady fealty, put them to rout. The classical text in this regard is in Paul's Letter to the Ephesians:

> For our struggle is not against human foes, but against cosmic powers, against the authorities and potentates of this dark age, against the superhuman forces of evil in the heavenly realms. (6:12)

.   .   .

It is submitted that no one who has stood at the Pentagon or any of the centers of abomination where nuclear death is in prospect, and presently holds sway—no one can take part in events there, and not feel to the heart, the clutch and terror and malevolence of the spirits.

Nothing prepares for the awesome sense of something gone terribly awry in the soul of things. Neither forty years of gelid war nor a feverish pursuit of "security" nor east-west tensions; none of these taken separately or together can exhaust the meaning of our plight. A spirit ranges at large in those corridors and rooms; a spirit in opposition to creation, to humanity, to life itself. A blindness, a certainty, a willful procedure in favor and pursuit of death.

.   .   .

ACTS 1: 5-8

John had insisted on a "greater than I" "who would baptize with the Holy Spirit and with fire." A limiting metaphor: bathed, immersed. (Cf. Luke 3:16.) Maybe the truest note, surpassing the metaphor, is universality, a constant theme and struggle in *Acts*. Or equally of note today, the "boldness" Luke insists on, empowerment of one's self and others.

.   .   .

Vv. 6,7 have the character of a general instruction, reproving bootless curiosity, then and now. Faith is not to be understood as a matter of one's becoming a species of inside trader, a matter of occult access to "dates and seasons", whether conceived as holy interventions or pseudo-scientific "futurology."

In response to the intemperate query, the Lord shifts ground; a non-answer. It is not, for him, new ground. He simply offers a new, unimagined way of looking at things.

We have heard before, in Luke's Gospel, his weary impatience with the game of crystal gazing. The event around which speculation lingers, how far the disciples are from understanding its meaning, and how clumsily awry they put the question. "Sovereignty to Israel" indeed! They can scarcely imagine an event that will cancel rather than approve an impure past, a present ridden with violence and complicity.

God's intervention, the judgment, the final form of things, the banquet of the Realm, the Return—however the event is imagined, even as ineptly as here, one thing is certain. The shape and timing of the final day are removed from mortal hands; it lies beyond all scope or claim. It is, like the act of creation or resurrection, condignly superior to all attempts at control or seizure—including the control sought in tampering with "dates and times."

Consider, take thought, they are urged. Read the clocks right. Your sense of the times is out of kilter. A far different event than you imagine lies immediately at hand. It will be followed by a task, in the course of which a different conception of time itself will prevail. Your lives will be spent in a kind of "meantime."

Thus an end is commanded of vain speculation, romanticism, magic; and at the same time, an end of the stodginess and fear and despair that have all but swamped them. Gift and task lie ahead. These are godly realities; they offer a "way" in place of an impasse, a way to live—and die.

.   .   .

"Power" and "witnessing" are the key realities of the "meantimes."

The power Jesus speaks of is an altogether new reality. The world rolls along, seemingly irresistible, riding under all who stand willing or witless in its path. The chariot rolls on. This is the ancient (as well as the current) conception of power. It is mindless, clever in its own interests, blind to its direction, indifferent toward life. It is in the last instance the power we name death.

But something new is in the air. It will halt in its tracks the rake's progress of empire—and the heart's dark urges, whose symbol is this runaway will of conquest and control.

.   .   .

ACTS 1: 9-11

"He was lifted up...and a cloud took him from their sight."
(v.9) We are within sight of an old mystery in which holy ones
are "taken up" as was Elias. And the holy cloud brings to mind
the *shekinah* of Exodus (13:21), as the Israelites made their
uneasy way through the desert.

We have thus symbols of simultaneous absence and presence. God was with the people, at their side, under the cloud.
And yet he is taken up, taken away.

As we mortals experience God in the world, or do not; as we
despair of knowing, know only God's absence, distance, powerlessness—surely God seems "taken up" from us! At the same
time, the cloud passes before our eyes, another more awful image of absence.

Images, all said, of faith itself. We are left—where we are.
We make do, or we do not. But if we are wise to the original
event, we do not give up—there is more to come. There is the
Spirit of Jesus who, as we shortly note, waits on those who wait.
And that mysterious surcharge of "power" follows, a Power
equal to the awesome task enjoined.

"You have seen him go, so you will see him return." (v.11)
The "standing there, looking up" is scarcely to be equated with
the later scene of the upper room. There, we are told, they abide
at prayer; no false hopes, no feeble anticipation of a short-term
"return."

But here a different matter is under way; it is subject to reproof from the messengers. The implication is one of false expectation, dawdling, missing the point, longing for the quick
solution. And none of these, it goes without saying, will be
forthcoming.

At the same time, their presence at his departure is a kind of obscure guarantee. They have had to undergo a kind of second death after the first: his going forth from them. And this, even though they already have had part (not a very laudable part, to be sure) in a momentous crisis: his death and resurrection and glory.

They, or some of their tribe, will see another event, the Return. The first is guarantor of the second. Perhaps this is a clue to their delayed greatness; the eleven have undergone so much, events have broken them to pieces; they are all but beyond human mending.

.   .   .

We summon their condition, bewildered and lorn, their hopes assaulted. They are as yet torn between two worlds, they hear two rhythms beating at ear. The first is the old unexorcised longing for vindication on the world's terms. Are they not to be instruments of national glory, to take a rightful place among the new satraps of David's kingdom? Did Jesus not come to assure this, were they not his friends and supporters from the start?

Then the second rhythm, obscure and dolorous in the extreme, like a muffled drum beat. It is that "other" horrendous way of the cross.

Of this they know only a little, and that bitter beyond words. His Word of the cross, more, his way of the cross has stolen away their best hope, has brusquely swept it aside. And worse; he reproached them bitterly for clinging to it, as though to a spar in the mauling sea of that week we name holy.

.   .   .

Of all the vexed questions opened by this scene, surely the "Return" has offered most grist for the mill of speculation. Today we are overwhelmed by technological terror, drowning in images of catastrophe. God too is invoked in bizarre fashion; it is as though judgment, condemnation, and the wreckage of creation were God's sole intent from the beginning.

In such a welter of contradiction, of false prophets and their wares, of the real and present possibility of nuclear destruction, it is all but impossible to give place to the word of God. To ask, how has Christ imagined the end time? And yet, we must; for the sake of integrity, for sanity itself.

.   .   .

There are two elements here, closely aligned. The first is the theme of judgment, the second, of fulfillment.

Christ imagines a world completely other than our own. The Luke of *Acts* and the Luke of the third Gospel are at one on the theme. The old world of privileged power and casual murder and noisome injustice is finished. It is summoned to judgment, declared null and void.

A new world emerges. Mary, at the beginning, had ecstatically announced its dawning. (Luke 1:46-54.) The "mighty works of God" are hailed in anticipation. The "proud and all their schemes" are routed. Tyrants are toppled from thrones, the lowly are raised, the hungry filled with good things, the rich sent away empty.

In such shocking ways, technique, which had claimed control of the last day, is revealed for an absurd upstart. Technique could change nothing, reverse nothing; it could only cast the future in the one form it knew, power, concentrated violence. Technology thus has become the magisterial form of violence itself; it must be summoned to the bar, a very god of presumption, a master idol.

Judgment vindicates the new, even as it casts down, once and for all, the old. Through the long awaited justice of God, the "new city of God, Jerusalem, descends." Then it is that images of triumph, celebration, joy may flourish.

Thus the imagination of Christ, much given to parables of the end time, offers a very garden of Eden in prospect. The harvest is abundant after a painful and unpromising spring, in which every prospect was bleak. The pearl of great price is redeemed, the lost coin found. Indeed, a wedding feast is in progress, celebrating the union of God without humanity. The mustard seed, lowly, all but invisible, has issued in a great tree; in it the birds of the air may nest. The treasure buried in a field is recovered. And after a long night of frustration, an immense haul of fish is drawn in.

Thus is the moral economy of history vindicated at last. Nature and our humanity, all living beings, the earth itself, recovers its true face: a paradise.

.   .   .

With a difference, however, of enormous moment. Nothing here of romantic backward looking. Quite the opposite. Judgment again, the reality that alone can clear the way for the advent of a new world. When the drift of history is criminal, someone is responsible. This is perhaps the underlying sense of the atonement theology of the late Middle Ages. The form of payment is as simple as it is costly. Someone, that is, pays the price for the recovery of a lost human sense. Christ makes the payment; he takes into account, takes to himself the tragic history of crime, wars, hatred, mass murder—our history.

Thus Christ carries through the long night of existence the faint endangered flame of a human sense, a sense of justice. He is violated and despised; yet every age knows a moment of truth, reads in his fate the condemnation of its own crimes.

For ourselves, the "payment" is a reproof and summons against our appalling technological savagery. Its text reads simply: "Thou shall not kill."

.   .   .

This is a command which in the night of omnicide burns brightest. Bearing it forward, holding it up boldly to the gaze of generals and technocrats is the perilous vocation of the saints. Often as not, it goes without saying, they are jailed or murdered for their moral pains.

.   .   .

It matters not greatly to their seemingly impervious state of mind that the eleven had been offered many "proofs" of Jesus' rising from the dead. (1:3) The Event of events seemed unable to exorcise their somewhat childish personal anticipation. How could it (in their lives or ours)? It is death, not life, that counts in the scales where we balance one "way" against another.

Rarely indeed do we take our chances on imponderable, chancy life—as contrasted with that ponderous hoof coming down, crushing all arguments and visions: the "proof" named death.

.   .   .

"Therefore, choose life." A rare choice indeed; so rare that it awaits the outpouring of a Spirit to whom they are, as of the present, utter strangers.

(Yet in this plight, where human calculation leans strongly toward its own selfish interests, they are hardly to be thought of as different from ourselves.

(Enough said. We too look wise when we are merely clever, and calculate our chances, and grant death the upper hand.)

.   .   .

He goes, and yet he returns; and the manner of return is *houtos eleusetai,* one with the manner of his going. Which is to say, each is a mystery, beyond our gimlet eye, searching out the seasons and times. But they have "seen" the "going up" and are free to draw, or not, the crucial inference as to the return.

.   .   .

ACTS 1: 12-14

It is the time of return, time also for a second naming of the tribe. The first naming (Luke 6:13-16) must be corrected, for a sorry interlude has preceded this assembly, as all are aware. Betrayal most grievous has been followed by the death of the betrayer. And within the ranks of the (former) twelve, what disarray! Only John and the woman have stood with the Lord in his last hours.

What now? Their best hopes are dashed. He has declared how widely, consistently they have missed the point. The point of friendship, then the wider point of vocation.

A deeper question assails: what point to it all? why were they chosen?

Israel was their realest spiritual boundary. And not so spiritual at that! In time and place they saw only as far as her constricted, humiliated borders. Up to the day of his departure, the prospering and restoration of Israel were the only questions that occurred. Would Christ not at long last play the game—the might that makes all things right?

Indeed, was there any other "way" to liberation than the one consistently put forward, whether by Temple collaborators or violent insurrectionists—by those who would connive in a craven peace, or those who, intent on revolution, would risk everything?

.   .   .

He refused the dilemma as presented. That was the rub.

It would become the nub of the indictment against him. He pleased no one. He walked in calm of spirit the narrow gantlet of this world and its choices. And he signaled: No.

According to conventional wisdom, including the wisdom of conventional religion, there were but two choices. Resist and take up weapons; or buckle under and make do. Those who chose the former disposed of lives not their own; those who chose the latter, made much more than "do."

Each of the two parties was massively persuasive, lined up to right hand and left. They represented in fact two regnant sensibilities, two interpretations of history (how, through whom this has come to pass), as well as two ways of confronting an intolerable situation (what must be done).

He heard them out. He debated them fiercely and close. And he signaled: No.

.   .   .

Let us grant for the moment that each of the two factions is making the best of a sorry impasse, the hateful Roman occupation. Each might be called emblematic of the effort of humans (then as now) to survive, to work change, to achieve a modicum of decency and peace in tumultuous times.

But Jesus would have none of the above; that was the long and short it. His refusal struck like a lightning bolt. The insurrectionists turned away in contempt. The Temple establishment sensed on the instant the threat to its hegemony, and so sensing, proceeded to move against him. Both reactions were of course predictable; he spoke of the outcome calmly and even scornfully. It was as though he sensed a beat of doom in his prophetic bones.

. . .

The question that clung like a lamprey to its prey, and drew blood, was: what of the twelve? where did they stand?

He was shortly to learn, as acquaintance ripened into uneasy friendship, and the question clung; it was like the shadow of a lamprey in defiance of high noon. His "third way" of the cross, of submission and patience and the suffering of wrongs—this was beyond them. It seemed that no effort of his, neither example nor parable nor works of wonder, could bring understanding.

More time, more time? more experience of sorrow and setback, of humiliation and self-knowledge, of failures in the breach, even of tergiversating, equivocating—these might at length move lives that seemed (so like our own) for so long, impermeable to simple truth.

Or was the truth so simple? Despite all, for the sake of all, Christ must be patient. Patient in death, patient in his rising (strange virtue of glory!), patient now in departing. They did not understand. Must this be their epitaph?

.   .   .

They were "constantly at prayer." (v.14) The Greek has a strange accent; they were also of one heart. Later we are told, as the decisive event nears (2:1), "They were all together in one place." There is a tone of insistence, as of an achievement already won. An achievement of the Spirit to be sure, since despair and betrayal had all but prevailed in their midst.

(Yet prayer and life together won out after all. At least for a time. And this evidence, given the course of events today, remains precious beyond words. How many communities, marriages, friendships, projects claim for themselves a pentecostal moment—without a pentecostal discipline! The outcome, more often than not, is lamentable.)

.   .   .

They had their mandate: "Bear witness for me...even in the farthest corners of the earth."

But before the grand design there occurred a remarkable hiatus, a pause, a moment between two heartbeats. The world movement is delayed, another rhythm is born. It may seem opposite to the grand scheme of universal love, may even seem in opposition. But it is neither.

They are sent into the great world. And the first stage of their voyage takes them into—solitude. This is how they came to understand the mandate. They are to grant first place to the exigencies of their own spirits; solitude, the truth of their helplessness.

They obey, circumnavigate the immeasurable spaces, all unknown, unexplored, of their own hearts, and land. Another world indeed; they enter an upper room, apart.

Their Pentecost is under way. They sense it in the darkness. Memories, and by no means remote at that; the scalding helplessness, ignorance, disarray, scattering of the painful week of the Lord's passion. And now, knowing nothing of what lies ahead, indeed, having absorbed so little of the teaching patiently offered, they must receive help "from on high."

How far this "help" must lie beyond the Temple religion and its paragons! No help from that quarter! It was at those hands Jesus had suffered; their narrow-minded self-assurance, their hardness of heart, their intolerance of tentative and searching spirits—of whom the Spirit of Jesus is a disturbing animator—these had assured his doom.

.   .   .

The eleven gather. The question of betrayal is harsh and horrid and intolerably vivid in memory. It must be raised.

"Of necessity," we are told.

Dei: in the Greek the word is twice repeated. Two events are indicated. The first falls under the ironbound necessity regnant in a world of sin and death. Under that sign of woe, betrayal too found place, even had a certain inevitability. It waited there in shadow, like the derisive leer of a gargoyle, mocking human goodness. Jesus endured that grimace in the world; the stone grin came to life. Then he met his opposite number, friend, doppelganger, shadow; the mocker of goodness, the betrayer.

The second *dei* (v.21) refers to a new world aborning. The old world has (of necessity) passed into the void, the grave. The Victim is risen, the betrayer has perished. Another form of necessity now holds. It is the grasp, the loving pressure and claim upon the soul of the community, exerted by an old tradition and its symbols. This "necessity" is sweet indeed, is akin to air and water, in favor of dearest life. It is the very opposite of bondage;

rather a form of containment, of vessel and boundary. The soul is a vessel which the symbols fill, its proper element. As we "must" breathe, as fish "must" move in water, so the spirit is in its element that beckons, cherishes, withstands, holds it fast.

Thus the symbols proffer a hope of redemption, extending far beyond the individual. The number twelve is one such extended symbol. The twelfth apostle together with his companions stands for a complete humanity.

·   ·   ·

It must be thought that only the bleak necessity of death makes the scene of election necessary. Someone has died and must needs be replaced.

Death has indeed occurred in the community; but no ordinary death. A shameful event shadows them all.

·   ·   ·

A reflection, as the betrayal touches on ourselves.

One cannot, as is said today, expect everything of everyone. The saying is commonly proposed as useful in a bad time. The times being such that far from "everything," very little is commonly expected of one another. Our hops are lowered, almost to the vanishing point. Mutuality, affection, sacrifice? They are all but lost arts. What counts in the new economic dispensation is something quite other: bullishness, aggressive self-interest.

Such days as we endure prove a cruel and cunning instructor. They persuade us without a thousand tongues, that we "know what is in man" [sic] Prudence dictates in consequence, that we humans act with a measure of calculation and forethought. To wit: what is in this, for me? The question has all but acquired the dignity of a charism. It is as though frivolity and selfishness had been named gifts of the Spirit.

In a climate of moral desolation, betrayal of principles and people shortly becomes a horrid commonplace. Betrayal is simply built into the structure of things. It is a badge of political office; it rules the bear pit of economics. It carries no trace of stigma, provokes no reproach.

The world of officialdom is organized according to a tight (inevitably male) hierarchy. According to the social compact, some command, others obey. In church and state, in the mind of those who signify, embody, and dispense authority, the compact holds.

The arrangement has great, all but awesome power; it is thought of as simply a fact of nature, a law, like gravity or thermodynamics. Serious questions are not encouraged, few impeding second thoughts occur. The top-down scheme is considered useful, beneficial, expedient. This is the world according to its movers and shakers; indeed (for them) it works.

The world is so arranged for the sake of the majority, it is said (for the few, nearer the truth). For the good of the "faithful" (or the elite). For the "prospering of institutions," those amorphous omnivorous behemoths. For "principle's sake." For reasons cloudily referred to as "religious." The litany and its casuistry are wonderfully elaborate, like the incantation of a demiurge or a fakir they evoke nightmares or nirvanas, draw genies from bottles. They feed on atavistic dreads, on guilt and bad theology.

With skill the "soft sell" treads softly past an issue which a certain priest, a very paragon of decadent logic, evoked brutally: "It is more to your interest that one man die for the people than that the whole nation be destroyed." (John 11:50.) The high priest, Caiaphas, was of course a punctilious observer of the canons of this world. According to the rules he respected, he was correct; and the machinery of destruction moved on Jesus. It would perhaps be naive to conclude that such reasoning, with such consequences attached, had ended with the demise of this ecclesiastic worthy.

.   .   .

A different social compact, implying a far different human-ism, has been proposed by Jesus. "Serve one another." (Mark 10:42.) In effect: "This is the way that best responds both to your nature and to the will of God. Moreover, and of equal import, this is the 'way' that most sharply sets you off from the brutalities of secular power."

Historically both church and state have, in the main, rejected his instruction. The grand inquisitor has proven more persuasive by far. He knows, better than his holy Adversary, the nature of power, chameleon as it is, vermiculate, the steely smile coming and going.

This word of Jesus, it is tacitly agreed, were best put aside. Other matters, closely concerned with the patronage or punish-ment attached to things as they are, other matters press close. The Gospel, admirable no doubt but incontinently naive, were best consigned to a future that may arrive (here the timing becomes vague) or may not.

One sees with a kind of chagrined wonderment how badly the word of "authority as service" has been received, how seldom adopted, whether in Jesus' time or now. Let it be admitted: the word is unpalatable, unmanageable, beyond translation in action, an undiscovered Dead Sea scroll. And we, like wrecking illiter-ates, huckster the precious parchment at some flea market or other.

We mourn the almost universal neglect of the command to "serve one another." We suspect moreover that obedience to the word offers, even apart from obedience or faith, a way of living and working in a non-betraying way. And for the saints, something unimaginably more.

. . .

ACTS 1: 15-22

Peter's homily before the assembly, while particular to the occasion, sets the tone and method of conveying the faith. He draws on the only resource available, the Hebrew Scripture.

We do well to recall the events which led to this address, so dispassionately reported by Luke, as well as the part played in recent events, not only by dead Judas, but by Peter himself as he suddenly rises in his place to speak.

We start with the Lord's death, and his no less shattering emergence from the grave. More, we recall how Peter and the others, with the exception of "the women and Mary His mother," quickly vacated the scene of catastrophe.

. . .

The emotional charge of Peter's words! Surely Pentecost is already under way, in the stiffened spines and knees of the speaker. And something more—we sense a kind of code language, conveying as it does his sense of being forgiven, of a new start.

Only by pondering the circumstances from which it arises, one thinks, can the somewhat self-justifying tone of the address be rightly assessed. Peter, recalling as he does the terrible death of Judas (an outcome confusedly spoken of here and elsewhere), walks a perilously thin line. Judas and himself; the laconic summary might have applied to either. Only one lived to tell of it.

"Judas...was one of our number and had his place in this ministry."

Which is to say, Peter is conveying indirectly his understanding that there—Blood Acre, Akaldema—but for the grace of the risen One, went himself.

.   .   .

"One ...must now join us as a witness to His resurrection." Surely a key sentence, implying a precious self-understanding.

Who is the "one," what the task? And who would lightly step into this burning inner circle? Privilege, pride of place? Let the self-deceived or self-aggrandizing vacate the scene; they risk death by fire.

Witness, "martyr." The Greek is sufficiently austere. The reality, the risk, the slight edge given life over death, these will shadow not only the twelve, but all those who in many times and climes would step into the dangerous circle.

.   .   .

"Witnessing to the resurrection" is not to be thought of as a physical presence, either at the cross or the tomb. (The disciples had simply taken themselves elsewhere, as prudence dictated. And had they been present, what event would they have "eyewitnessed"? A light that stunned the guards, a boulder rolled back?

Peter is speaking, knowledgeably or not—or perhaps out of half knowledge, a hazy insight into the path that lies ahead. He stands before the others, he bears a new and commanding look. Never again to be shamed, having dealt double, never again to buckle under. He girds himself, bids them be bold for the start of a very Argonaut's voyage of whose outcome he knows nothing.

And he speaks with an insuperable confidence, the confidence of the newly innocent, or the newly forgiven. Perhaps the two are one.

. . .

The assembly is to cast a vote for a new member; all are to prepare for they know not what. We, high on our perch of history, know Peter spoke a truth that set history moving—in our direction.

Seven labors and more, Herculean. What terrors, journeys, dangers lie ahead! Paul, named Saul, late born, will write of them: "...in difficulties from all sides, but never vanquished; no answer to our problems, but never despair; persecuted, but never deserted, injured but never killed...."

. . .

All this, but first the betrayer must be replaced. There shortly follows the casting of lots. We note in the act, and will note repeatedly, how intervention from on high mingles unselfconsciously with quite pedestrian action. God chooses, they choose.

The choice at hand is momentous. An apostle, one "sent," for service of others, of the world. No chancy cast of the dice must rule the outcome, but an action of the Spirit they both invoke and await.

. . .

Thus in the first recorded speech of *Acts*, the Jesus event is contrasted with two others; the Judas event and the Peter event.

The community will have cause without end to decry the crimes of "the nations" against its members. They will be imprisoned and vilified and tortured and executed. Herods, Pilates, Caiaphases aplenty! But no crime wreaked by unbelievers will match the betrayal, despair, cowardice of those within, of Judas, of the eleven who foregather. Especially of Peter. He too is risen, from a near hellish outcome.

May not the most favored be capable of the worst? More to the point of hope, and this scene: may not those capable of the worst, also be saved?

TWO

What transpired in the upper room,
an event momentous, a presence.
The consequence to the twelve.

ACTS 2: 1-13

The next episode is removed from the grasp of the twelve. They have done what was possible, even what, given their unpraiseworthy history, seemed highly improbable. After a grievous, destructive scattering, they are together once more.

We recall, we wonder. A charge had exploded in their midst. Of all tragedies they might have conjured in nightmares, surely the worst would be the seizure and destruction of Jesus.

Death had undone him—and themselves. It was over, done with, that improbable venture. The dream gone on thin air. Death the undoer. Luke recounts how on the evening of Easter, a pair of somber recusants trudge away from Jerusalem. The others huddle away in hiding.

And then a rumor, and more. He stood in their midst. He was no haunt, no fabrication out of air. His words were oil and ointment upon their wounds. Underlying his greeting, his breaking bread with them, he pressed an urgent message, tender and yet firm; a new start was possible, was in fact under way. "Peace be with you." Even with you.

And they, the failed protagonists of a drama of shame, turned a new page. And there saw, astonished with wild surmise, a consummation beyond this world.

.   .   .

We turn a page too. That so-safe past we see enshrined, can-
onized, in place in the pages of *Acts*—the Lord risen, the Spirit
outpoured—this is their unsteady present; they must pray and
hope on. Things will perhaps go better for them, perhaps not.
The future is untidy, improvisational. What to do?

We read; they do nothing. Or better, they do the one thing
necessary, the thing most difficult, most counter to the later,
driving purpose. The thing most intense. They gather, concentrate, turn within, longing, emptying, letting go. "Prayer," someone has said, "is a bold, even arrogant effort on the part of the
community to hold God to her promises."

They confessedly can do nothing more.

And then, something happens. Something neither they, nor
all the king's horses, all the king's men, could have brought to
pass.

.   .   .

Can do nothing? An event they could not bring to pass? Such
statements, given technological arrogance, violent and presumptuous and headlong as it is, are passing strange. Who of us in
North America, backed by an establishment armed to the teeth—
who of us has felt "helpless"?

The feeling is utterly foreign to us. It may be native elsewhere; we despise and pity the helpless. For our part, confession
of helplessness, vulnerability, shame would require that we renounce (as a mockery of the judgment that lies heavy on us) the
credentials of common stock and summoning; our might, our national glories and achievements, illusions of moral excellence,
probity, benevolence.

. . .

Let us venture on a difficult exercise. Let us conjure for a moment the image of a beleaguered Salvadoran peasant. His life and that of his family are precarious. Death, to be sure, is nothing new to them. Starvation has made stalking skeletons of his ancestors while they worked the earth, has brought them low before their time. Now the Guardia and its hired killers offer a like service, only more quickly, cheaply.

But this is not the whole story. Our Juan, being quite helpless where he stands, has sought help elsewhere. Better, he has been forced to seek his hope beyond the mischance of this world. Indeed, were his hope drawn only from the facts of life, it were as shallow as the soil he belabors.

Behold that deeper hope. He is literate. The first book he learned to read, perhaps the only one at his disposal, is the Bible. More; he belongs to a *communidad de base*. His friends and he, through diligent study, have come on a precious insight. It takes in account the possibility, indeed the likelihood, of death by violence. Small matter, great matter, there you are, death being by no means the only word that reaches them, nor the last.

The promise, the Spirit. Juan lives by the promise of the Spirit. This, he will tell you, is enough to live by, to die for, if required.

Providence is a large word, perhaps he does not even know it. But he believes, and hopes on. God will have care of him and his people. He has only to take seriously the word of God, to love and cherish his family and friends. That will be sufficient, on the Day.

This is Christianity, one might say, stripped to bare bones. Helplessness, then a mysterious "power," the power of the promise, irrevocable, lived by.

.   .   .

For ourselves, another power looms. The Bomb, that nefarious symbol of the power of death, threatens more than our lives. It symbolizes what the Bible calls the "second death," the death of the spirit, of self-understanding, of very sanity. It threatens these precisely in virtue of its claim to all sufficiency, to protect our misbegotten spoils, to vindicate and justify, to require of us nothing of remorse or moral change. It leads us radically away from God.

.   .   .

At Pentecost a baleful continuity is broken. Obsessive failure, weighing heavily, has been declared of no import, forgiven, forgotten even. Failure of nerve, scattered conscience, childishness and ambition, even betrayal, these are healed and canceled. They become a "before." The past is done with, healed.

It is as though in a dusty album one came on a faded tintype of a youth or child. Could it be—myself? One regards the image with a certain detachment, a chastened tenderness even. Or it is as though one held in his arms a wayward child, reproving its errancy, and holding it close. The first compassion is toward one's self.

And now, an "after." The disciples are truly included, within; including too: others, task, the world. Free so to live and so to die.

.   .   .

All this has not happened abruptly; or it has.

It would seem that Luke's account of Pentecost concentrates a long passage of moral rebirth, into a single hour. This may be so, or may not. What is essential to the scene is not the instantaneous or gradual character of the event. It is the outcome, which, whatever the timing, remains the same: the new woman, the new man, in the new assembly.

Which is to say, all romanticism and narcissism and pretense and blustering and fear put aside, they are ready at length for their world. In their possession is a precious charge; a message to issue and stand by, a combat to the death; a death, as the message grows more insistent, all the more likely.

Readiness for the task implies the defeat of the empery of death within. Implies the healing of a despair that, alert to save its skin, so ill-served them and their Lord. The restoration of a faith that had so easily yielded, in the high wind of crisis, to unfaithfulness. (The healing of what we know of ourselves; and yet so dimly and partially known, and with such wealth of excuse, so finely tuned a pride, as not to know.)

.   .   .

The story of Pentecost is told under a barrage of ancient symbols. The small gathering quailed and bent as in a firestorm. And so they were renewed, and undertook a fresh start.

.   .   .

Pentecost was no magical event, nor was it once and for all done with. The Vessel continues to pour out the largesse of God, until the Spirit reaches ourselves, our lifetime. If this were not so, how could Luke's words hold meaning for us? Indeed if we know something of our savage century, we know the all but terminal illness that afflicts us, the always present threat of our falling away, back into the "form" of the world.

Insidious or overt, by no means invariably resisted, that siren call: to conform, to show ourselves "really no different," to ape the structures of control and compromise that serve worldly self-interest so well.

·   ·   ·

The Spirit came "as though," we are told. The event was beyond all direct narrating; we can know of it only through analogies of wind and fire.

The Spirit comes as though in a great overriding wind.

Come then Creator Spirit, blow over us, within us once more!

Cleanse our dwelling, lest the habitation become a veritable Augean stable, filthy with dross and debris, ill-seeming wealth, possessions and pride of place.

And then, "as though" with tongues of fire.

Dare we pray: Come, Creator Spirit, judge us? Heal us of deceit and lying and compromise and fear. Grant us to welcome "other tongues," other truths and ways, other cries!

Grant the truth a welcome in our midst, in our temples and hearts, even as our world is given over to untruth, to propaganda, a babble of hatred, violence, contempt.

Dare we pray: Make us new, O God, who makes all things new?

Pentecost: an event that dares us. To pray, to hold fast. Dares us enter the world on our own terms; truth-telling, courage, steadfastness.

The event is a rebuke to all arrogant suppositions. That national pride and status in the world—that these can bring the healing of our humanity.

The rebuke is abrupt as a wind, and fiery. In order to become human, to be healed of our inhumanity, we require an intervention. Call it grace, call it aid, Pentecost, Holy Spirit, friendship with God, voice from heaven, thunder, blindness and then relief from blindness, dream then awakening. Luke speaks of all of these, metaphors, happenings, hints, false starts renounced, promises kept.

They come to the same thing: a plight, then a liberation.

.   .   .

The coming of the Spirit is one with the death of Christ and the conquest of death. No one of these can be considered *in vacuo*. The death, taken as it was by the disciples in disarray and panic, in isolation from its outcome, summoned before them only a borrowed grave and a shameful memory.

So with the resurrection. Considered apart from the condign punishment of Christ, the "victory" is a cheap grace, ignorant and fearful of death. In a community that takes so unreal a victory for its motif, there lies heavy on the air, in homilies and private prayer, a cozy sense of being elevated above the fate of others.

We are told that the Spirit comes not to the proud achievers, but to those broken by the powers of this world. Luke refuses to mince such matters. The people of original Pentecost are helpless as stones of the road to turn their lives around.

Bones, dry bones. Then they are joined inexplicably one to another. They hear the word of the Lord.

.   .   .

They came to a new understanding and practice of the human. This is indeed a mysterious subject; at the time of Pentecost it was by no means clear that they had become "new women and men." Time and experience would show it plain, the shape of the new. In the chance and mischance of life together, at worship, in jail and court, even there they "doubled the heart's might."

It is an aspect of the mystery we do well to remember and draw on: the indispensable character of that much used (and abused) word, community.

.   .   .

The Spirit freed them (and frees us) from worldly systems of retaliation and revenge. It is the Spirit who justifies, but in a way hardly compatible with the culture. The new community, then as now, is the enemy of any and all enmities. It admits of no war or warmaking—least of all, of the monstrous race to oblivion called nuclear war.

.   .   .

There is a caveat here, much to our point. The symbols, we are told, the "strong, driving wind, a noise which filled the whole house," these warn and remind us of the "last days." something final is in the air. In consequence the community is not to live as though a given culture were empowered to set for us the canons of moral life, norms, counsels, directions, guidance.

What indeed is our sense of the times? If we knew the Lord's return was near, and every worldly power shortly to be summoned for judgment, perhaps something of our political stance would be altered, and sharply. We would stand aside from such spurious normalcy as is being widely huckstered. A gesture would be evoked: call it divestment, resistance, outcry, the drawing of a line.

.   .   .

Another gift of the Spirit: a communality of understanding. "Each one heard his own language spoken." Surely we have here something more than a breakthrough of language, however miraculous. Something of far greater import, call it a common understanding with regard to matters of life and death. No need to start yet once more from "first principles" to clear away accumulated ignorance, fear, blindness. The truth wins an eager hearing; the word of God does not hang empty on the air.

More; common symbols can be invoked. For centuries to come, one act will be repeated, an act of mutual recognition. "When he had sat down with them at table, he took bread and said the blessing. He broke the bread and offered it to them. Then their eyes were opened, and they recognized him." (Luke 24:30-31.)

It would be so with water and oil, blessing and exorcism. The symbols stand for a noble ecology; creation is infused by the Spirit.

.   .   .

Be it noted also, the Spirit promises no relief from the tyrannies of the world. Quite the contrary. Prior to the conferring of the Gift, the disciples had fled the consequences of their vocation. Fear ruled. Then, "all, all is changed; a terrible beauty is born." They shortly underwent in full force the rigors prepared for challengers of imperial law and order. They were branded enemies of the state; finally they underwent plenary punishment.

The hostility shown toward them is properly Biblical. It is not that the disciples advocate the overthrow of the imperial state. Its prospering or fall is simply not their affair. The point of the conflict is other; their message is incompatible in practice with the worldly ethos of divide, conquer, break, enter, control, condemn, amass, punish, seize, torture, deceive, deride: all the armaments of Mars.

No working arrangement is possible. The issue is clear (on both sides). From the point of view of the Gospel, those in charge of the imperium have pre-empted the sovereignty of God.

.   .   .

Who indeed shall play God? It is an old story; the state's pseudo-divine charade. According to its rules some shall die and some kill, always under sanctioned orders.

The Spirit of God, to the contrary, would have believers play another role entirely. Shall we call it—playing human?

In any case, for several centuries, up to and including our own, far from taking part in the imperial game of kill-be-killed, believers in considerable numbers have died at the hands of state authorities. Faith in Jesus is weighted with consequence; it implies a discomfiting edginess, brings many to costly decisions, to the razor's edge of an either-or. Believers also refuse such part in public life, whether in armies, courts or temples, as demeans or compromises their understanding of divine authority. Hence the troubles, unease, conflict. And the beat goes on.

Come Spirit of unease, trouble, conflict!

.   .   .

ACTS 2: 14-36

The narrative is interrupted for the first of many times. Indeed someone has computed that Luke includes some twenty-eight sermons and speeches in *Acts*; the majority of these issue from Peter and Paul. The addresses, homilies, defense elocutions comprise almost a third of the text. We are thus moved by the text itself to reflect on the literary method of Luke, a method considered essential to the message and apt to convey it.

(And we wonder that so few convey in our time the passionate conviction that made combustible the lives of these faithful ones.)

.   .   .

Peter rises to address the crowds. The phase in the upper room, by turns stormy and calm, is ended. The public life of the church is under way.

The tone of the sermon is astonishing. Here we have the words of a fiery ecstatic, a very Daniel of apocalypse.

All, all is changed. And the change, in virtue of the Spirit outpoured, according to Peter brings the human venture into its "last days."

.   .   .

The signs of this? They could no be more exultantly dwelt on by a tent revivalist. Perturbations in nature and the human family, portents bursting forth in heaven and on earth. Blood and fire and pall of smoke, the sun turned to darkness, the moon to blood.

. . .

What to make of it? Can it be, for instance, that our present ecological plight goes beyond a mere catalogue of disasters, becomes a "sign" of something impending? Certainly the words of Peter imply more than an arbitrary whiplash of divine anger. The word regarding the world of nature goes beyond nature. It points to human irresponsibility and consequence.

Thus a linkage is forged between "signs," whether in heaven or on earth, and the conduct of humans. We are left with that; no denunciation follows. Instead we are told in general terms of the rousing effects of the Spirit on young and old. Far from being reproved as mere recalcitrant sinners, all humankind is presented as a race of prophets. Humanity erupts with gestures of uncontainable truth and its wild telling.

In such times as Peter imagines, everything predictable in human conduct is stood on its head. It is not the aged who prophesy, it is the young. And the old in turn spin the dreams traditional to youth. Everyone, it seems, is renewed, every eye blinks, somewhere between disbelief and belief, astonishment and hope. Intuition, imagination, chaos, anarchy, loss of foothold, new terrain, spelunking in the dark, dancing in the noon—what words are adequate?

. . .

We may choose a safe way, a rather cowardly comfort; to look about us, smile gently, perhaps cynically. Ecstasy? prophecy? We are something other than those cited by Joel and Peter; comatose, media ridden, passive before a fate we seem helpless either to interpret or oppose.

And yet, and yet. Perhaps we look in the wrong direction. The "servants and handmaids" on whom "my Spirit is outpoured"—can it be that we look only to the old world that passes away, and so miss the new?

Let us say only this. The evidence of Joel's words concerning prophecies and visions and dreams is before us. The portents stand in our world, in our land. If the imperial apparatus is stalled, and it most certainly is, if the official necromancers and magic men are paralyzed and the politics stale beyond bearing— these are not the point of the prophecy, nor need they detain or dismay the eye of faith. The prophecy concerns others than these leaders become misleaders. Joel's "sons and daughters" go about other affairs, properly scriptural, consistent and courageous.

They dream. They act, for others, on behalf of despised justice and violated peace. Thus they ensure, despite all official incoherence and havoc, that dreams come true. Dreams of a temperate, gentle world, apt to receive, welcome, nurture the unborn.

.   .   .

Toward the end of his discourse, the language of Peter shifts somewhat. Earlier it was of "prophecies, visions, dreams"; now it is of "miracles, portents, signs" in our midst. Through Jesus of Nazareth.

The motley audience had not witnessed such wonders; they only heard rumors swirling through Jerusalem. A Wonderworker, or One who claimed to be such, was detained and executed by the authorities. Who he was, what the affair could mean to anyone, was far from clear.

Now the challenge is laid down, direct.

Through the attesting of God, approval is bestowed on One who lived, died, rose again in our world.

. . .

The story, as it reaches us centuries later, is jostled and challenged by other stories, equally horrible, equally wonderful. Preachers weary of the story Peter tells, as do many believers; often both are only half-hearted in granting it airing.

But at the time of Pentecost, as we sense to our chagrin, even our shame, the story is new, urgent to mind and tongue. The blood of Christ was fresh on the altars, his memory green among the people.

More; Peter has a long tradition in his favor. His argument, that this is the story of all stories, that on the truth of this story all literally depends, is drawn from history, the people's own. It is as though the story of Jesus were drawn from their very entrails, an event renewed, made vivid, made present in liturgy and Scripture reading and instruction.

The story concerns a Jew, it is recounted by a Jew, to assembled Jews. In the nature of the promise, they are told, a promise which entails the truthfulness of God, it could not be that "death should keep Jesus in its grip."

Therefore, "allow yourselves to be saved." Passive in voice, urgent as to the initiative of Another. Does Peter sense it? His hearers are in a pre-Pentecostal state. They are as helpless before God as, shortly before, were Peter and the eleven. Now a mightier chorus must arise to heaven. Come Creator Spirit!

. . .

Peter's sermon makes much of the prophet Joel's ecstatic treatment of "that day." But Peter changes the earlier text in a quite remarkable way; he speaks of "the last days." Which is to indicate that after Pentecost, something has happened to the time sense of believers. The Event of events has erupted. We and the early community need await nothing more in the way of spectacular intervention from on high. Where are we, who are we? The Spirit of Christ is in our midst; this all but sums up our place and time in the world. Christian Life will flow strongly through the centuries, like a stream weaving its way within a sea of time; cold stream or warm, a saving and opposing stream, touching all shores.

·   ·   ·

The story flows onward, straightforwardly. The stream will touch all lands, temperate and torrid, in one way or another affect all creation. The preaching and example of those who first drank from that stream, the "strengthened ones," will be joined by generations unborn. They will combat the Principalities, speak truth to power, persevere in worship and witness.

The fullest sense of the human is thereby proffered the little community (who in time will offer it abroad). The sense includes an admission of powerlessness and more; the bitter falling away, the all but unbearable losses and betrayal of the immediate past. Then, only then, could the Stream touch their torment, healing, offering the "new power." The possibility that dawned! They can despite all come together, heal the horrid memories of failure and moral destitution. They can reject the voices which spoke only of the impossibility of a fresh start.

·   ·   ·

The human is transfigured, we are told, "in the last days." Class arrangements are overthrown, slaves grow vatic along with their masters. The young grow visionary, the dreams of the old are quick and vivid. The world of nature—that is something else. "Portents in sky and on earth, blood and fire and columns of smoke." Creation is hardly in consonance with the presumed new order of humanity. Nature, wounded to the heart, also grows vatic, raises a cry. There are as yet ecological crimes to be renounced!

We are reminded in ways that are profoundly disquieting, of that unfinished affair of our history, the Fall. An open would lies on the body of creation, afflictive and tormenting. It is as though nature were twisting in a fire of our stoking, as though a massive contempt were turned against living beings. And finally the entire organism of life, like a brilliant, teeming rain forest, is threatened, torched, and sent crashing to ground.

·   ·   ·

We cannot but note in *Acts* an unattractive atmosphere surrounding the pronouncements of our founding fathers (sic), a rather constant, high-minded self-justification. Peter, quickly seizing (or quickly granted) the initiative, might be challenged in this regard. He, and at a later point Paul, seems intent on occupying a high ground of impeccability, and addressing lesser mortals from that elevation. Is this the price, we ask in our braver moments, of new authority: that an unpleasant past be put easily to one side, and the present be turned like a whetted blade against others?

What then of forgiveness, compassion stemming from the vivid memory of one's own rather grievous backsliding? We may be forgiven for wondering.

Possibly Luke is offering us a subtle clue. We are hardly meant to conclude that every word issuing from the mouth of Peter is to be taken as approved of God. Peter remains human and fallible, however little he seems to take cognizance of the fact. Luke's task, it would seem, is to set down the facts with reasonable verisimilitude; not everything he records is stamped with his (or God's) approval.

Nor are we to read of such events, words, such lofty tones and *pronunciamentos,* as though we had dispensed with all critical faculties. Or as though Pentecost had wiped the human slate clean of the memories that create ambiguous tendencies, peccadillos, and worse. As though we were being presented in fact with a race of supermen (sic) newly sprung from the brow of a Jovian deity.

Peter in other terms remains Peter, for all the new Spirit upon him. Nothing more electrifying, more edgy, than the fervor of a new convert! Of his former estate, so seldom referred to, both he and we know much, not all of it laudable. It would seem in sum a matter of good sense to cast a cool eye on one who in former times so exercised the patience and forbearance of Christ. Thus we are, perhaps rightfully so, puzzled, somewhat askance, as we witness Peter's new avatar—his tendencies toward triumphalism and harshness.

. . .

At the same time, it would seem fitting to summon a measure of mercy in our judgment of the "authors of our faith," those who early on were seized by an all but irresistible fire. Understanding how that fire burned hot and bright, all but consuming them. Hardly to be wondered at, that the early stages of so austere a "Way" are presented in stark, take-or-leave terms.

. . .

The danger implicit is in the method. The truth may be so starkly presented, a matter solely of either-or, salvation-damnation, that a sect emerges, irritating and self-enclosed. We have had enough of this, then and now. Then and now, as we are appalled and aware, we are involved in a continuing disaster. *Acts* tells of its initial rumblings, the Judaic-Christian split, a sectarianism gaping wide as a lavic eruption, hardening, permanent.

.   .   .

ACTS 2: 37-47

The discourse ends neatly. The point of the sermon of Peter as well as the larger evangelizing purpose of *Acts* are served in the question of the audience. "What are we to do?" they ask, "cut to the heart."

Peter's response will suffice, for then and for now. He sets in place the community's understanding in this crucial matter of repentance, change of heart. Is our freedom the crux, or is God's initiative? The question will not be answered here; in a sense, it will never be "answered." We are faced with something infinitely more puzzling than a mere human conundrum.

Let us say only, as the church has been obliged to say on many a boisterous occasion, that in this matter of conversion, the initiative of the Spirit is joined to the freedom of the neophyte. The one is hardly enemy of the other. Nor should the fact that God moves mysteriously and freely, clearing the path, suggesting the next step, indeed making a next step possible—all this ought not be construed as an assault on ourselves. Quite the contrary. Let us be free by all means; but at the same time, let us grant God place.

In *Acts*, the initiative of God in such matters is clear. The story is told again and again; a light must dawn, impetuous as in the case of Saul, usually a more modest flame. (As in the present episode, the change of hearts of many, consequent on Peter's teaching.) That light, small or a wildfire as may be, is the work of the Spirit. It flares where It will, against all human expectation, striking down pride of place, arrogance, routine, life at even ebb, things as they are. So impetuous a Spirit, need it be added, is not invariably welcome.

We cannot prevent Its coming, any more than we can seize the time of the Spirit, anticipate, manipulate.

Therefore the imperative mood of Peter's instruction, "Repent," is best understood in the context of a kind of moral helplessness, incapacity, a pre-Pentecostal mood, before the onset of the compelling Wind.

.   .   .

As I set down these notes, in the Fall of 1989, we of the Plowshares Eight have received notice that the Supreme Court has turned thumbs down on our appeal. Thus a ten-year judicial process grinds toward its close; Pennsylvania is now free to move against us.

Is this to be understood as a pentecostal moment? It is clear that, in somewhat the manner of the early disciples, we are launched once more on the unknown. In the darkness of a nuclear world, a nuclearized judiciary prepares to deal with us. Nuclearized? The courts have bowed before the nuclear demigods, their honors are severally polluted with collusions, are positively aglow with chagrin at such as ourselves! How dare these impetuous spirits invade sacred precincts, bearing their blood and hammers, intemperately occupying the nuclear shrines! Down with them! Off with them!

THREE

Of the first healing,
and of its puzzling outcome,
the arrest of the healers.
In no wise reformed,
they pray for renewed boldness.

The first of the "signs and wonders" promised at Pentecost impends. The occasion is deceptively simple; two of the disciples make their way to the Temple "at three in the afternoon, the hour of prayer." In them the worshipful roots of Jewish discipline are intact.

But something utterly untoward is under way. A power not of this world has entered the world, and in the persons of two inauspicious people.

. . .

The Temple, to be sure, signifies far more than a place of prayer. Worship and prayer are an innocent guise under which other, less salutary matters proceed. The "house of worship" is the setting and headquarters of an awesome caste, as Jesus knew and the apostles will shortly witness. Among those who control the place are a chief priest and his family and coterie, a controller, various intellectuals, Saducees and Pharisees. These comprise in effect a worshipful body of collaborators with the occupying power, Rome. They are powerful agents of law and order in a time of enormous political unrest.

In the Temple precincts the hours of prayer are celebrated as usual, and morning and evening sacrifices, and the great and lesser feasts. With aspects of these, the new community will have no quarrel. Quite the contrary, one has the impression in the beginning of *Acts*, of the easeful sense of at-homeness amid the symbols, liturgies, communal prayer of the Temple. The root and ancestry have happily not yet been severed; Jewish followers of Jesus are members of a vast family, both scattered and gathered, that honors Yahweh and the prophets.

Too bad that other considerations of moment must shortly impinge.

.   .   .

It is by no means unusual that near the Temple, a number of beggars assemble to plead for alms. No objection is lodged by those in charge, as long as the suppliants do no grow unmanageable as to numbers or boisterous as to conduct.

At the same time, certain limitations accruing to the Temple and its management suggest themselves. Let us say that the beggars are free to live off the worshipers' plenty—as long as it is understood that alms express the limit of the mendicants' hope. A neat substitution of charity in place of justice is thus in force. One can assume, moreover, that no one of the physically or spiritually disabled comes to the Temple to be healed of his ailment. The coterie of priests and sycophants are unskilled in such preternatural arts.

Nor, least of all, would one dare enter the place in order to stage a social protest. Unthinkable! The Roman troops are at hand to quell any such incursion; likewise the priestly caste, largely occupied, beyond liturgical niceties, with canonizing the status quo.

Thus is the charity of the pilgrims blessed and set in place, along with the displayed limbs of cripples, inviting and awakening pity. Need it be added: also distracting the worshipers from a truer, hotter issue, that of social injustice. A game shortly to be challenged.

Our two friends approach. Luke recounts the event with altogether delicious sense of detail; ironies, humor, sparks that fly. The scene of healing is, as usual, public; it could shortly become chaotic, as word of the wonder and the workers of wonder is spread abroad.

Another option was open. Could Peter and John not have taken the unfortunate one aside, healed him in some dim corner or other, and dismissed him quietly?

They act otherwise; there is a point to be made.

It is troublesome, that "point." The implication. More, the provocation; the power invoked. Does one heal by invoking the dead? Certainly not. Restoration of life or limb is wrought in the name of one who stands sound and alive on our ground. We are to make no mistake of that. And in the tic of an eye, the authorities make no mistake of that.

.   .   .

The pith of the matter: Someone declared dead and buried, disposed of, capitally punished, entombed, his tomb sealed and guarded—that same One walks abroad. His followers swear to the fact.

Their word of course could easily be gainsaid did it presume to stand alone, raving into the wind. But there is an embarrassment; witnesses, a multitude of them, witnesses of a fact both dangerous and enticing.

And what are the authorities to do? They are skilled in dealing with the would-be founders or followers of this or that ragtag sect; they simply round them up, discredit them, dispose of them. The way has lately been applied in plenary fashion to a certain Jesus, as is known here and there.

Such methods, altogether legal, also serve warning to others, malcontents or dreamers. Let them mend their ways, lest worse befall them, including the present duet. The event is a sputtering fuse set alight at the Temple gate.

.   .   .

But will the old way work, in these unprecedented circumstances? And the one so recently healed, what is to be done with him? He has by no means fled or hidden out; in court he will stand boldly at the side of his benefactors.

.   .   .

We know so little of him, not even his name. We wish we did. He would be an admirable figure to name our children for, this one who endured some forty years of helplessness, at the mercy of others, from friends to indifferent passers-by.

His story, but for an unprecedented moment, an intervention, is unremarkable. For years he crouches there, passive as a stone of the road, in the way of his kind.

No hint of something precious, dazzling, building like a jewel within, from the abrasive gritty matter of his life. It will be known, though it is long unknown; under those limbs of his, useless as a ventriloquist's doll's, within and within, he guards his soul like a prisoner in a keep. He is his own man, as will one day be manifest.

He begs, for one must live. Beggary is also a useful front; a charade. It keeps the contemptuous good-natured crowd at distance. But his heart's desire vaults free. It will have its day. Luke knows it, tells it.

.   .   .

The scene as described is notable as well for what it does not assert of the disabled man. There is no sin impinged, no sense that he has betrayed himself or anyone. He has never yielded to blind destiny, to the fateful loss of autonomy, though everything in his damaged makeup might have so tempted him. Hopelessness would have rendered him blind, dumb, dead as nails. Live off the pittance, begrudged or otherwise, of others, die a little each day. Behold your portion, as it is and shall be. Thus went the temptation, held out to him in the grudging hands of life itself.

Hopelessness? The word was not in his lexicon.

A countervailing sense of himself rejected base blandishments, invoked discipline and will. The tags tied to him by careless looks, wagging tongues, rotted and fell away.

He keeps his own counsel, maintains his dignity; in his soul he walks upright. This, though worshipful conformists surround him, use him as the occasion of their pharisaic virtue. Toss him a coin, God will reward!

.   .   .

Later he stands with the prisoners in court. There could be no better measure of his healing; he is reconciled with the community of healers. More, he stands by them. He has become one with the "witnesses of the resurrection" who have stood by him.

.   .   .

ACTS 4: 1-31

There occurs a muddled, hastily called court proceeding. The law is unprepared for such as Peter and John, its champions are incoherent and distempered. What is the charge? It is by no means clear. Indeed, what statute has been violated? Equally unclear. Something about "proclaiming the resurrection from the dead by teaching the people about Jesus."

Resurrection? Insurrection? Disturbing the peace? A properly religious matter, at least as recounted by Luke, is made the occasion of a charge under the law. This is the most we can make of it, and it is not much.

The charge bespeaks bad faith and consequent public tremors. Memories are stark, and hardly comforting. These judges of Peter and John are, if not the same, in league with those who made recent decisions regarding the fate of Jesus. Their decisions were arrived at with a view toward "ending the matter." He is disposed of, dead and buried, level with the earth. The dossier of Jesus Christ is closed. And what may be imagined to come of that—a shameful death, a guarded tomb?

This precisely. The healing of a man born lame has come of it.

.   .   .

That Name is fast becoming a dreaded incantation, bespeaking a mysterious power at large in the world. The Name (which his enemies hardly dare pronounce) invades forbidden precincts, brings a word of life (and indeed an act of lifegiving), brings people to pause in their tracks, induces felonious thoughts, changes minds and hearts. And in the process, the Name confronts unequivocally the bedrock claims of the establishment.

Those claims have stood firm for centuries, the "squared blocks of Rome." The *Pax Romana,* one phrase, one boast, says it all, sums it up. That awesome machinery of torture, war, ego, sweet promise and brutal performance, invasion and occupation (and local hegemony on a tight leash), splendor and prosperity, bread and circuses, slaves and captives—this is the very model, progeny, progenitor of Big Brother, more terrible than Assyria, more merciless than Babylon, a ranging imperial eye, a sword on the ready. Who shall withstand?

These two, Peter and John, by all accounts.

.   .   .

The first business before the court is presented as a criminal matter. The charge is adroitly trumped up; it is designed to criminalize, separate the defendants from the populace, stain them with obscure infamy.

But Peter has words at his disposal to define their case in its true light. His speech is a masterpiece of defense strategy. "If it is about healing we have offered a disabled man, and the means by which he was healed, this is our answer." And so on.

Thus is the matter laid bare, not only for the defense, though that is a capital point, but for sake of the listeners, of the readers, of the future. For the sake of a truth which by presumption, the forces of temple and state, the prosecutors, are desperately unwilling to convey.

.   .   .

This conflicted view of the case—a criminal matter according to the prosecutor, a compassionate act according to the defense—is the index of a deeper conflict. Then, now, the centuries have not served to resolve it, even in the most enlightened societies.

The conflict appears beyond resolution, then or now. The legal system (then and now) is designed to validate and enforce the imperial imagination, to embody, protect, maintain the imperial world view. That view, *ipso facto* justified in the courts, seldom varies in any significant way; foreign conquest is the objective, together with domestic order maintained intact.

Thus at any point of time, the imperial image must stand firm, no matter what the provocation, the alternative, the disruption, the despair.

For citizen-subjects, the message is clear: the present, whatever its immoral tactics, its wars and pillage, is their lot. It is also an image of their only future. The prophet long ago warned Israel of the consequences that follow on the imperial sellout. Give us a king, the people clamor, that we may be as other nations. A king they are granted, and along with him taxation and levies and armies, slave labor and more levies, feverish prosperity and recurrent misery, the erosion or instant canceling of human rights.

.   .   .

And what of the future? According to the authorities, the future is one with the present, only writ larger, more grand, more monstrous. There will be more conquests, invasions, more victims and slaves. Above all, more blindness, more foolish pride. On the occasion of foreign military adventures, the citizens will be roused to a livid pitch of patriotic fervor. Flags will be displayed and venerated like religious icons, deviants will be pilloried.

Do we say "will be"? It is all too familiar to afford much consolation.

.   .   .

But lo, come these two, Peter and John, bearing no credentials, and yet denying "with boldness" the imperial charges. And more. The more, the intolerable more comes to this: they offer their own version of the events in contention. Their version is artfully modest, canny, monosyllabic. Worse, it is backed by the witness of the one healed. He has indeed grown "bold" as his benefactors.

The story, whatever its merits, is dangerously germinal; others, many in number, are listening and drawing conclusions.

Hence a dilemma. Manifestly the truth cannot be denied, though they would with all their corrupt will deny it. What other expedient then?

.   .   .

It is notable that faith is never presented as an alternative. Faith is simply unthinkable; then and now, it lies outside the range of the proceedings. Too much is at stake; to believe, the Temple officials must step down from their eminence and declare themselves one with the people "from below," the believers. Temple officials must think the unthinkable, must become believers in the One they have recently condemned.

What to do? They content themselves for the present with a mere threat, veiled, shelved in some dark dossier, one day to be summarily unveiled. For the present, let the defendants look to themselves; they and the others are to "refrain from public teaching and preaching in the name of Jesus."

Any but these eminent figureheads might have known it. One might as sensibly forbid these incorrigibles to draw in and exhale the air of day.

The response is quick as a drawn blade. "Judge for yourselves whether it is right for us to obey God rather than you."

.   .   .

Thus the defendants introduce by inference a most delicious
irony. Is not the supposition upon which these mighty thrones
rest, as upon bedrock, that they and no other mortals stand surrogate for the will of God? How then shall the two religious duties, obedience to the priests and obedience to God, two which
God has made one, how shall these be separated?

And yet at a stroke Peter and John have separated them. Or
more precisely, the defendants, uneducated commoners, with
sovereign boldness, have declared the two realities, temple religion and the will of God, already long separated. Those who
purportedly embody and convey the will of the most High must
be disobeyed. It is a postulate of faith, as binding as "Thou shall
not kill."

Where might such breathtaking effrontery lead? The defendants have spoken, not as insurgents rising up against lawful
authority; rather, as those whose task it is to unmask a truth
long, laboriously, skillfully concealed. A bankrupt system
stands self-betrayed, given over to the powers of this world.

To be sure, the powers, the debased sacred and the violent
secular, dovetail cunningly. There is no telling in such a court-
room, who speaks for which; where the special interests of the
one may be thought to end and the other to start. Equally of-
fended, equally threatened.

Offense and threat! They proceed unaccountably from a
ghostly presence, a presence that refuses to vacate the world, a
presence literally unkillable, though the wiles and tools of empire and religion have been mustered in its destruction. Offen-
sive, threatening! Jesus, the name is proscribed.

A crisis is at hand. A veritable lightning flash of intuition, self-knowledge, worldly insight is granted the defendants, and the church. The powers have once more gathered, the charade of justice known as a Temple court has assembled. In truth, the rulers have made common cause against God and God's messiah.

.   .   .

Since this is so, since the powers have grown overweening and militant in their assault on God, let us, implies Luke, name names. The list of those present and in charge is deliberately exhaustive; the defendants, and by inescapable inference the throng of converts, cannot, in obeying "the rulers, elders, scribes...Annas the high priest, Caiaphas, John, Alexander, and all who were of the high priestly family," cannot be thought to obey God.

Quite the opposite. Quite a reversal.

.   .   .

Let the generations take warning. Let us take warning; for Scripture is by no means a record of high crimes renounced, crises resolved once for all, empires converted to godly ways, the nations streaming into the sanctuary. Scripture is for our perennial instruction, our unease. Christians standing in the dock, whether in that or this century, bear witness to a dolorous truth: while time lasts martyrdom never is done with. Empires remain themselves, then, now, always. They are skilled and willful instruments of legalized murder. Thus they resist the blood spent for their sakes by heroes. Then and now.

.   .   .

It is like a threnody, a closure. The Scripture tells of it, mourns and instructs and witnesses. Empires pass, come and go, wreak their worst, peddle their wares, entice and enlist, stroke their sycophants, dispose of their adversaries. And whenever they mount the cockpit of history, from the first empire to our own day, kings and shahs and pharaohs and presidents and chiefs, along with those who serve and cajole and stroke, they learn from their dead predecessors—nothing. They, each and every one, are born blind and inflated with pride.

These are requirements, credentials of office: blindness, pride. The illness is congenital.

. . .

The smell of brimstone is by no means a pollutant of our times only; it stains the earliest air of Christian history. In that air, the supreme skill of the demonic is displayed: its ability to conceal itself.

Thus a certain political-religious arrangement, presenting itself as God's embodied will, was unmasked in the first chapters of *Acts,* our genesis. The Romanized Sanhedrin was declared early on, indeed before the word of God was dry upon the page, no surrogate of God. Indeed, quite the opposite; two obscure believers turning the tables, indict the eminent body as the enemy of faith, obedience, justice.

Even to this extremity of wickedness. The Sanhedrin's priests and rulers hold in thrall both conscience and worship. So, addicted as they are to public favor and secular subservience, they prosper.

Thus it follows in virtue of a perverse logic: if they are to perdure (and to them perdurance is everything), the sword is first blessed, and then drawn. The unsubdued must be destroyed, beginning with the Christ. And by no means ending there, by no means to this day.

.   .   .   .

The subsequent action is predictable, given the actors, given the crisis. The authorities are of course unconvinced of the truth. Indeed were they to be convinced, they could no longer exercise such authority as they claim.

In what follows, Luke grants them short shrift, scant attention.

Indeed the outcome has about it an air of simple dismissal; these persecutors, in spite of every stratagem, bring themselves to grief. And those who must walk the cruel gantlet of crooked minds, are honored beyond all telling. Another, holier than they, has gone that way.

.   .   .

The apostles have come through, tested and true, unrehabilitated. It is not to be thought wonderful that when they rejoin their companions, the assembly falls spontaneously to prayer. Nor is the tone of the prayer surprising, taking in account the mettlesome spirits who pronounce its words. The prayer turns juridical maltreatment around, turns to God in thanksgiving for very misfortune.

The prayer is Jewish: in its invocation of the Creator, in its plain stubbornness. All creation, and the Creator, are summoned: "Maker of heaven and earth and sea and everything in them..." It is as though the cosmos, in its vast variety and beauty, must be summoned to stand witness, to celebrate the moral efforts of the newborn community. The world of authority, ethical understanding, moral efforts of the newborn community. The world of authority, ethical understanding, moral ecology must also know its pentecost, be made new. Thus the pentecostal community joins itself "boldly" to a larger picture, a larger history. Not easily, not by chance or velleity; in strenuous testing.

And they do not, despite all, stand alone; in them the Creator creates anew.

The spirit of the prayer and its petition are one: "boldness" they seek in word and work.

We could hardly discover better teachers in the matter of a prayer that seeks to joust with the world rather than to be granted refuge from it.

FOUR

Of property and money,
of deceit and consequent death.
Also of growth and
further legal jeopardy.

The matter of the economics of the community must shortly be taken up. It is not, to be sure, the most savory or satisfactory issue, then or now.

Luke begins with a delectable hyperbole. It is a device to prepare readers; a letdown is to follow. In this instance, the shock will follow shortly and with unexampled abruptness.

We are told, in the first instance, of a truly laudable spirit of unacquisitiveness, permeating the trade and trafficking of the community. The apostles are appointed to yet one more responsibility, an uneasy eminence. They not only preside over the assembly in its deliberations and directions; since no member possesses anything in title absolute, the apostles must also act as dispensers of its largesse. Shall the spiritual and material easily conjoin, even granted the neophytal fervor of the community?

Yes and no. A certain Barnabas (whose name, "Son of Encouragement," Luke is careful to translate for us, needy as we are in that direction) is briefly praised. Epitomizing the economic ethos of the group, he sells his estate and brings the proceeds to the apostles for gift giving.

This good Barnabas, we are given to know, stands with a majority. His act is not dwelt upon; it merely exemplifies a general standard. When all are good, goodness is not to be thought startling.

The opposite is startling: evil, backsliding and deceit. And we are immediately and in gruesome detail offered a startling tale.

Not now the chicanery of politicians, judges, priests and their clones. The malfeasance of its own members afflicts the community. Then death enters the garden of innocence, so recently and eloquently praised.

But we are born skeptics, or our world makes us such. Of what use such a tale to us, of a garden inhabited by wide-eyed innocents, stuck as we are, blessed or cursed as we are, planted in the real world as we are? Are we then to take hope, reading of another, radically different world, fastidiously placed at distance from us, peopled by superior humans, innocent of our paltry crimes, our deceits and betrayals, and itching after security, property, empery?

.   .   .

Would that we could imagine ourselves, each and every one, a Barnabas in a community of the unselfish and untrammeled! Would also that Ananias and Sapphira, that utterly likely pair (like us), did not dwell in our midst, indeed, lay claim to our hearts, their little stash of gold, their fetching equivocations, their conniving how to dole out to best advantage their paltry plenty, keep a little, yield a little.

We know them too well, they are ourselves. To this extent: we read of Barnabas and his kind, and our hearts sink. It is all beyond us, beyond our history, our inheritance, our hopes for the children, who above all (and for the most part unacknowledged) we wish to live in the world, no different from ourselves, to "pass along a little something, a nest egg...."

. . .

We read of the doomed pair, and by the strangest twist of things, we nod in understanding. Strangely, knowing on the moment that we are in the company of our kin, we take heart. Taking warning, we take heart. At the least, as we attend to the awful story of the two who wheeling, dealt and so died, we are warned; ahead lies the dead end named death.

We sense the truth, the displeasing truth; the piratical consumer-ridden economics of the empire have no place in the Christian community. And further, if such is granted entrance among us, we too, along with the culture that adores the calf of gold and despises the creation, we too shall be struck down.

. . .

The story of Ananias and Sapphira has overtones strongly reminiscent of the Genesis story of the fall. With notable differences. In *Acts* the woman is by no means scapegoated as the temptress of the male. Turn and turn about, each party is summoned for judgment, each is equally dealt with, as each has entered in the pact of deception.

Is the story an allegory, told for our instruction? Is it rooted in fact? In any case, it sits strangely in Luke's history where mercy and forgiveness have played so large a part in the pedagogy of Christ.

Peter's role as judge and prosecutor sits uneasily on one whose delicts were so enormous, whose need for forgiveness was lately so acute. Why, as ask, were husband and wife not granted time and occasion for repentance? Why the summary capital sentence?

The questions are valid; more, they are pressing. And in the final analysis, they hover unanswered. We are left with—what we are left with; a feeling that the outcome is disjointed, that we hover uneasily between the spirit of one testament and another; that we are plunged into the ruthless story of Judges or the law of Deuteronomy.

. . .

That admitted, further reflections occur. Granted that the story reveals much of the sensibility of the early believers, of conduct condemned and outcome so harsh, what was to be conveyed in the telling? Surely something of degradation is implied in a marriage founded on an economics of selfishness and deception. A marriage so entered upon or pursued can, with fatal ease, issue in the death of the parties.

Something, too, of the seriousness with which honesty in financial matters was regarded. The faith has immediate and practical consequences: candor, honesty, accountability.

. . .

ACTS 5: 11-16

Now and again, *Acts* reads like a rags-to-riches success story. Luke once more injects a dose of glory into his plot.

He thus opens an unpromising episode with a grand flourish, as though writing "success" vaultingly in the blue heavens, redeems what sorry episode is to follow.

Perhaps the stamp of "success", that awe that falls on those around, the spectacular increase in numbers of believers, the spontaneous healings that emanate from the apostles, an aura, a glory, perhaps this approval from on high must redeem episodes that in commonsensical terms end badly.

A touch of *deus ex machina* does no harm to those (like ourselves) who know, in like evangelical tasks, little success of any kind.

.   .   .

Thus today do we also fumble about, and get ourselves arrested, and sit out the times, in jail and out; when out, clumsily weaving tents or performing other inauspicious tasks for a living. Tasks that go nowhere, evangelically or in worldly wise. Knowing meantime, to the chagrin of ego, that we are doing little to "redeem the times"; that the times, with or without us, wear a most unredeemed look indeed.

.   .   .

Luke lifts a veil. There is a truth, hidden and humiliating, beyond the brute facts that so defeat and devour us. There is One who witnesses, takes in account. The success story, so endearing, so contrary to the common experience of the vineyard crew, is a metaphor. Let the one who reads, run. Full speed, and no giving up. A divine glance rests on the unavailing labors, on the holiness and truthfulness of the work itself, longing to burst forth, groaning in its birth pangs.

An element of humor saves the day.

Here we go again, say the equable in good humor. After the awe and foregathering and unity of mind and heart and high public regard and increase of members, after the easeful healing, as though healing were as native to nature itself as illness and incapacity—after all this, the healers and truthtellers are simply rounded up. The arrests are in their own way also a fact of nature; thus Luke's cool-handed treatment.

Here indeed, nature's scope is widened and worsened. It now includes the official malevolence that follows ("naturally") on the doing of the good. The arcane ways of the law, its irrational logic, are here nakedly revealed—and what a blessing!

.   .   .

ACTS 5: 17-32

If this were all, we were condemned indeed to dwell behind the looking glass. We are not. Or rather, another species of wonder restores sanity.

The apostles are jailed; and rightly so, as any judge will intone on demand or remand. Then an angel intervenes; this splendid being, unlikely and promptly at hand, expresses in the springing of locks a divine logic superseding the human, which has become, all legal niceties nicely observed, intolerably overbearing.

Not only does the angel liberate; the same being bears a message, which in the circumstances would seem to have issued straight from headquarters. Go, the disciples are told, return to the scene of the crime. Repeat the crime.

They do so, straightaway.

Confusion is shortly compounded. The prison is undoubtedly intact; and no prisoners within. And of what use an empty shell designed for durance vile? It is a bird cage empty of singing birds.

There ensue fuming and fretting unaccustomed in high places; commands issued in all directions: Go find them!

They are discovered in the familiar place, surrounded by crowds, issuing the same, still forbidden message; they are rounded up, once more.

.   .   .

But the denouement would be lacking in much of its delicious irony were we to neglect the character of the mysterious visitant so dear to Luke, so near to his point. The angel is beyond doubt a mischief-maker; we must imagine his face wreathed in a half-smile, a mere brush stroke of the mirth of God.

An emissary, no less, of a recusant God, of God the resister, God of the unrehabilitated, God of those who simply keep going without respect to outcome, success, proofs patent, self-justification or bastardizing success. Of those who keep going out of their soul's conviction, and require no other approval: the goodness and truthfulness, yes even the beauty, of the work at hand. It is the work that detains them, the angel's sovereign finger points—to the work, appoints it to them, them to it. Hand to tool, tool to hand's skill.

Again and yet again. "Go, stand...tell the people all about this new life." The truth must be told, no matter the penalty. No matter success, no matter barren outcome. No matter anything, except the matter, the truth. It is this fierce single-minded concentration, this mystical implanting of one's life in the heart of things, the heart of reality, of vocation, of faith, of task—these are commended.

The angel is more than the bearer of a message; in fact, a gift giver, sent from One who endows an otherwise incomplete humanity with its true and burning entelechy, the fire that fuels and impels, that knows no destruction or depletion. The angel bears a burning coal from the brazier of pentecost; touches them. Now they are plain enduring men, they stand somewhere. Thus they confound the powers, as with sprung locks and empty cells. This is their prevailing. And ours.

.   .   .

The acts of the apostles, our acts. A paraphrase of the above event has occurred; it is based on actualities surrounding the trial of the first Plowshares group in 1981. Eight Christians, it will be recalled, entered a General Electric plant in King of Prussia, Pennsylvania, armed (disarmed?) with household hammers and vials of their own blood. They proceeded without hindrance to a "high security area." There, to their dumfounded awe, they beheld a number of nose cones of the Mark 12-A, a first-strike nuclear weapon. The weapons were stacked and packed for shipment to Amarillo, Texas, there to be armed with their nuclear payload.

The eight proceeded to "disarm" the weapons with hammers and anoint them with their blood, in token of Isaiah's oracle concerning the "beating of swords into plowshares." They were subsequently brought to trial in 1981, and convicted.

A paraphrase of chapter 5, verses 17-42, suggests itself, referring to events surrounding the Plowshares action and trial:

"Someone came in and informed the court: 'Those you put on trial are back at General Electric, talking to the people.' So the captain and officers went and brought them into court, without violence.

"They brought them in and stood them before the judge. And the judge reproved them fiercely, saying, 'We strictly charged you not to act again in this manner, and here you are, filling the countryside with your talk. I even hear that you seek to implicate this court in what you are pleased to call nuclear crimes.'

"But the defendants answered, 'We must obey God rather than you. For it is true; you are complicit in the threat of nuclear crucifixion of the world. You stand convicted, even though through us you are offered access to the truth of nonviolence. We hereby invite you once more. Resign this unworthy office and join with us in the work of resistance. And know that it is in reality the Holy Spirit and not us, who issues this invitation.'

"The judge on hearing this grew furious, and said to them, 'I wish it were possible to send you all to a Puerto Rican leper colony or a Siberian prison camp. Short of that, I sentence you to the maximum allowed under the law!'

"Now the judge had a friend on the bench, who witnessing these proceedings took him aside. 'Judge,' he said, 'I urge you to cool these matters. We have a hard dilemma here. By coming down so hard on the defendants, you are ensuring an outcome opposite to the one we seek. Take my advice; minimal sentences; long drawn-out appeal. In this way, we can hope that the entire movement may peter out.'

"The judge nodded. He called in the defendants once more, gave them a tongue lashing. He referred to one among them as 'a so-called priest. a wandering gypsy.' He warned them against repeating their 'irresponsible actions,' and put them all on indefinite probation.

"The eight and their friends left the court singing. And in the weeks and months following, each of the defendants could be found at nuclear laboratories, bases, bunkers, resisting once more. They were clearly irreformable."

.   .   .

ACTS 5: 33-42

Much has been made of the virtuous intervention of Gamaliel, "a Pharisee, a teacher of the law." It would seem at first glance that Luke registers his own encomium: Gamaliel is "held in high regard by all the people."

Except that with Luke, subtleties are the very pith of style. We may well be advised: watch closely, judge narrowly, for this admittedly "good man" exhibits the limits of a certain type of goodness.

We are presented with an example of highly refined prudence. In such lofty circles as Gamaliel enhances, the virtue might be thought of as—serviceable, a surrogate for faith. But prudence is not to be confused with faith.

The commentators are of interest here, if of little practical help. One among them seizes the high ground, homilizing away. Thus Gamaliel is viewed as a reproof to those who would "think that membership in the academic and religious establishment automatically disqualifies one from any shred of righteousness." The comment of course misses the point, the subtlety of Luke's telling.

His point being, not the virtuous potential lodged in the establishment (or absent therefrom) but the more or less evident limitations of Gamaliel's logic. His distance from faith can be measured by his commending to his peers a canny game of watching and waiting upon the outcome of event. This, implies Luke, is the best response human genius can summon in face of the beckoning obscurities of faith. Let us bide our time; let us see where all this goes.

Thus too the high and mighty are contrasted with the many, the many who take the salutary leap. Or rather, in this instance of a learned, high-minded teacher, the mighty set themselves against the many. The speech of Gamaliel is the self-revelation of a blind Oedipus.

.   .   .

His prudence waits upon the fruits of a method before passing judgment on the method; the "if" is the rub; "if what is being planned and done is from God...." The reasoning of Gamaliel is autumnal, wise in the way of the world, much given to rumination, takes no chances, weighs and waits.

Faith to the contrary is a matter of heart; it has its own reasons, is impetuous, steps across lines, is often intemperate and instinctual and at a loss to explain itself. Simply: "It is good for us to be here."

Faith is a virtue of the early season, the springtime; it bends to the labor of planting, takes its chances on season and outcome.

The disciples in sum are faithful; Gamaliel is logical. We are not moved to join him.

.   .   .

The proceeding, let it be added hastily, pace our commentator, is not set down in order to demean Gamaliel or his establishment, or to consign such worthies to outer darkness. So are they all, all worthy men. But hardly are they to be praised as faithful men; nor does Luke so praise them.

The confreres of Gamaliel, we may be pardoned for pointing out, are hot in pursuit of the condign punishment of the accused.

Praise therefore, within limit, is due Gamaliel. His prudent temporizing, for all its limits, has its uses. He saves the lives of the apostles.

.   .   .

As the accused set their course and make their willful re-
cidivism clear, the penalties increase.

The eminences who yield before the prudence of Gamaliel,
we are told, have cooled as to earlier combustion; but not entirely. Capital punishment is presently abandoned. But still, they
will have if not their day, at least an hour. The apostles are
flogged, and only then released. The savage illogic of the decree
has the character of a pre-emptive strike, a warning. *Caveat
fideles!*

.   .   .

The apostles remain unswayed from their purpose, it goes
without saying.

It goes without saying, we write. After the fact is easy. And
yet what a marvel of steadfastness is implied in the words of
Luke. We are being instructed as to what is extraordinary in
Christian conduct, and what a matter of common behavior and
life.

It is, for instance, taken for granted that the believing community will be marked by a calm righteousness of purpose, a
certainty of the "way." No matter the impediment, no matter the
cost. (Then certainly, but now?)

They are also to stand the law on its ear; its worst punish-
ments become occasions, not for discomfiture, disarray, mourning, intemperate tending of wounds (literally or in figure), but
for rejoicing, celebration.

So we are told, laconically, they went on with their tasks
"every day, steadily, in the temple and in private houses, telling
the good news...." Luke is detailed, diagnostic; he would not
have us miss a beat. The message, the work is publicly commit-

ted to them and publicly taken up; it is their dignity and vocation. It is also a clue to their state of soul, fervent and lively as it
is.

The message, we would say, is indeed the media, themselves. As they are resolved to stand by the word they offer,
even to die on its behalf, they also live by it. (Is the "also" not
redundant?) We must think of the word of God on their lips as
an essential of life itself: bread, water, air.

. . .

So many words hovering about, claimant and clamorous,
demanding attention, subservience, like noisy spoiled children;
come-hither words, buy-me words, sell-me words, huckstering
words (appetite, money, power), patriot words, promissory
words, religious words ("Come Home for Christmas" messages
put in public places, along with abortion words, liquor words),
words hot from the barrel of a gun.

There is only one Word. It is none of the foregoing; it is of a
different order entirely; it is of God; it issued from the tongue of
Christ. Love your enemies, return good for evildoing.

The word must be attended and obeyed, or we die—as
surely as though air were withdrawn from us, or water, or bread.

Many are dying.

FIVE

Of the first martyr;
the politics of faith.

ACTS 6: 1 - ACTS 8: 3

Stephen, the first among the new deacons, is also the first to underscore, if not to aggravate, the simmering controversy between the new community and the older Temple establishment.

This tempestuous spirit brings wonderment and perplexity in his wake, even to this day. His dramatic tirade before the council, his absolutely burning conviction, the violence with which he argues for a radical revision of Jewish history: these make him the prototype, not merely of the martyrs, but of the racy line of Christian apologists. In Stephen, the new community issues its defiance, signifies its willingness to live and speak up, no holds barred; and, if required, to die for the truth given in its charge.

What is perhaps less considered is that Stephen is in the direct line of those, beginning with Jesus, who are determined to call the covenant people to accounts. (Would he not today likewise call us Christians to account?)

. . .

In any case, the theme explored so relentlessly by Stephen is by no means his alone; his speech before the Council echoes the lengthy tirades of Jesus recorded in John's Gospel. Jesus too had assailed the substitution of law for tradition, the Temple worship gone stale and worse—gone idolatrous. Stephen is in good company, his shout is also an echo: "The most High does not dwell in houses built by men." Jesus had issued a summons for a new worship "in spirit and in truth."

.   .   .

We must tread ever so gently on this dangerous ground. It seems evident that if the lengthy, detailed indictment laid down by Stephen is plucked from its circumstance, it becomes dangerously apt for misuse. It must be recalled that the community of Stephen was a minority, persecuted, heavily set upon by the powers. Luke sets down his *Acts* after the fall of Jerusalem and the destruction of the Temple. *Acts* is his attempt, as a Jew confronting Jews, to come to terms with the disaster, a catastrophe which in its own ways raised (for both Christians and Jews) dreadful questions.

.   .   .

Once raised, the questions reverberate throughout Jewish history. We have heard them in our own day, as Jews continue to agonize over the German holocaust. Has God abandoned us? Why must the children suffer and die? Where, Who, is God when God's people are devastated?

To transfer the diatribe of Stephen to the mouth of today's powerful Christian church, guilty through much of its history of persecution of the people of Jesus—this would be a bizarre exercise in the method of special pleading endemic to the powerful.

. . .

Let us have no part in it. Let us acknowledge that time and again we have stoned the prophets who arose among the Jews in the course of "Christian" history. We too may well have had the tables turned on us. In many ways, we have become, with regard to the Jews, the faithless who kill, who refuse with fury the truth offered us.

That history of ours, scathingly revised by a latter day Stephen, would show small cause for pride; little by way of peacemaking, generosity of mind; a paltry residue indeed of the spirit commended to us in the Sermon on the Mount and bloodily verified on Calvary. Little fidelity to our own prophets, little of spiritual, truthful worship.

. . .

More, we might dare ask our souls in fear and trembling, is there no connection between historical Christian crimes against Jews, and the current crimes of Jews against Palestinians? We might require a sense of the underlying violence that fuels the conduct of institutions, that is passed provocatively from one age to another, a pandemic "quick fix" throughout history—this would perhaps illumine understanding—how our crimes invite criminal conduct on the part of others, even as the same crimes violate the gospel we claim as our own.

. . .

The speech of Stephen casts his audience into a paroxysm of fury. And no wonder! The underpinnings of authority, authenticity, self-esteem, control of others, ego—these are shaken by a verbal earthquake. Worse. They are held to public scrutiny, derided, and scorned.

The outcome is predictably violent. How thin is the veneer of law and order that fictionalizes, even while it lends credence to, such officialdom! Reactionary vengeance is never far distant from such as these. Rational argument, when it undercuts and exposes the roots of illegitimate power, is quickly swamped by more convenient, speedy ways of "dealing" with those who dare.

No more pretense of a judicial hearing, condemnation, sentencing; these go under in a hurricane of wrath. Stephen is dragged from a chamber, and their Honorables of the Sanhedrin transmogrify into a lynch mob. Stephen is stoned, witnessing in his last moments a vision of the welcoming Jesus.

.   .   .

We have seen equivalent scenes in our lifetime. The crust of legal punctilio thins and collapses under the hammer blows of unsubdued conscientious defendants. These are shortly dealt with, if not by stoning, by savage prison sentences, at the "discretion" of distracted and irascible judges.

A more than passing tribute is fitting here, to such noble spirits as Father Karl Kabat and Helen Woodson, officially "stoned" by an iniquitous judge, sentenced to more than a decade of imprisonment. Because they, in the manner of Stephen, dared assault American pretensions to rule the world through a vile nuclear hegemony.

.   .   .

What is worth living and dying for? The question implicitly raised by Stephen, raised again and again in our lifetime, seems to many simply absurd, extremist. Yet in the early church it was very nearly the only question raised. Raised publicly, dangerously—dare one add, politically?

Quite a contrast. Today most Christians live quite peaceably with the narrow, fatuous "values" huckstered by the culture; valueless values, if truth were told. We squander our lives, rather than giving them over greatheartedly, in accord with a tradition honored by the "cloud of witnesses."

To live selfishly, heedlessly, is, measured by our gospel, never to have lived. So to "adapt" also implies in the strongest terms that one finds nothing in existence worth dying for. Thus life and death are reduced to a paltry, colorless affair: boredom, distraction, and appetite.

.   .   .

We also become strangers to our own Scripture. Stephen, Philip, Paul, what can these folks be about? We lose a sense of communality of spirit, of admiration and awe, pondering the heroism of our own bloodline.

In proportion as the cultural icons become our idols, we even become inclined to quarrel with the martyrs. Indeed the word grows suspect; it takes on an aura of extremism and judgment. The *media aurea*, which might be translated inelegantly as "anything goes," is the cultural rule of thumb. Then the martyrs appear only as strangers, even to their own. Sociology, psychology are invoked to trivialize and explain them away.

Hearers of the word, doers of the word? We neglect to seek in their example our chastening and judgment, the grace of emulation.

.   .   .

[from a letter of murdered Fr. Ignacio Ellacuria, S.J.]

"The description that we are utopian comes close to being accurate.... It is true that we aren't politicians and that, in that sense, we are more utopian than pragmatic. We are people of the gospel, a gospel that proclaims the kingdom of God and that calls on us to try to transform this earth into as close a likeness of that kingdom as possible.

"Within such a system it is difficult to accept unbridled capitalism, because the evils it has produced in history outweigh the good. As the bishops of Latin America stated in Puebla, Mexico, in 1979, 'We see the continuing operation of economic systems that do not regard the human being as the center of society, and are not carrying out the profound changes needed to move toward a just society.'

"It would be better to accept systems that better confronted the problems of the poor, and gave them the special place bestowed on them in a gospel vision. Such a vision emphasizes the common good; it calls for liberation, not just liberalization.

"In the case of El Salvador, the Jesuits here have condemned institutionalized and repressive violence, and we have done all that we could, including calling again and again for dialogue— to avoid and diminish revolutionary violence.

"We have endured a good deal during these recent years; one of us, Rutilio Grande, was murdered, and the rest of us received an ultimatum: Get out of the country or be killed. We decided to stay. Since then our home and our university have been bombed fourteen times."

SIX

Of the enticement of magic;
a warning.
Also of the charm
and candor of a new convert.

ACTS 8: 4-25

A rather humorous incident, though taken seriously; a reminder that the gospel is by no means amenable to magic. (And yet magic men [sic] are constantly "working" the gospel for all its worth. Today as well.)

Alas, *"plus ca change..."* In our own time, the gospel market is clearly bullish; charlatans intemperately flourish, and a weird cult of "communication arts" ensures such of both prosperity and progeny. To the detriment, one can only conclude, of the Word, which seeks a hearing in modest, hidden ways and places, worlds apart from the technique of mammon.

Such reflections bring one to a certain uneasy sympathy for the well-placed magician Simon. It is the sympathy implied in recognition; we know our own. Despite all disclaimers, such con men are our own. If Paul and Peter and Stephen have their progeny in Christian history, so does this mysterious eminence, whose descendants today grace the airwaves and tubes, even as they disgrace the word of God.

. . .

Simon allowed himself to become renowned as "the power of God...the Great Power." Whatever the meaning of the phrase, it bears the implication of ego mightily inflated and noised abroad for its own ends. The fame, unchallenged, uncorrected, indeed encouraged by a silent acceptance, became in effect a claim. The title became a telling form of untruth. Simon climbed to his pedestal; he became, in the eyes of his followers, a species of superhuman.

In a culture which deifies its rulers, can it be wondered that a number of demigods arose? Why strive for the merely human, when the divine, with its perquisites, rites, honors, is grandly available?

.   .   .

Simon, we have suggested, is by no means unique, in his culture or ours.

Indeed the inherent modesty of Christ's Word is not easily borne; according to some, it must be amplified, ventriloquized, rendered irresistible, subjected to the principalities. Then, alas, it becomes one with the fall of creation and the world of death. It offers no resurrection, even as it captivates with its promise of cheap salvation and emotional big returns.

Luke is nothing short of surgical in his analysis of the ploys of Simon and their large success;

"He captivated...with magical arts, making large claims for himself. Everyone high and low listened intently to him. 'This man,' they said, 'is that power of God which is called the Great Power.' "

And, as if the point must be driven home:

"They listened because they had for so long been captivated by his magic."

The captivator bears watching. What does he offer, what awakens a sympathetic echo in the heart, and starts serious mischief? This is the resolve to manipulate, control, and own the power of God.

.   .   .

Magic defines that power far differently than the gospel. For us, the power of the Word is the cross of Jesus. Such understanding introduces, to say the least, an array of impediments against the good life, defined as the culture would define it (and would have us define it).

That "good life" has, of course, a price attached. It implies on both sides, the signing of an implicit compact: the acceptance of political indifference, and irresponsibility. One hands over crucial decisions to others, consents to a gag of silence—even though it is known that crimes are in progress, or at least being contemplated.

Thus one collaborates with "things as they are." Including the violence of things as they are, the "filthy rotten system", in Dorothy Day's salty phrase. Enticed by special interests, one accepts the system as metaphysical, descended from on high, announcing itself as an irrefutable humanism.

.   .   .

Jesus refused. The great refusal placed Jesus on the cross. He must be done away with, in the nature of things; the nature of things being—things as they are. It could not be borne, this refusal of His, His rejection of the ironbound "nature of things." It could not be borne that He turn things around, defend the victims, heal the afflicted, launch an assault upon the perfidy, greed and duplicity of the ruling powers.

The logic of the system decreed that He must be disposed of.

Such a decision surely did not stop with the disposition of "the case of Jesus Christ." Let activity comparable to His, imitative of His, be indulged in then or now, and a like fate awaits.

The cross is peremptory; it would snatch from us the benefits of the crime of silence.

Simon offered money. Peter exploded. "To hell with you and your money."

·   ·   ·

We are in considerable wonderment at the *fioretti* that lie so gently, like pressed flowers, here and there on the pages of Acts. (C.8,vv.26-40) Angels opening prison gates, angels speaking familiarly to humans, the Spirit hot in pursuit of unlikely converts! Heaven and earth are abuzz with the to and fro of the vital unknown!

The atmosphere is vastly different from that of the gospels, where the signs and wonders are worked by a Human, dear and familiar, one of us firmly planted in our ground. More, gospel healings are an occasion of bringing together a larger community. Once the twelve are chosen, there is little or no attempt to enlarge the circle. And once restored, the healed generally go their way; the call to conversion of heart is issued as a matter quite different from the call to discipleship.

·   ·   ·

If the Spirit is active in the gospels, that Spirit is altogether subsumed in the person of Jesus. In Him the Spirit is palpable, but not as another Person. Only as the Spirit of this Person, Jesus. So we dare say, when He speaks, we understand; a human stands before us, uttering words that reach and wrench the heart.

The mystery of the divine comes down and down, dwelling as it does in Him, acting through Him, speaking through Him. The word of God is humanized and localized—in Him.

We forget our awe, our distancing; we come near, as though a friend were beckoning, one of us.

And we are right. So He is.

.   .   .

Then we open *Acts*. With delicacy and discretion, Jesus quickly vanishes from human sight; that is to be our history: his absence. Or rather, a new kind of presence (or so we are told), one rife with talk of Spirit, acts of the Spirit, such interventions, interruptions as bewilder the mind. We are brought up short, at sixes and sevens as to what is transpiring, who this Spirit might be, what this breath or wind or tongue of fire may mean to us mortals, unfiery and tongue-tied as we often are.

And in Luke's community, such dwelling and concentrating on the Spirit is highly unsettling to some. And to others the episodes are apt for mystification and the multiplying of charlatans, magicians—all claiming "the spirit."

.   .   .

As *Acts* would have it, that "Spirit" is as close to the activities of Christians as Jesus had formerly been. Innovating Spirit, Truth telling and impelling Spirit, Spirit of boldness, Bestower of eloquence and plain speech, Spirit of responsible living and dying, Spirit of judgment and irony. There is prodding and interfering and advising, as well as healing and the interrupting of death and daring rebukes hurled at the powerful. All, we are told, under the hot breath and compulsion of the Spirit.

．　．　．

Indeed believers, it is implied, would conduct themselves in the world in a far different manner, were they not "subject to the Spirit." We have only to think of the authorities they encountered whether in church or state; those who objected strenuously, sometimes violently to their words and actions, those who wanted them (and eventually ordered them) summarily removed from the earth.

Different indeed, conflict indeed. But for the Spirit, Luke's community would have simply given up their absurd claims, fitted in, acquiesced, been assimilated, ground into the world's gears. They would remain only an archaic footnote in history; obsessives who recanted their ways, faulty citizens who came to their senses, made their peace with Caesar, fell in line.

Deprived of the Spirit, Christian resistance would be unimaginable. The martyrs also, no more than a momentary faltering of the irresistible machinery of things.

．　．　．

Another image. Deprived of the Spirit, Christians would be a kind of supportive cable in the complex web of self-interest and greed and ego and violence that, then and now, is named "the world." Christians in the armed forces, Christians sitting high and mighty as judges and prosecutors in the courts. Christians with access to the ear of Caesar.

In the beginning, such eminences would have been simply unimaginable. Too strong sense of Christ, too vivid a memory of the kenosis of God, too close a reading of the great command.

But for such boundaries and taboos, Christianity would have been a disappearing act, a curious matter of the rise and fall of yet another bizarre sect littering the world's history. All this, but for the Spirit.

. . .

Then and now, a capital point. We too would easily be melded into a far different moral world ("dwellers upon the earth") were it not for a Spirit Who keeps interfering, seeing and telling, interpreting, suspecting, Who keeps us skeptical of the world's claims and concealments, keeps (unwilling as we are, and stubborn) instructing us—as to delicts as well as new directions, both. And all this in spite of our contrary longings, appetites, urges.

Indeed if the leading of the Spirit remains uninhibited and vigorous for a long time, for years and years, we look back in a kind of wonderment. How is it that life took this direction, that one has taken a path he could hardly have foretold or mapped beforehand? I chose and did not choose; I chose and was chosen.

. . .

Who chose, and why? We conjure up the two defeated men who set out on a Sunday morning for a distant town. They were bent only on one thing, and of that they could hardly be proud; picking up the shards of their broken lives.

Then they were joined, we are told, by a third. He walked along with them, sympathetic and silent in manner. Struck by their defeated mien, He slowly insinuated himself into their lives. Strongly inclined to friendship and listening—an outsider, one apt for their confidences, by no means likely to overwhelm them with an Easter epiphany.

In such wise, a certain dear normalcy gradually dawns on them, defuses the terror, the mystery, the all-but-unbearable event.

. . .

This is an approach to the rub, the difficulty. That Friend has vanished, as Luke relates, His place taken by the Spirit. Once we could look the Friend full in face; we must now, as we are advised, "discern the Spirit," often unsure as to the method. Nor, as we know to our discomfiture, are we guaranteed a right outcome in an equivocal matter.

Where once a friend's word stood unequivocal, his presence at our side taken for granted (for what else does friendship imply?), riposte, rebuke even (a friend's uneasy privilege)—we have now a multitude of spirits contending for attention and advocacy. Certain among them, risen from the culture, blow on us fiercely as a coven of eumenides. Others arise from we know not where, it may be from our own darksome hearts. We confess to being bewildered by the onslaught. Are we to understand that enlistment in the spirit world (even the enlistment implied in inertia) is somewhere considered crucial?

A battle of the spirits, on human ground. And the holy Spirit, the spirit of Jesus, advising, impelling, even insisting on—let us say, this painful conquest, the tackling of this temptation, despite fear and trembling, the venturing on a dreaded step, a much feared vocation. Enabling. Enlarging the scope of the possible, where beforehand we could have imagined only—impossibility, unlikelihood.

And yet the step beckons here and now, my thing to be done (better, our thing to do), perhaps the crucial act of a lifetime. Though at the time, beforehand, it seemed ridiculously beyond me (us), absurd in the eyes of others, leading nowhere, apt only for ruin and disarray. Or so warn the spirits of fear.

Then despite all, another, far different Spirit prevails. Enabling us, on such and such an occasion, to overcome. To surpass and supplant those other spirits, whose choral ode is greatly magnified; No, Never, Surely Not You.

.   .   .

There comes a time even, when the Spirit of Jesus becomes the very breath and exhalation of our prayer. Not merely the occasion of prayer; of something named, perhaps carelessly, a cliche, the "life of prayer."

We mistrust this, we shy away from this life, for the Spirit is colorless and formless and cannot be summoned in images; only in images of an image; breath, fire, tongue. The "consolations of the Spirit" are, more often than not, a species of cold comfort; a kind of neutrality regarding ourselves, a bearing with, a confession that our life is no matter of self-congratulation, rather something of merely detached interest, acceptable, neither absurd nor shameful, making now and again a modicum of sense.

We need reminding, at times, that something is being accomplished through us, even though we rise to no mood of satisfaction as to process, conduct, outcome. Let it all go, is our unspoken motto, the prompting of this Spirit, who seems at times a very buddha of offhandedness. Scuttle it, let it go.

And yet we need reminding; the Spirit is also our friend and advocate; therefore, Rejoice! Celebrate!

.   .   .

ACTS 8: 26-40

The same Spirit, or an angel closely resembling the spirit, shunts Philip about. (C.8,vv.26ff) Go there, come here! Little choice, less place for caviling; he comes or goes, as advised.

And on the occasion presented here, encounters a most engaging personage.

We picture the Ethiopian seated or standing in his chariot, being read to aloud by a servant. The text from Isaiah (C.53,vv.7ff) is arcane to his understanding. A mysterious personage, so the reading goes, is undergoing the harshest, most destructive treatment. Innocent as this person is declared to be, he (she) is haled into court, suffers condemnation and punishment. And it is through such suffering, so ignominious a death, the word continues, that the mysterious victim is enabled to liberate many.

. . .

Let us confess it; not only the unnamed Ethiopian is perplexed by the Isaiah episode. We are in no wise favored with particulars that might illumine an extremely puzzling oracle. Philip, we are told laconically, "told him the good news of Jesus"—presuming that the Christian assumption is a simple one; Jesus himself understood that his life and death were foretold in the passage.

With that we must be content. No responsibility is assigned for the crimes, presumably sanctioned judicially, against the servant. No hint of outcry, accusation, protest arise from the lips of the condemned; nor indeed is the issue of responsibility raised by the prophet who recounts this terrifying fate. Pure, un-

bearably pure is the image of wickedness unrelieved and innocence put to naught.

Philip is undaunted. In main, crude outline, unrelieved by
helpful detail, his apologia proceeds. Jesus is servant of God.
The systems of this world, wicked to the heart, have thus dealt
with the holy One. And in this unheard of way He responded; by
refusing to respond in kind. Such was his saving activity, of
such surpassing merit as to bring tears and a change of heart, if
not to his executioners, to the multitudes who hearken.

.   .   .

The story is austere, single of mind. Philip is faithful to Isaiah in applying the servant song to Jesus; no one is summoned
to account, neither Pilate nor Herod nor the Sanhedrin. It is all
quite straightforward, the point is simple; faith, its sudden eruption, the Spirit hovering over. Faith means clinging to this One
whom all have abandoned. Faith is conduct and mind and ad-
herence entirely at variance with those who condemned the just
One, those who vilified and scorned, those who fled and betrayed, those who cannily circumnavigated the murderous scene
and cowardly kept their counsel.

Faith in sum is one thing; the world and its tactic another.
And the two, in a drama of consequence, meet and clash in the
figure of the Servant, whose fate is left at that; unrelievedly
tragic, a waste even. Dostoevsky could have offered no more
terrible image of the cost of a faith that challenges the principalities.

.   .   .

But defeat is hardly to be thought the final episode. The servant is rehabilitated in those who read His fate differently, who

choose for themselves in courageous reaction a moral stance far different from that of the persecutors and the inert silent majority. To speak up and pay up, is faith.

Faith reverses for all time the unjust execution of the just One; even as "I believe in You" justifies the one who utters the phrase in the teeth of the world's vengeance.

. . .

Isaiah spares nothing. We are stricken with awe at the driving power of so stark an image of the Holy. Is it the nonviolence of Jesus that wins the heart of this exotic solitary pondering man, pursuing his destiny along a desert road? Does the hungering hint awaken in him, that he has come on an incomparable icon; God in our midst, mysterious and dear beyond telling—the human, isolated in its tragedy and splendor?

The Ethiopian cannot, any more than ourselves, have been acquainted with humans comparable to the One described by Isaiah; royal courts being what they were, governments what they are. What is helpful and striking is the daring with which the text of Isaiah is simply plucked from its roots in one age, and transplanted to another. Isaiah's mysterious one is verified in Jesus, destroyed and risen. The wonder is that the essential features of the servant easily undergo so drastic a transplant; new ground, new person. Root and branch, the original stock is hardy and adaptable; the holy, the human take root, other noble shoots arise.

. . .

Isaiah and Jesus are never finished with. The seeds of noble servanthood are loosed on the winds of time. In new soil and setting, the servant image flourishes abroad, to this day.

Romero, King, murdered nuns and peasants and Jesuits, victims known and anonymous—suffering servants of our lifetime.

Under the millstone, in the wine press, the nonviolent ideal endures. Little else does, as a persuasive version of the endangered and elusive human.

SEVEN

A giant is born,
the church is shaken.

ACTS 9: 1-31

Up to now, in prospect of one who is shortly to come onstage, we have met with only minor characters in the drama entitled The Spirit of Fresh Starts. We may have thought them giants, protagonists. And how right we were—up to now. God's *kairos* is at hand. Every act and scene, everyone who declaimed, endured, spoke passionately of the new faith briefly stunned us, contended, momentously moved our hearts, launched winning images of heroism, everyone who was welcomed and emulated as a governor of major events—all must now shift places, move over.

It is as though on the vast shelf of world literature, without prelude, a volume marked *Shakespeare: The Complete Works* were to appear. No one can explain the event; few are tempted to do so; fewer still succeed. This coming is as mysterious as the message of an angel traced on a tyrant's wall.

Every other name, every page and volume on the shelf must shift, make room, be valuated anew. For all the calm of that act, the simple placing of a few fresh volumes in the storehouse of art, the pages whisper like tongues and pass the astonishing word; the vast treasury has suffered an earthquake of genius. A cataclysm scatters all former, neatly placed, critical judgments.

A new measure of greatness has appeared. Nothing will ever
again be the same; no one, whether of ancient times or times to
come, but must be measured anew.

.   .   .

Saul named Paul.

This greatness was once a great wickedness, a stinging lash.
It was armed and malevolent and darkly bent on that vengeance
we name the law. A man of the law, summing him up, wrapping
him as though in a shroud. Obsessive, driven, an exterminating
angel, he left a mark of blood on every Christian lintel, created
suffering servant upon suffering servant in the new community.
They cowering under the lash, raising a cry to heaven: when, by
what power, might this scourge be withdrawn?

.   .   .

He was the dark force behind the oracle of Isaiah. He would
have murdered Jesus and been content. He was determined so to
bind the law to his purpose that he might remove from earth the
abomination, the unbearably deviant "Way." In this he was law-
less, stood literally outside the law; as does every such instrument of literal law, law as vengeance.

The crime of the Christians? Their Way stood against his
way, the only way. Those who so stood were a scandal, a stone
in the shoe; they must be removed, cast aside.

.   .   .

He was, as he later confessed, a very paragon of his kind.
(Cf. Ch. 22, vv. 3ff.) Which is to say, he acted always within the
law. With punctilio; he "went to the high priest and applied for

letters...authorizing him to arrest any followers whom he met, women or men...." He is frenzied to stand within the charmed circle of law, for there he is *justified,* and by virtue of the law. Justified in any action, any crime. Is he not the law's champion and exponent? This is his highest praise, which he confers on himself.

"I was thoroughly trained in every point of our ancestral law.... And so I persecuted this movement to the death, arresting its followers, women and men alike and committing them to prison, as the high priest...can testify.... I was on my way to make arrests at Damascus and bring the prisoners to Jerusalem for punishment...."

(The law as justifying humans, be it noted, is also the pivotal renunciation he must make after the event of the Damascus road; and in his letter to the Christians in Rome, he will expound the matter with devastating thoroughness. Faith in Jesus, not the law, gives access to grace.)

.   .   .

But for now, Saul is the one whom, according to the intractable ideology of the law, the law has made perfect. Behold the perfection; he has become an executioner. No higher exemplar, a very doctor of the law, of the truth he is later to explore so relentlessly; the law as vehicle and instrument of death.

Nothing, no resource in the community he pursues, can avail against him. They have no weapons; they desire none. When summoned, they utter equably the most unlikely convictions: they live by a different law, something known as the Great Command.

.   .   .

The Christians walk gingerly on ice; the sun of power has thinned it to a crust. So to live, so to die, must appear harmful to their cause and contemptible to Saul's. What could be less to the point of law and order in this world than that a benighted knot of believers take for literal charge the love of God and one another?

Indeed, what God has joined the law has separated, these two, God and the neighbor. And to the good estate of each; so says the law. No human power shall henceforth join them; thus saith the law. For the law is above all, the instrument of love of God. And for the integrity of that supernal command, all other love must be put to the test; the test of the sword.

A harsh and dreadful love, and he, Saul, its instrument! The Christians have violated the love of God, invoking as they do, a strange God. They are no better than the heathen; worse in fact, for they claim to stand, they and their Jesus, within the Tradition. Standing treacherously there, they subvert the Tradition utterly. The abomination must be contained, put to the sword. Thus saith the law.

.　　.　　.

The Christians cry out to their God. Does no resource avail?

The community, for all its weakness, is gifted with a supreme Resource; it is governed, not by the law, but by the Spirit. And the same Spirit that creates martyrs of mere women and men will avail to bring the persecutor to knee. One and the same Spirit!

A nice balance between the works of the Spirit, the making of martyrs and the changing of hearts—this is not invariably maintained in history. The martyrs multiply; the persecutors raise the sword with venomous fervor. The martyrs cry out: How long, O Lord? Does the sword govern all of history?

It does not. We are granted in the episode of Saul named Paul, a precious relief, a *kairos,* a glimpse of that which may be, the realm of God. That which could not be, which no human power could have brought to pass, has come to pass, here and now. It is a solitary glimpse, but a crucial one, of things to come. The tyrant is transformed, the sword sheathed. At least once in our tormented history.

Thy kingdom come! No sword in human hands, no tyrant to wield the sword!

But not yet. Thy kingdom not yet come.

.   .   .

It could not be, and it was. An impregnable tower tumbled to the ground. The law, the law! No more the edifice he built and inhabited with such pride. It is the quondam Saul who would write, addressing his fellow Jews, "While you take pride in the law, you dishonor God by violating it."

He is addressing himself, his former life, and that murderous mood in which, as champion of the law, he violated the first law of all. He played God. He refused love.

The law fell, the elaborate enslavement wrought by temple religion was broken. An entire system is placed in question; the great command lies once more unequivocally at the center of conscience and history.

All other law must henceforth be judged by this law; the love of God and neighbor. Does the ancillary human law aid and abet, hinder, obscure the central command? Christian ethics must stand or fall in relation to this question. Christian scrutiny of human law must likewise stand in judgment on that lesser law; it stands or falls, is to be observed or violated according to a simple (but so difficult) rule of thumb: the coherence of human enactment with the great law.

.   .   .

Let us not delude ourselves; the hold of the law upon humankind remains none the less lethal. Capital punishment looms
as the law's final word, clutch; death's claim on the living. So
does war; for the victims, no less than for inducted soldiers. So
does abortion, the law's cruelties extending to the unborn as
well as the mothers, hapless and victimized as all are by a murderous social and economic system: the law of the market: a
disposal drain for the unwanted and unproductive.

.   .   .

One must be modest, even in hope. Jesus and Paul and other
great objectors notwithstanding, today Saul, not Paul rides tri-
umphant. The law is hardly placed so deeply in question as to
abrogate its power; by no means. Who would seriously claim
that the law has died of its own weight and tyranny, has lost its
hold on us humans, has been replaced by the "great law," the
law of the heart's rhythm and cry?

.   .   .

At least one can maintain this: the law is revealed for what it
is, in the stupendous intervention of God whereby Saul became
Paul. And for that we take heart. The crimes of Saul are clarified
in the act of conversion from crime. Those crimes were justified
by the law, executed by a fervent son of the law. They were legal crimes, each and all, imprisonments, executions, meticulously legal.

Thus the law itself is revealed as murderous, for it legitimates murder and clothes the murderer in a cloak of unassailable justification.

.   .   .

Let us be more precise as to this matter of the law as instrument of death. The law is the murder of Jesus. But the appetite of the law is scarcely satiated thereby. Not content with having removed "the Lord of life" from the world, the law forms a posse to pursue and prosecute his followers. The Name, the least trace of the divine one, the teaching, the example, the power that refuses to die, these must be expunged from the earth.

It cannot be said too often, or repeated to greater advantage; it is all done within the law, all legal. There can be no doubt of this point; the effort, successful in the main, at least for a while, to legalize the murder of Jesus and (legally) to extirpate the little community.

Paul addresses at length the Jerusalem populace:

"As a pupil of Gamaliel I was thoroughly trained in every point of our ancestral law. I have always been ardent in God's service...and so I persecuted this movement to the death, arresting its followers, men and women alike and committing them to prison.... It was they (the high priest and the whole council of elders) who gave me letters to our fellow Jews at Damascus, and I was on my way to make arrests there also and bring the prisoners to Jerusalem for punishment...." (Ch. 22, vv. 3ff.)

.   .   .

It is all there, the skeleton articulated, rattling menacingly, this admirable, self-enclosed, self-justifying system. Saul will not proceed on his way without authorization; the highest au-

thorities are compact with the enterprise; papers are drawn up
and signed. On Saul's hands the blood of Christians will lie, but
by no means to his condemnation. Rather, to his honor; for is he
not the instrument of an insatiable platonic reality? He and the
high priest and the Sanhedrin are but "doing their duty." They
are the earthly servants of a higher law.

Of the nature of this "higher authority," both surpassing and
vindicating worldly authority, a godlike power to be honored
and obeyed, of this Paul later wrote. It is notable that he identified this mysterious supremacy, writing to the Christians at
Ephesus, in the course of an imprisonment. Indeed jail brings,
then and now, an unwonted clarity of mind.

In that letter he identified the faith of Christians (their faith
and his, as struggle, drama, *agon*) unequivocally. The drama of
faith is not to be understood as the world would understand it.
The faith knows itself, its task and ethos, with a clarity the
world ("flesh and blood") can never reveal.

The faithful, that is, are not simply a "flesh and blood" adversary of "flesh and blood." The faith is not an element of this
world, however spiritual. Not as joined to the world can it be
pitted against the world. It comes to this: the weapons of faith
confronting the weapons of the world are totally other, which is
to say, nonviolent, the very "weapons" of Jesus. Paul names
them, in some detail: truth, integrity, the gospel of peace, salvation, the word of God.

.   .   .

And Paul names the adversary as well; in so doing, he de-
nies that the world can know itself. "Flesh and blood," ignorant
as it is of the nature of faith, cannot even know itself! —cannot
know that the world is enslaved, utterly bound over to a higher

power, the adversary not only of the faithful, but of its own good.

From these higher powers emanates the malignant power of the law, the law that holds "flesh and blood" in its bond, and would possess the faithful as well. One great swath and roundup, all bound over to death. Ourselves bound over.

.   .   .

Bound over to what? to whom? When he attempts to answer, Paul becomes unusually bleak. Phrases, names familiar to no one (least of all to ourselves) tumble from his pen. "Cosmic powers, principalities of this dark age, superhuman forces of evil in the heavenly realms...."

Stupefying. But let not the language put us off. Let us simply ponder an insight that as many believe, then and now, is central to our understanding of the faith, of our task. We also struggle against something vastly more ominous, momentous, than "flesh and blood."

.   .   .

It follows that the race toward nuclear oblivion is not to be understood as a merely human deviation, a going awry of political, social, military arrangements. This is the language of "flesh and blood," stone blind as to its own predicament.

Nor is the nuclear arms race to be thought of as a "problem" to be set right by experts, diplomats, the dissolution of the age of war, a cannier distribution of the world's goods and markets. The great powers are quite skilled in rearranging the world, even to admitting the existence of a less violent world, should the new shuffle accord with their interests. They might well arrive at an understanding that nuclear weapons are an anomaly, a waste. And so must be eliminated.

And nothing of reality would change. Neither on behalf of the beset poor, not in the plight of the enormously more beset rich.

.   .   .

The arms race is to be understood by Christians as a mystery of that evil we name death. It is the expression and symbol of the activity of "principalities,...of this dark age,...the superhuman forces of evil in the heavenly realms."

To assert this is by no means to acquit human forces of the evil they sponsor in our midst, in our time—they and their atrociously abused freedom. It is rather to indicate their enslavement (and ours as well), to the powers of death at large in a fallen world: powers alert to delay, to becloud, to deceive, to win over, to enlarge their claim and dominion.

.   .   .

We are not dismayed (though we are) by the divagations of humans in search of some absolute—gods, a god who may be thought, all unconsciously (or perhaps consciously enough), to justify their (our) worst instincts. Indeed the absolute, so it is commonly thought, sanctifies those instincts. They are like a sword doing double duty, one sacred, the other lethal. The sword is first placed on the altar as guerdon of holiness, then is taken away, for use. Thus in one form or another, all do obeisance to the power of death. Some are to take warning, others to take heart.

Saul took heart; the warning was not for him.

. . .

And then, in a sense classical and tragic, the hero's fortunes tumbled. Of that moment Paul is born. And the community so recently in his power, hunted down, imprisoned, executed, dares breathe again.

The conversion deserves the much abused name pentecostal. It could not be deserved, anticipated, organized—any more that Pentecost. It underscores the dependence of all, even of those whose god is the law, upon Someone other than the law; Someone whose power, intervention, saving grace, stand apart from all calculations, claim, observance, virtue or criminality, religious observance, ancestry, tongue, color, sex, genius, weakness.

. . .

We would like to believe in this God, who stands above human law, and from a mount higher than Sinai, issues the Great Command, and then is silent. We would like in our better moments to live in accord with that Command. So we say, and all but persuade ourselves. And for the most part, alas, we live in a far different fashion. Our institutions are protected "by law." The statement pretty accurately sums up our "faith"—in whom (or what) we place our hope.

So the institutions are granted an altogether displacing and distracting greatness. They stand surrogate for the faith itself. In their prospering or not, we read the only "signs of the times." It is as though one scrutinized for oracle, not the prophets, but the stock market.

Thus our conduct gives faith the lie. In the breach of history, as has happened time and again, institutions, the laws that surround them with immunity and unaccountability, assume a monstrous prominence. They tower like an Everest and cast a shadow at noon, obscuring the Great Command, as it touches on the fate of our neighbor.

. . .

Still, despite all, we record our relief and joy; we take heart. The early church, vulnerable and newborn, was relieved of its nemesis.

. . .

Our era is something else, so interminably cunning in its legal strategms, so morally dim. Saul and his generation continue to raven about the world; Paul is desperately slow to get born. So many die; so little relief is apparent. The Spirit breathes where the Spirit will—or does not. So we are told, cold comfort at best. And we voice, as best our grief allows, the plaint of the martyrs in Revelation: "How long, O God?"

. . .

What is the source of such hatred as then and now steeps the world in blood? Is Saul's hatred unsheathed against life itself?
And more to the point, what power could one day so transform the Sauls of the world that their hatred of life be transfigured in love?

. . .

Saul named Paul. No character in the church's history is so ambiguous as this changeling: so loved and detested, so combustably debatable. The centuries have not served to cool his ashes; they glow away in the darkness, unquenchable. If he had written nothing, if the sole record of his life and death were the *Acts* episodes, still he would tower on the horizon of the centuries like a Himalaya, would continue through many conflicts to speak in the organ tones of genius.

.   .   .

But those letters of his! Giants have wrestled with them, chapter and verse, a trudge up a Himalaya never finally bested. Faith, grace, Jesus savior and servant, the calling of Israel, the Spirit, baptism, resurrection, the nature of authority, the law, community and its sources and resources, terrors and rewards of ministry, rigors of prison, sexual conduct, lawsuits and the courts. Essentials and local trifles, he takes on all comers, this fierce oracular mediator and arguer.

Is there true teaching, and false as well? He praises the one and excoriates the other. Do questions fester on the air regarding duties of new converts? He will settle them, if not in a letter, then "when he comes"—a prospect only less daunting than the return of the Lord Himself. Is condemnation according to Christ? Then he will first pay the price and offer the example, writing the flock from his own "Birmingham Jail."

Are women to attain equal voice and place in the assembly? Are wives of equal dignity with their husbands? Here his vessel strikes a shoal. By no means, he insists. In this matter, vexed then as now, he is irreformably Jewish and misogynist. Conversion has failed to convert the corner of his synagogal heart where the woman huddle apart, veiled and voiceless.

No question too great, none too picayune. He must have been a terror; he probably, now and again, was a bore. To loose the scroll, to read aloud one of his letters in a local congregation, was like loosing on hapless heads the thunders of heaven.

Were they, the local churches, worthy of praise or blame—or both? They would shortly, unmistakably know.

Letter upon letter, details were set side by side with the vast questions that would furrow the brows of the ages. Mites crawled under the great vault of heaven; principalities wrestled among the planets. And he, observer of insects and their habits, recorder of the planets in their course.

.   .   .

The church as we know it would be unimaginable but for Paul. He is one of those pivots upon which our world, nicely balanced, was made to turn.

The conversion scene has passed into the lore of the tribe. Three separate times he returns to the moment on the Damascene road. He cannot loosen it from throat and mind; it lodges there, both credential and confession. The church, the pagan world must hear of it again and again; the fall, the confusion, the cloud of obscuring dust, the voice audible to him alone, "Saul, Saul, why are you persecuting me?" And he at wits' end, stuttering, "Who are you, Lord?" It was an impasse of understanding when the proud mind is newly humiliated, dark at noon; and on the moment is flooded with light. Like one bereft of wits, he answers his own question: "Lord."

Conversion, its epitome and nub—greatness brought low. No one enters this lowly gate proudly caparisoned, "breathing murderous threats." he must know what he has done, the shambles he has made of lives and of his own life. He must see the fine irony; the net he cast over others closes on him. He is brought low; the hunter becomes the hunted. And more to come. One day the champion of the law, in a better cause, will fall afoul of the law.

.   .   .

Miraculous means, the *fioretti* of the first generation, the memory of the tribe, the passing on of its story. The story is of an unlikely survival, an even less likely flourishing. The book of *Acts* continues in this vein.

.   .   .

A series of interlocking visions follows. One has a delicious sense of a holy, under-over rendezvous, of a two-tiered universe, earth and heaven swift with a game of hide and seek. Jesus appears to a new disciple Ananias to announce a meeting arranged in supernatural fashion, between himself and the chastened convert, blind as a bat at noon. Ananias, in prudent fashion, protests the errand; is he being sent into a trap baited by this fierce *poursuivant*?

The account is artless and direct. Jesus, high above mortal estate, but by no means relieved of the ordaining of earthly matters, is induced to explain the celestial strategy. The response takes the form of a notable encomium. Saul, the Lord insists, is an entirely special case; no wonder then if he requires special treatment, to wit, this intervention.

Gifts are distributed lavishly from on high. Ananias, heretofore unknown, becomes on the hour a healer. He seeks Saul out, relieves his blindness and confers the Holy Spirit.

.   .   .

The lion has found his thunder, his scope. A new phase, which merits the conferring in all sobriety, "new creation"; Paul, not Saul. Of what renown a lion who knows but one skill, that of ravening?

This lion surpassed his kind. From king of the beasts he has been transfigured—now he is regnant among humans. His voice will reach from end to end of earth and time. He will offer an utterly new possibility to others as earthbound as himself. They too against all chance may be reborn, as surely as they once were born.

.   .   .

To be reborn. To become, while nature stood aghast—human. Like a Beethoven or a Shakespeare, Paul will embody and celebrate the human. Afterward, so fierce a light cast on the humanity of God, such a shift in world understanding—it will be as though the human had not been before.

Now we know after the stupendous fact: the original Saul was a mere simulacrum of the human, a mockup; under the mask of law the inhuman lurked, writ large, writ dangerous.

King of the beasts, he is now greatly human. The glory, the shame, the grace and disgrace. "I myself will show him all he must go through for my Name's sake."

EIGHT

The Community moves out and out.
Of Peter and his works:
the healed one heals others.
Death shall have no dominion.

We leave Saul, the mighty newborn, to take his first steps in the new world.

He has a twin, Peter, though in different fashion reborn. Peter's moment of truth was, as we can infer, the earlier Pentecost. And his main function for the present, is that of healer: lest we forget in the rush and thunder of Saul, those dear and modest gifts that touch with unguent and word the ailing human body, our own.

Peter, be it known, can touch the immobile to life; the lingering paralytic Aeneas, the modest, workaday woman charmingly named "Gazelle," untimely stilled in death. Thus it is inferred: death in all guises must take warning: An invader is within; no limits to the disruption of the dark kingdom.

.   .   .

Tolstoi and his tales, the folk tales of any people, from Ireland to Russia and beyond! The raising of the woman is told in simplest words; the images stand clear, the emotion unfeigned. The words of Luke conjure the scene: an upper room, the body of a dead woman. Her friends stand about weeping. For proof of goodness, for entreaty, for sign of grief, they hold up before the eyes of Peter "the shirts and coats Dorcas had made while she was with them." They are irresistible. Peter sends them outside, kneels, commands the dead woman. She rises.

One might say, in light of such episodes as stop the heart in its tracks, Christianity was obsessed from the first with the bitter fact of death in the world. Here was the true, bare contest. Just as obsessed, or more so, with the sweet fact of life; there resounded in the bones of believers the call to take sides, to stand for the one against the other.

"Mors et vita duello conflixere mirando." "Death and life in awesome conflict joined." Peter, like Jesus, must enter the house of death which is the world; and against all expectation, raise the dead.

.   .   .

This was the heart of the matter. The resurrection of Jesus was their talisman, their credential, their warrant. They were like sheriffs sworn to break and enter the house where death had claimed the living. They entered and searched out death. And the dead walked again—because He was risen.

Life was thus, then and now, granted a slight edge over death; though the conflict would go on, bitterly, and without massive final outcome—until the Outcome, which is also sworn to.

Thus we have signs to walk by.

.   .   .

Death by napalm, death by carpet bombing, death by starvation, death by sorties, death in prisons and precincts, death by disappearance, death by the inadvertence of power...we know the horrid, necrophilic catalog of the century. And we know too a slight, all but invisible, all but voiceless alternative. By this we shall know it; it will not join the crush and rush, not climb aboard the death train, not sign up for the ideology, not join ranks, not fall into step. It has another word, a mere whisper to pass along and along:

Life; consequence; fear not.

.   .   .

Our book of *Acts* might be otherwise entitled, "The Book of Hectic Signs," or "The Book of Messages from the Muttering Cloud."

Or "The Book of Wonders." It has taken wing, voyaged the centuries; then, alas, it has landed in an arid place: the Church of Few Wonders Or None At All. No wonder that, so to speak, the book molts its pages away under our prosaic eyes! What, after all, are we to make of spirits, signs, wonders, healings on the instant, veritable resurrections, voices from on high, the Spirit impelling, napkins teeming with creation descending, tyrannical and otherwise unpromising spirits tamed, prison doors unaccountably opening, the prisoners sprung...?

It were best to admit it: we are spiritually out of our depth. Tamed if not housebroken, our church grown pale of visage and dim of action before rampageous nation states, our bishops and elders, ministers and priests and popes generally frantic or half coping or plain misreading the signs, our liturgy a shambles of trivialities. No wonder rote and rot are the daily portion of most, that we languish rather than cry out or gutly groan, that we expect for the most part that the heavens will stay shut and ourselves breathe shallow in the world—and all this, though celestial beings continue making shocking earthly weathers, portents, changes of heart, in an effort to win distracted attention.

NINE

Of signs and wonders.
How against all chance,
a persecutor is summoned to salvation.
Also how Peter,
much against his inclination,
is enlightened.

Wonders proceed space. It is hardly to be reckoned that the miraculous introduction we have been privy to in the story of Paul would go unmatched in Peter's. Turn about is fair! Peter, for all that he has grown pentecostally alert, stands anew in the charmed circle of beginnings, where all things marvelous grow possible, then probable—and finally make a bold epiphany before the first Christians' (and our) eyes!

We have a seven-fold drama, no less. Well for us, we are more or less used by now to the custom of heaven, casting as it does unexpected, not to say unlikely, characters in leading roles.

.   .   .

Here, for a start, a Roman officer. As to unsuitableness, he rates near peerless. He is under military orders, a jackboot of empire; his command sits heavy on a victimized people. Nonetheless, Luke is tireless in repeating word of his piety, alms, prayer, as though the centurion were in rather constant need of rehabilitation; or perhaps as though we were being required to take a closer look.

Cornelius is in any case, to that close look, an apt instigator of Peter's continuing adult education. We shall hear more, much more of this officer of note.

.   .   .

The first scene is of Peter at prayer; there follows a trance, and the wondrous episode hereby entitled, The Groaning Napkin of All Creation Descending.

At sight of this teeming bounty, Peter is urged, once more by a voice from on high (we have heard it before), "Take, kill, eat!"

Peter is a good Jew, he recoils. The napkin for all its plenitude, includes a menu notably, widely, perennially forbidden.

It is a weighty matter that lies before him, and ourselves also, in the disputed area of understanding. Peter shakes his head, No; he has been known before to stand bullish against heaven. We, for our part, are not to regard the scene lightly, or dismiss Peter's refusal as a matter of sectarian pique.

.   .   .

A tradition is at stake; for millennia, survival of the tradition has been indissolubly linked with survival of its vessel of election, the tribe. And closely bound in with the tradition, stand the dietary laws, and their close categories of "clean and unclean."

The matter of what one admits to mouth and guts for nourishment or delight is perhaps taken too lightly among us. A tradition of fasting has all but died out. So by and large has its counter, the joys of the groaning board, the banquet as image of the coming, straight from the kitchen of creation, of the Realm of God, Provider and Host.

The church no longer in effect teaches, invites or forbids in the area of diet; we are left to our own taste, which one is tempted to remark, often borders on the bizarre or downright lethal. We are also left other, less noble ways of satisfying hunger; we dine lonely and hasty, distractedly, often as not from frozen offerings.

Are we now to await, as image of our destiny, the advent of Fast Food from Heaven?

Among us, as is known and even taken glumly for granted, eating is often a joyless chore; and more among us die of gular and related ills of obesity and heart, than of hunger.

. . .

Thus we are ill equipped to understand the reluctance of Peter; his refusal strikes a discordant note in the ears of those prepared to consume creation to the lees, rather than banquet in honor of the Benefactor.

. . .

Not To Consume. It was the original command of Genesis. To eat, on occasion to banquet; never to consume. The former provides for need and invokes delight; the latter, only disaster. According to the horrific word of *Revelation,* consumers properly pursue their course on a battlefield; the image is surreal: scene of carnage becomes a kind of banquet hall of the damned. (Rev. 19:17-18). There, amid kites and vultures, they (we?) skirmish for a menu of dead flesh.

The image is a complex of the incongruous and irreconcilable. Yet there it is, as best we can understand; a battlefield-banquet, an anti-banquet of the realm, an anti-eucharist of the last days.

Fellini could do justice to it, or Cocteau. The ultimate consumers are warrior-cannibals.

.   .   .

We have seen Peter stand stubborn in other matters, lesser and greater. For the most part lesser. We have also seen him recusant in large matters badly grasped. One must concede (he would be the first to concede), he has shown himself in the Gospels to no great advantage in regard to wise choices and modest claims.

Here once again he takes his stand. On the rooftop, his prayer interrupted (or perhaps answered) the heavens opening like a cornucopia, it could be argued (and he so argues) something of moment is at stake, quotidian though it appears at first glance.

.   .   .

It seems important to examine, even to vindicate his refusal. The fact that he will shortly stand corrected in no wise undermines the seriousness of his objection.

He refuses, three times, which would recall earlier events from which he emerged shamefaced and subdued. A man of conviction to be sure, even when wrong. Here, by no means wrong. Nor so self-willed as not in time to yield. But in his own time.

.   .   .

The vision signaled an end to the old division of things, "clean and unclean." The voice said, "It is not for you to call profane what God counts clean." There are to be other ways of clarifying who one is, who the community is in the world, in the ages. The way of clean and unclean no longer serves; it serves only to enlarge the scope of dispute and exclusion, to extend areas of suspicion and sinfulness.

.   .   .

In Peter's time the division has widened to a ruinous degree. Now the law of clean and unclean casts a cold eye, a denouncing finger on humans also; the unclean include women and lepers and Samaritans and gentiles. The tribe has tightened to a fist. Yahweh, God of the nations, is reduced to a tribal god, a god of exclusions. Only members of the tribe and keepers of the law stand in the narrow orbit of salvation. (Including, it goes without saying, the keepers of a law which, rightly understood, has little to do with approved or condemned foods, and much to do with approved or condemned humans.)

.   .   .

Peter is puzzled; his noonday prayer is a shambles. He was praying, it is implied, for anything but this! A crisis of understanding has intruded. Who can this God be, who lets down the napkin of creation like a heavenly ark, everything tumbled about confused, good and bad together—and then utters a kind of preprandial grace, and bids one set to?

Who is this God? One ascends a roof in order to address the Deity at prayer, with reasonable assurance as to Whom one is addressing, as to one's errand in the world, one's religion and its bounden duties. And then, to one's worshipful dismay, the gentle interlude, the easy communion, more—the very scheme and fabric, the yin and yang of a reality on which one had staked everything, are torn apart? Who is this God?

Was not this the approved way for centuries, that the good was crucial to the worship, that gestures of take or refuse, feast and fast, defined the day, the year's rhythms, the persistence of memory?

It is the larger question furrows the brow. What is the import of the teeming napkin? What can this question of diet have to do with the larger world, with neighbor welcomed or rejected, gentile and Jew?

. . .

"While Peter was still puzzling over the meaning of the vision, the messengers from Cornelius...arrived at the entrance." There comes a knocking at the door. As in *Macbeth*, portentous; unlike Macbeth, hopeful. In any case, an unlikely and yet so befitting clue. The Spirit summons; Peter descends from the questionable banquet to the no less questionable visitors.

Luke's skill in story telling! The one episode will shed light on the other.

. . .

It is finally in the house of Cornelius, before an assembly, that the light breaks on Peter's mind. He may perhaps be forgiven for making no mention in his account, of the rooftop event of high noon; the banquet of hoof and claw from on high, the unlikely arrival of a teeming menagerie. Would the story strain all credence? He passes over the puzzling vision, and comes immediately to the point of his enlightenment, just as though this had occurred in the most natural way in the world.

"God has shown me that I must not call anyone profane or unclean; that is why I came here without demur when you sent for me." We are invited in the subtle way of Luke to note the artless transition on Peter's tongue. His account goes from "anything...unclean" to "anyone...unclean." The passage slides along easily. Peter has gotten the point. But a more tumultuous voyage through the white water of the Spirit could scarcely be imagined.

"God has shown me"; he is forthright as always. Only the Holy Spirit at the helm brings humans and their frail currach through the treacherous shoals that encircle the human tribe.

We imagine the history of the taboo, how harmless it is at the start, even how beneficial. Then, left to time and inclination, it subverts a larger human inclusion. (It turns by the same token against those it was designed to protect.) The original command turns lethal; from forbidden foods to forbidden humans.

And more; the same perversity that altered the original, now urges the inviolate character of the new, radically enlarged version. Thou shall not eat becomes thou shall not make welcome.

The stranger at the gate has become the enemy at the gate. We have here a clue as to the degradation of covenant. The dead end of tribalism, apartheid in all its hideous, multiple forms— and all in the name of God.

It is unknown to us, what crimes we wreak in the world, all in the name of God.

Who is my neighbor? We hardly know. We know with far greater acuteness, who is my enemy.

.   .   .

The unknown neighbor? It could be argued, and was—we had always known. There was a time when we looked the neighbor in face. And yet we kept our distance. This was the meaning of the "other"; distance. And so distrust. We knew him too well (he knew us too well), which is to say, each knew only the worst of the other, and nothing of the goodness. Knew, or concluded one knew, the strategms, the coldness, the alienation. Then the fear.

And on bloody occasion, offense offered, they or we, or each simultaneously, as though in a mirror game, took up arms. The distancing, the ground between, a no man's land, invited hatred. No one walked there, conversed there, traded there. The time was ripe for other uses than the human; with treacherous ease the world became a battleground.

.   .   .

Religion played its part, a large one. That boundary, closely drawn, those rituals, their memories enshrined and recalled. That banquet; its approved or forbidden foods; then its approved or forbidden guests!

It came to this perhaps: the first and last question hammered home, in the liturgy, in the lessons taught children, in the wisdom of the elders passed. What is the price of survival? Then the answer: we must pay it, and others as well, bitter though the payment.

.   .   .

In time this happens. The price becomes a burden beyond bearing; it weighs people under, they cannot budge. Especially the poor, and women, and lepers, and Samaritans to a degree. The outsiders, who in the beginning and at least on occasion, might be allowed within, allowed at table, these are dismissed *in perpetuo*. The line that originally was drawn tentatively, and easily erased or altered, now is deepened and widened to a pale. Some are permanently outside the pale. Thus saith the law.

And all in the name of God, as goes without saying, and as the law stiffens, all the more frequently said. As though indeed, as things become more evidently inhuman, the divine must all the more insistently be incanted.

.   .   .

Let us pursue the matter to its end. Those who decree the burden themselves become the burden. They ride effortlessly and without payment on the backs of their victims. This is the conclusion of Jesus in his series of "Woes" uttered against the religious mandarins in Matthew's Gospel. (23:13-36)

.   .   .

Thus if we make much of a purportedly small matter, what is to be eaten and what not, it appears that God does so also. The small matter has become a great one indeed. What is allowed on the menu and what forbidden determines with the force of an oracle who is seated at the table—and who not.

The table is thus an image of the world. And the question raised by the image can become a monstrous one: who is worthy to dwell in the world and who not.

And then a disposition is made, something known darkly and terribly as a "definitive solution."

.   .   .

Thus a fatal line is drawn across the body of humanity; it is often drawn with a sword. The matter of a menu and its laws has become a great matter indeed, wide as the world, and bloody as a busy sword.

.   .   .

A chastened Peter has come step by step to a truth; from the unlikely napkin ballooning down, to the unlikely visitors at his door. And in time, on to table hospitality, and in a new spirit, to his work in the world. He begins, I now understand how true it is that God plays no favorites. But that in every nation, those who are godfearing and just are acceptable to God."

And so our story goes (and does not go, is stuck) to this day.

TEN

Strong bars do not a prison make;
Peter walks free.
For the tyrant, another outcome awaits.

Peter has his Herod, as Jesus did. Once again, capital execution threatens a capital figure.

Irony upon irony; it is the time of Passover, the anniversary of the execution of Jesus. Jews are celebrating their liberation from slavery. And Peter is in bondage.

In contrast with the passover of Jesus, there is a sense in the midst of the powerless community of a new power at their command.

It is "the very night before Herod had planned to produce the prisoner"; which is to say, Peter's execution is decreed for the day following.

But this is not the first Thursday we name holy. Then the holy protagonist underwent his *agon* alone in a remote garden, the disciples "sleeping for sorrow."

We are told of a momentous present difference: "The church kept praying fervently to God for Peter."

. . .

What follows is another unlikely liberation scene, detail upon detail. Could one doubt then or now (can Luke's beleaguered community doubt) that angels attend such prisoners as Peter—such prisoners as regularly are being (and shall be) plucked from their communities? More, can Christians doubt, in light of these stories, that imprisonment and death itself are the silliest fictions in the entire, absurd armory of tyrants?

. . .

Peter's cell is suddenly ablaze. He is chained, doubly secured, guards sleeping at his side, doors locked, guards at the portal. It is all a vain show; it all comes to naught. An angel stands there; every detail of what follows is scrupulously reported; events go as smoothly as though there had occurred beforehand, a heavenly rehearsal. A tap on the shoulder, a quick summons, Get up? and Peter's chains fall away.

Belt, sandals, cloak, doors opening of accord. Luke's prose has the surreal quality of a dream sequence, and Peter the dreamer. The pen wavers on the page; hilarity or solemnity? Plain bewilderment maybe: "Peter had no idea the angel's intervention was real; he thought it was a vision."

Such an event leaves not only Peter light of head. What are we to make of it all? Undeniably, on the phiz of the world's tyrants and judges and jailers, an iron look abides, then as today, and bodes ill. Their locks hold tight, their guards are vigilant. We require, alas, no instruction as to the methods of Herods or their historical pertinacity.

. . .

Their architecture? Prisons, interrogation centers, execution chambers are the dark extensions of centripetal flying dreams. Bridges of sighs are inevitably raised between the great chambers of state and the necessary dungeons. There the traffic of misery is heavy and constant, a muffled drum of doom.

. . .

Of Peter's liberation, so unlikely, so abrupt in the telling, we may at least say, it sends a message in two directions: to the tyrants and to the church. To the first it speaks of the absolute fatuity of their crimes. The swords are not only obsolete, they are wooden simulacra. And to the church, it speaks of the hope that stretches beyond this world, a hope that now and again, breaks into dungeons with the word: Fear not, come out!

. . .

Still, the community fears mightily for Peter's fate. It could hardly be otherwise. The friends take to prayer. It is a last ditch measure; it has the tone of a vigil for the dying. Peter is to be "led out" like an animal to the slaughter, in the morning. What else than prayer can they turn to, when no swords are at hand to forfend Caesar's sword; more exactly (and more justly to this community), when none are sought?

They expect only to hear the news of his death; that perhaps, and the slight chance that his body will be delivered up to them. Minimal favors from on high; and all connected with death, its inevitability.

And then there comes a great beating at the outer door. Peter has made his way through the midnight streets to the "safe house" where they are gathered. And they cannot believe it, his deliverance. The maid is swept away in the rising tempest of his coming. She leaves him there at the gate, stumbles into the dwelling to tell the impossible good news.

144 Daniel Berrigan, S.J.

. . .

The assembly is at prayer, they hope for an outcome of prayer. What the outcome might be, they are hard put to tell. And perhaps it is better so, not dwelling on the outcome concentrates the heart on the prayer itself. Peter, they believe (they hope), is in better hands than theirs.

But wait. They miss something, as believers in sore straits commonly do. They do not grasp the reality of prayerful hope (any more than ourselves). Which is to say, of hope against hope. They do what they can; not much, as the world would account for it; prayer.

For they too are bound over to the law, unable to give immediate succor, let alone to liberate their friend. They must learn a hard lesson, a bitter; what Christians can and cannot do, what lies in our power (even in the power of our prayer) and what does not.

The best outcome they can conjure, even at prayer, is a good death. Let us pray: That Peter might have a good ending. But his deliverance alive is beyond the scope of their prayer, of their hope. Even at prayer, death is the issue, not life or deliverance.

. . .

Luke, one thinks, implies all this: the limits of the prayer, even of the prayer of the saints—even of those who shortly before suffered the death of the apostle James, then must witness the arrest of Peter and his imminent execution; and what these horrid events portend for them: the shadow of the tyrant, a presentiment of doom.

We think of a prayer that looks for a minimal return, petitions minimal favors. Or refuses to grow peremptory. Or so announces its plea, as the Savior prayed in the course of his passion: Let this cup pass from me. But adds the clause that leaves the outcome in other hands: thy will be done. The choices are wide, the space for the heart's speech generous.

.   .   .

The tradition honored here is old as the book of Daniel, and older. It concerns the strange empowerment of the powerless, the exiles and slaves upon whom God's compassion rests. It is enough that "the church made continual prayer for him." The Spirit offers the form, the words—as well as the surprising outcome.

.   .   .

We have prayed, many of us for years, that our brother Jesuits in El Salvador might be spared. They were not spared. On a certain night, their bodies, mutilated, defamed, were "produced in public."

And the prayer did not cease. It took on a new urgency. The point, I take it, was not to insist on justice from the unjust; we leave that perforce to the God of justice. The point of the continuing prayer is to attempt to bring a halt to the mass killing, of which the Jesuit deaths were but one horrid example.

Our prayer took many forms. Some were arrested at federal buildings, others at the Pentagon and White House. At the latter, friends brought vials of their own blood, mingled with the earth of El Salvador, earth that received the blood of the murdered Jesuits. They mingled the earth and blood, and anointed the portals with that sign of guilt and forgiveness, for all to see.

.   .   .

It is typical of Luke's sensibility that the Episode of the Unlikely Return is bathed in a mix of awe, lightness of heart, delays and alarms, absurdity even. The condemned one, free as a night bird, stands at the gate. Too good to be true? It is a resurrection scene in a minor key; too much happening, minds reeling, quick quick, take it in! (It cannot be taken in.) Reason, tried beyond measure, between tears and laughter cries instinctively, this cannot be.

What cannot be, is. We are invited to rehearse or recollect— the resurrection.

. . .

From the deliverance of Peter to the death of the tyrant; for Luke this is a short lyric leap.

Herod's dungeon is rendered irrelevant; its locks are sprung, its prey at large. As Herod stands for pure threat, pure exploitation, pure violence (and he stands for little else) he is already countermanded by a greater power; he is dead as his edicts.

Enough therefore of the "Acts of Herod." There remains only to tell of the manner of his death, to adjust its details nicely, in view of the scope and sense of the book—the Acts (in the present instance) of Peter.

Peter and his community have shown one way of coping, with threats, with prison, with death itself. They simply speak the truth and pay up; they go to prison and risk death. It is all quite simple: the truth is worth the price. The fate of the faithful is in other hands than Herod's; in submission is strength, the steadfastness of the saints.

. . .

There is another way of responding to Herod and his kind. it is not Christian in the heroic mold of *Acts*. It implies little of understanding and less of strength.Yet to many, it is perhaps the only way available in the circumstance; or at least people have concluded so, not merely in Caesaria, but elsewhere.

The tyrant, we are told, traveled once to the beleaguered towns of Tyre and Sidon, there to hold court and consider the fate of his suffering subjects. The cities are starving; the hope is that the ruler will take their plight seriously.

But his name is Herod. In accord with his kind, one topic only is of point, the advantage of his rule. What shall his message be? Peace or war?

Herod addresses the people; we are told nothing of his message. It is, Luke implies (and how Luke loves speeches!), of no interest. But to the starving people who have gathered to learn their fate, only one recourse seems apt to evoke mercy. Flattery.

Herod speaks; shortly he is interrupted with a burst of hectic fervor. "It is a god speaking, not a man."

Tyrant that he is, and fool, he takes their foolishness kindly, takes it to his foolish heart. His demise, Luke says, follows on the moment.

He has been dead for so long! "Instantly an angel of the Lord struck him down, because he had usurped the honor due to God; he was eaten up with worms, and so died."

.   .   .

The slate of one tyrant is wiped clean, his words words words are written in water. We have heard them, we hear them, we shall hear them, a mad declension of folly and fury.

Pity is that for so many earnest citizens and sycophants, such words issuing from such a source as this, convey the very substance of meaning, history, citizenship, loyalty. Whereas such words are no more than a form of terrorizing nonsense.

Academics pore over the words of Caesars and Herods as though they breathed there a precious myrrh of wisdom. And the tyrants perish and achieve a kind of ersatz resurrection in their outlandish monuments; truth told, the cenotaphs of their victims.

Luke is nothing if not subtle. Reporting as he does, meticulously and at length the speech of the faithful throughout *Acts*, trustful as he is in the supernal power of the word, he gives not an inch to Herod's windy final utterance.

.   .   .

Herod laconically disposed of, the episode concludes with a muted paean of triumph—not for the death of the imperial adversary (living or dead, he is finally irrelevant to the task at hand). Luke's joy is for the flourishing of the word, all jeopardy notwithstanding. "Meantime the word of God continued to grow and spread...."

Even, be it noted, at the heart of the empire, the army. On Herod and Caesar notice is served. Not idly does Luke point out, but with a light elegant thrust of his rapier: the first convert among the gentiles is an officer of the imperial forces. Conversion? more aptly, subversion!

ELEVEN

More concerning Saul named Paul;
of voices and healings,
of comings and goings without end.

Once more the Spirit is heard, counseling the next move.

We are told nothing of mode or means, merely that the Spirit issued marching orders to Paul. Such a presence, speaking with such urgency, is all but taken for granted; to Luke it seems unnecessary to interpose a human voice or vote.

We are offered only a general pattern of the proceedings. A pentecostal sense was in the air, commending both fasting and prayer. Beforehand, the community prepares; afterward, they test the spirits. At some point certainty is reached, doubts erased. In consequence Luke can write, with an audacity that stops the breath, "the Holy Spirit said..." As on another occasion, "we and the Holy Spirit have so decided..."

We are unused to visionary intrusions, and being unaccustomed, would hesitate long before claiming it. Can it be that we have neglected the evangelical counsel of prayer and fasting?

.   .   .

To Paul and Barnabas it yet seems possible that the word will be esteemed among Jews. (We remain unsure today, and with reason, whether the same word is welcome among Christians.)

Their hope has its reason: a heartwarming reception awaits them in the synagogue of Pisidian Antioch.

The scene would make hope bloom in the wintriest heart. They are given a warm welcome by the officials, and an even warmer reception by the people. (And this after, not before Paul's sermon, which is uncompromising as ever.) Both Jews and Gentiles follow them out of the synagogue, we are told; and the missioners are invited to return on the following sabbath.

The audience this time is enormous: "Almost the whole city gathered to hear the word of God."

In a rare instance, we are granted a glimpse of what might have been. Friendship, comity, worship, one faith, one confession, the two stocks grafted in one, "neither Jew nor Gentile."

.   .   .

No one requires telling.

The burden is a heavy one; the ideal, the will of God—all was frustrated, stopped short. Instead, horrors, pogroms, ghettos, forced conversions, many a grand inquisitor, and finally, or nearly finally, in our lifetime, a holocaust. And for the survivors, inching ashore out of a history of bloodletting, Israel, a homeland.

And now the past rises up like a chorus of avenging furies, forgetting nothing, forgiving nothing: the uprising, the maltreatment of Palestinians, the brutality, the hideous distorting mirror held up, Medusa staring back, the grotesque crimes, the unsavory justifications....

.   .   .

We grow used to Christian crimes, we are horrified at Jewish crimes. This is surely a double standard, to be renounced. And yet, and yet, we cry out: have probity and innocence fled the world?

Could the ages have presented a different outcome, could the word of God have been presented as something other than a bone of contention, tossed hither and yon, creating of one people two warring factions? Could Christians have accepted the Savior's people from the beginning, knowing that all sprang from a common stock? Might history have worn another face than the bloodstained one we know so well?

Alas, the temperate season appears—and then is shortly blasted. Spring was an illusion of a day; merciless, winter descends.

.   .   .

Thus begins a pattern that can only harden, as a lava that first flows hot and then halts and hardens, sealing the earth. Special interests are at stake, so is ego. On both sides, though unequally at the start. The Jews are in possession, the "missioners" are few, and outsiders to boot. The new message is hard indeed, and presented in stony language. Almost a model, one thinks, of how to alienate others from a belief, no matter how dearly held.

The lost chance! the chance history does not hold out twice!

With Luke we stand at the beginning. There are as yet no intervening awful centuries, mutual recrimination, overlordship high and mighty on one side, victimization unforgotten and festering on the other. There is only—Jesus, the devastating matter of his death (and at whose responsibility?). And this proves enough, and more, to kindle the fires: like a self-combusting hell, to this day unextinguished.

The fires mutter and smoke, on and on; they and the two factions entrenched behind. *Procul esto!* let no one come near;

Auschwitz is ours, its earth is forsworn; it will never be yours, even as a place of prayer.

.   .   .

ACTS 14: 8-28

Meantime. At Lystra, Paul, still accompanied by Barnabas, repeats almost to a nicety, the earlier miracle of Peter at the gate named Beautiful. The eyes of the healer are fixed on a disabled man and he walks. Now we are in gentile territory, and the re-action of both the crowd and the authorities is wild with delight. Jesus is unknown here, healing in His name is hardly to be con-sidered a criminal act; quite the contrary. A storm of religious enthusiasm greets the two mysterious strangers; they must be venerated for the gods they undoubtedly are.

The scene that follows might have been incised on a classical Greek vase. "The priest of Zeus, whose temple was just outside the city, brought oxen and garlands to the gates, and he and the people prepared to offer sacrifice."

The proceeding stands at the very opposite pole from the persecution such healings as this have commonly aroused. The missioners can bear the latter with equanimity; but adulation that approaches adoration? The street is abustle with ominous preparation; it sets a panic rising in their hearts. "But when the apostles Barnabas and Paul heard of it, they tore their clothes and rushed into the crowd shouting, 'Why are you doing this? We are human beings, just like you....' "

There is an irony of note here. Was it not the Greeks who once for all diagnosed the sin above all sins, the pride that im-pelled humans to play god, thereby sowing wrath, and ensuring the destruction of the presumptuous hero?

And behold, two hapless humans here being victimized, two mere men pushed to the verge by a folly of enthusiasm. They are about to be raised to high heaven! And this when they know beyond doubt that the power moving through them is from Another—and they, no more than empty hands outstretched, to receive and give.

.   .   .

Thus went the fevered gentile response to a first exposure before the power of the Way. And thus we are introduced to the peculiar gentile temptation, far removed from the Jewish as heaven from earth. Paul will diagnose both in his letter to the Christians of Corinth.

To the Jews the new teaching is blasphemy; its announcement awakens only religious frenzy and reprisal. To the gentiles, as will be seen, the same word is simply foolishness; no right mind could take it seriously. In the present episode, the wonder that accompanies the word offers no telling proof of its power. Beyond doubt the healing is to be taken seriously, gratefully. But the word, the invocation of a god, a "Jesus" heretofore unknown, signals only a new error; two eminent members of the pantheon have descended in their midst. "Barnabas they called Zeus, and Paul they called Hermes, because he spoke for both."

.   .   .

Adulation, persecution; sometimes the two arrive together, and the fusion is combustible indeed. "Jews from Antioch and Iconium came on the scene and won over the crowds. They stoned Paul, and dragged him out of the city, thinking him dead."

.   .   .

There is a Greek myth, indeed an entire mythology, concerning the destiny of the hero. Oedipus must be self-blinded; even though ignorant, he has transgressed a taboo. Orpheus must be both honored and slain. His person is godlike, his guise human. Therefore, since he is both transcendent and immanent to humankind, two seemingly opposed responses are called for. The godlike one must be adored, and he must be slain, his bones scattered, his flesh eaten. The former pays tribute to his divinity, the latter brings into our entrails and heart, his sublime human virtue.

The incanting of the godlike Paul, and his stoning by the religious mob, are thus closely (and truthfully) juxtaposed by Luke. We are to take note of "primitive" responses that here, as in most instances, are not primitive at all; they merely play chameleon down through the ages. They are closer to our instinct and conduct than most are prepared to admit.

Both responses are forms of violence, powerful instinctive gestures of evasion. They are simply sins of omission, ritually performed. The stoning, be it noted, is as religiously conceived and ordained (it is after all, mandated in the law) as the worship whose intention preceded it.

What each attempts to evade is simply the human; indeed the rites celebrate the evasion. The evasion and its rites thus move in two directions; the Greeks attempt to raise the human to a species of divinity; the Jews would destroy the human when an unconscionably broad vista is opened before the human, in Christ.

TWELVE

Of burdens lifted, not imposed.
And of the well nigh intolerable
lightness of faith.
Finally, of dissentions.

ACTS 15

Then, we are told, divisions erupt among these communities of the Spirit.

Is this to be accounted news, or shocking? One would not think so. Mere humans, alight with pentecostal fires, undertake two rigorous tasks. Some sojourn afar, others nurse the holy fires at home. Everything has changed, nothing has changed. Which is to say that the advent of the Spirit has created the first Christian witnesses; at the same time, Pentecost has obliterated nothing of prior differences in vocation and temperament.

Some we are told, are chosen as gyrovagues to wander about the world; others are appointed to attend the flock once gathered. The choice, be it suggested, is no less a matter of the Spirit than of the spirit; being chosen does not preclude human choices. We have lurking here the very large possibility of "fierce dissension and controversy."

. . .

All sorts and manner of questions arise. What is to be done with regard to new converts? What burdens, observances, codes are to be laid or lifted? Is a gentile convert to be judaised as the price of becoming a Christian? Or at a deeper level, even more disturbing, who is the church anyway? Who makes it up, who rules, by what authority? Who obeys, and at whose mandate?

These are matters of some moment, with implications that shake the drum of time with a fierce rhythm—even today. Far deeper than temperament lies—choice. Which is to say, the untrammeled choice of the Spirit, blowing where and when She will, and on whom She will—this determines the *status quaestionis*. Nothing else. Neither admirable nor abominable character, liberal or narrow leanings, psychological strength or weakness, sexism or other proclivities toward domination—neither these, nor a humiliating or honorable past, moral worthiness or its opposite, a speedy or slow passage from darkness to light—none of these is to count for a feather's weight either in the conferring of baptism, or the moral code laid down.

.   .   .

The gentile world, new converts beating at the door. What price of admission, if any, is to be exacted? The issue was bound to rise. Under the world-encompassing vision of Paul, the small, local, rather hidebound Jewish community of Pentecost has been urged aboard ship and nudged into open sea. The astrolabe of Paul is scanned; steering is by the stars. The daring course, the unknown, the wind of the Spirit in the sails!

Too much has happened too quickly; winds are at cross purpose; bickering hampers the passage of the trireme *Ecclesia*, outward bound.

It is time, they judge, to haul into port, drop anchor and assess the situation.

.   .   .

Here and now they must decide on a question that touches them deeply (and ourselves hardly at all; indeed a question that seems inordinately parochial). What obligations are to be imposed by an almost totally unoethnic community, a proud, persistent and immemorially persecuted people, on the multiethnic converts who are crowding the portal, seeking admission?

The plight of the would-be converts is indeed darksome; it inspires both revulsion and pity among the Jewish Christians, but hardly what might be thought of as a fulsome welcome. Those who seek baptism are, after all, pagans; they languish outside the pale of salvation. They have in their favor neither promise, covenant nor torah; no temple, no prophets, no God.

And then, those inside. The massive symbols coalescing throughout history like coral on a living reef. Elaborations of divine mercy that in desert and exile made of bones dry bones, an articulated body of believers—Jewish, then Jewish-Christian—these have been denied the benighted peoples of the outer rim, dwelling as they do "in darkness and the shadow of death."

.   .   .

Or so it seems to those within. We for our part, are not overly patient with questions of rules and ethical demands laid upon hapless outsiders by those in possession, a price of entry so to speak; unworthy of both sides, those called, those welcoming.

Still it may be that our impatience is ill-timed. If we find the questions faced by the early community tediously beside the point, we may be taking for granted a settlement which can only be thought of as generous, indeed inspired.

.   .   .

A long-term question is implied in the immediate one. What ethical essentials are implied in the Great Command, at a given time, among a given people?

Such questions will never be done with; they ride on the living, questing prow of *Ecclesia*; they whisper in the sails. For every voyage, a sabbath ashore. Time and again, the ship must turn about and seek port, seek respite and recall. Again and again, such caucuses must be decreed as occurred here for the first time, between the wanderers and the fixed stars, in Jerusalem.

.   .   .

Thus the pattern is of import, the rhythm. Moral conclusions drawn anciently in Jerusalem no longer detain us, gentiles though we are. But the method endures. Here and there and everywhere in the church, expansion and ingathering, the breath of the body, alternate in the world's air. Early on, such rhythms of faithful understanding are set in place by these inspired sisters and brothers.

In this order: first the experience of those who labor afar is heard from. "Barnabas and Paul described all the signs and portents God had worked among the gentiles through them."

Then the Scripture and tradition are consulted. James sums up: "This [God's choice of a people from among the gentiles] agrees with the words of the prophets; 'all the gentiles whom I have claimed for my own.' "

.   .   .

One more note. The conclusion they reach is a generous one: "To lay no further burden upon you beyond these essentials...." How sensible it seems, after the fact! Jewish law is not to be imposed on non-Jews. And joy fills the hearts of the community. The converts are integrated with ease; the welcome from Jerusalem is wholehearted.

.   .   .

Shortly thereafter we are told unflinchingly of a parting of the ways, of dissension in the high command, the missionary front line. Paul and Barnabas fall out disastrously.

Hard to take in! We are long accustomed, if not inured, from our catechetically stupefied childhood, and on through later pulpit inanities, to searching the Scriptures solely for ideal types. Yet a common experience of life would urge that we pause. The world is larger, wider than a communion of "ideal types"! Or better, the Christian ideal itself is wider than a certain kind of religion would allow.

Make room, make room in mind and heart! Give place to the untidy, unfinished, brusque human! Alas, we are ill-prepared by our mentors and preachers to heed the complexity and strength of character, daring, imagination, required in order to hold the tiller firm, to steer the ship like an arrow, straight into the storm.

.   .   .

Two great men go separate ways. Whatever the immediate loss, the breakup of so stupendous a partnership, the tenor of what follows offers a tempered assurance. The decision was a sensible one. Doubtless, to change the image, the church has need of both Barnabas and Paul; but the idea of two eminences, not one, each so to speak in tandem command of the ship *Ecclesia,* one fore and one aft, or one captain by day, the other on night watch—this is hardly imaginable, let alone practicable. The decks would buckle and break under the command and countermand of two such giants.

THIRTEEN

A dream is taken seriously.
Luke passes from author to protagonist.
Also of women in the church.

ACTS 16: 1-10

The Spirit nudges the ship away from certain shores, for reasons that remain obscure. Finally, a momentous night vision determines the next port.

Like it or not, we have had airborne napkins by day and angels by night; and more than once, voices from clouds, and a mysterious Being variously referred to, now as the holy Spirit, now as the Spirit of Jesus.

This time, a night vision erupts, a personal visitation; not, according to Luke's text, a dream. Or perhaps a dream, but one of superior and solemn content. Its person too is unique; no heavenly being, but a corporal man stands before Paul, a Macedonian. He knows the dreamer and his work in the world; he pleads, *Come help us.*

Something to give pause. Only one form of help is possible and that, of course, totally unknown in the land of the vision. Can the plea for "help," uttered in so general a way, indicate the primordial yearnings of a humanity as yet incomplete, longing, awaiting through Jesus its final crown?

We come on these hints and starts continually in Luke's story: what one might think of as the theory and practice of the human, suggested, adumbrated among the world's tribes; taken in account, violated at times, again clear, radiant, announced, celebrated.

Our humanity in Jesus. That icon of humanity, luminous in the darkness, walks the waters toward yet another shore. And the humanity of the Macedonians stirs like the unborn. Come, help us! The people are by no means to be left to shift for themselves, forever prenatal, doomed to their own prehistory.

Salvation is near. Macedonia too is reverenced, will be evangelically nurtured. The word of salvation will be carefully translated in view of time and place, language and custom. The people will be and become—themselves. Themselves in Him, in whom alone we can be—ourselves. Divinely linked, one to another, genealogically sons and daughters, sisters and brothers.

Something of this the vision implies—headily, one adds, especially in view of maladaptations and frictions that have marred the vision elsewhere. And, alas, will continue. It could hardly be claimed, in view of the realism of Luke, that the acts of those who follow (or indeed the primary acts of the apostles) have invariably brought in their wake, unity and healing.

.   .   .

We have not had account of such a vision before. Humans do not in Scripture commonly make epiphanies one to another, at least not with divine warrant. Thus the vision of the Macedonian has all the force and urgency of a summons of God. And it is dealt with and honored as though the Spirit herself were beckoning and entreating, not a mere human.

"As soon as Paul has seen this vision, we set about taking passage to Macedonia, convinced that God had called us to take the good news there."

A sense of the human erupting! A human instigates the next move! "We set about...we sailed...here we stayed...." Suddenly Luke is at center stage.

We have had nothing of the kind in *Acts,* nor in any of the gospels, where the common mode is that of third person recording of event, an outsider's view of personage and time and, now and again, of meaning.

.   .   .

Now it is as though a meticulous and subtle author has grown impatient with his bystander's role. Why merely record momentous days and nights, when one is in fact planted deep amid it all? Why not scotch, at least for a time, at least now and then, the fiction of the "sympathetic third" whose only task is the precise setting down of a story enacted by others? When as matter of fact, one is enduring the same chills and fevers as the protagonist, one is aflame and icy with a like hope nearing, a like hope deferred. Why not emerge now and then from the page, declare one's self, say it straight out: I, Luke, together with Paul and Silas, we made this voyage, endured this, rejoiced at that....

It would seem that the occasion of this momentous decision, to step forward on the page—is the vision of the Macedonian.

Let us venture something. Surely Luke heard from Paul of the night vision, for it was the basis of their next move. And the vision worked a further wonder in our scribe; it changed utterly his stance and style.

.   .   .

Our Acts, as well as the Apostles'.

Do we have a hint offered here, and more? The book, we have suggested, is still open, and we too are urged to pass (if ever so slowly, clumsily) from reader, meditator, scribe, recorder, admirer, third party, bystander—to the authentic, difficult, responsible "I" and "we" of the *Acts*. The book open, the acts still unfinished. Let all emerge from the shadowy protection of the "she," "he," and "they."

All, all is changed. It is as though the book had reached toward us, like two hands responding to a tentative gesture, had embraced us, one by one. Included us. And lo! we too have lines to speak, choices to make, actions to dare. I, we, have part in the momentous narrative, the beginnings, the large setbacks and small triumphs, the tragic and comic episodes, the contemplative hours, the pell-mell, headlong conflicts. Part also in the outcome, for better or worse. Page after page clank as a newborn face, awaiting the time, and me, and us.

. . .

Thus Luke also, now "I," now "he," turns and turns about; a tease, a dramatic changeling.

. . .

ACTS 16: 11-40

The episode at Philippi is a sorry reminder of the small place held by women in the community and its story. It seems almost as though the twentieth-century plight of the church (which is by no means the plight of women alone, but of all) is here adumbrated.

Why a sorry situation should perdure so stubbornly, why arrangements so inhuman, un-Christlike, abide so persistently, why a dishonorable and by no means benign neglect and denial is the common lot of Catholic women, why a sinful situation is accorded the dubious dignity of a dogma—indeed the *mysterium iniquitatis* cuts all answers short.

.   .   .

The plight of the whole church. Half the church legislates; the law is enacted for the whole church. Not only that; half the church ventures solemn moral opinion on economics or peace, on behalf of the entire human race. A truly wondrous innocence governs such pronunciations. It is as though peace and justice were commended to the world by half the church—even while that same blithely violates the same virtues and realities in its own communion.

Of late, half the church is moved to venture on an even sorrier exercise, one more nearly related to the other half. The hierarchy writes a letter concerning women in the church; as though indeed women were the problem, and not the hierarchy itself (and the lowerarchy as well).

It is as though a male, white government, afflicted by the illness of apartheid, were to issue a lengthy statement regarding "the problem of blacks." We would perhaps be neither instructed nor amused, the problem being so badly placed.

.   .   .

The story of Paul and Silas at Philippi and the women they encounter offers nonetheless a momentary and charming relief. The vignette takes in the mind the form of a heart, the heart of a woman. There occurs a tender encounter near the river: two strangers seek on the sabbath a "place of prayer." They find women gathered, speak with them of the good news. One among the gathering, Lydia, embraces the faith.

Whereupon the missioners are invited into her home, her open heart.

The missioners alas are not for long left at peace, intruders as they are in many ways, bringing in their wake a wind blowing adverse to the stale and sanctioned atmosphere of the city.

A mixed economy rules, compounded of magic and greed— and official eyes are steadfastly closed to both. Sooner or later it is bound to happen; the strangers will strike up against the industry of magic, to the wrath of the authorities and citizen-consumers.

Alas for the haven, the heart and hearth of Lydia? A familiar venomous sequence gets under way. The missioners dare bring spiritual relief in the form of exorcism to a young girl whose soothsaying makes her a profitable slave. Mob fury and official vengeance and the swift criminalizing of the healers follow. They are seized, flogged, and cast in prison.

. . .

And then in the night, an awesome liberation; no angel this time, creation itself is aroused, an earthquake shakes the prison. But Paul and Silas take no advantage of the sprung locks. A question detains them where they lie; the fate of the keeper.

Newly awakened, that worthy is seized with despair at the supposed loss of his prisoners, a disgrace that invites condign punishment.

But no. The warder has become prey of another sort. On his account and no other, the prisoners refuse the freedom offered them. Shall the captor not now be liberated, the first urgent business of this stupendous night?

He is freed: of his past bondage to Caesar's dirty work; and of his present fear, which has reached suicidal pitch.

Plucked from his own dungeon, the warden finds that his heart melts within him; he tenders the prisoners the compassion of a woman. He washes their wounds, then "conducts them into his house, sets out a meal, and rejoices with his whole household in his new found faith in God."

.   .   .

As sometimes happens, the magistrates conceive in cold dawn, second thoughts about the punishment meted out to the strangers. Their qualms, one concludes, are hardly to be thought of as ethical; they are more in the nature of salutary fear of repercussions from on high. Have they perhaps acted precipitously, even ill advisedly, in ordering harsh reprisals for dubious crimes? In any case, what was hastily done can be as quickly undone; let the prisoners go.

But not these prisoners, by no means. Their dignity is intact, it has suffered no diminution at such manhandling of official brutes. They will go, but by no rear door; proudly, bearing the wounds of their flogging, publicly, and by dint of official apology.

All of which transpires. And the unquelled duo makes its way once more, a long way round indeed, back to restoring and healing, to the heart and home of Lydia.

FOURTEEN

Of Athens.
The sterility and frivolity of academe.

ACTS 17

And on to Athens. The intellectual heart of things? So we are informed. Athens, as well, one might judge, the repository of Paul's dearest hopes. Here at length, he will encounter a scene apt to match his genius to the full.

In vain: Pauline eloquence and presence seem to have made only a light ripple. Indeed the heat of debate and contention engendered elsewhere fails, and falls to ash. We are at the center of Greek pride and accomplishment; to the searching eye of Luke, a dead center.

To him, the buzzing of the agora is witless as a shaken hive of bees. No harvest of honey can be thought to accrue; Paul is in the presence of a cloud of drones. Luke comments acidly, "All the Athenians and the resident foreigners had time for nothing except talking or hearing about the latest novelty."

Heads askance, skeptical or stoic or epicurean, they hear him out.

For Paul, the experience is galling, humiliating. To be tolerated, or otherwise put down, by frivolous minds! The humiliation is deeper by far than stripes or jailings or the raillery of wicked judges.

More: physical punishment, inflicted by the unjust, eventually brings in its wake only honor. But to be ignored, cataloged, dismissed—as though the truth one lived by were no more than a diversion for idle minds!

Not that the torpid spirits of the Athenians remain entirely untouched. If some topic of Paul's may be said to rub them wrong, if unease, distaste, dissension surface, it is at Paul's mention of the Resurrection. It is the nearest his speech comes to wounding the mind's eye.

Nevertheless the moment of disaffection is quickly dissipated. The listeners shrug, then depart in view of some other distraction. The Christian harvest, even the planting, is distressingly and unaccustomedly thin; a man and woman are named as converts, "with others beside." Thus far Athens.

FIFTEEN

In Corinth and Ephesus, small returns.
Despite all, a vision urges: *Keep On!*

The moods rise and fall! They remind one of a fever chart; there are highs and lows, moods of good sense and no sense at all, devastating rejections, promises from on high, reunions and departure—but scarcely a "normal" word or deed to be found; if by "normal" one is to summon merely passive lives, poise without risk, assimilation. None of these—but the journeys unending on the road, on the high sea—the new faith is hardly an armchair exercise!

The present episode begins peaceably enough. Paul is in Corinth, in the home of friends, Jewish refugees from Rome and emperor Claudius. One has a sense, here and elsewhere, that it is from "safe houses" like this that the ragtag envoys, Paul and companions, take heart to go forth and endure. The present hosts are tentmakers, and Paul works along with them; a capital point with him is physical labor and the independence it brings. The scene for a change is domestic and endearing; it is also austere.

On the sabbath, synagogue bickering seems to be the rule, in Corinth or wherever the winds deposit the voyaging preachers. The contention, wherever it occurs, could not be called attractive, nor greatly to the taste of later Christians like ourselves. Cannot these perfervid believers live and let live? Is human variety the enemy of God's love, or its evidence? The questions arise on their own, our world being in the image of Noah's ark, a teeming variety with its inevitable give and take, pelt, claw and tooth (but also the heart's outreach).

.   .   .

On the occasion described Paul, one judges, ascends the podium as usual to state his case. His message wins small sympathy; and we can hardly wonder. It is the word of a Jew confronting Jews. Superiority in numbers, a settled unified community, pride of possession on the one side; and on the other, the primary, rather unprepossessing fervor of a convert from that same community. He has been won to another sect, locally unknown; and where known, found suspect. Could it be found astonishing that the contest will be adroit and heated?

To speak of Paul's style here, it would seem that neither the meekness of Christ, nor confidence that truth will prevail on its own, is the tactic or ethos of the protagonist. Nor are such attitudes current among the synagogue worshipers. What animates the scene, if we can judge from its like elsewhere, is the hurling of scriptural thunderbolts, back and forth. It is a contest of titans vying for the same turf. The bolts harm no one, neither do they strike their intended eye. Rather they tend to a kind of mutually assured destruction, neutralizing in mid-air, leaving only a whiff of brimstone and frustration on the air.

Has Paul perhaps confused his own function with that of the Holy Spirit? Has his sense of vocation gained so heavy a hold, that the unyielding faith of his adversaries, their communitarian stubbornness, is to be laid like a tonnage on their conscience? We cannot know, much less condemn one whose life is so clearly on the line—but the questions seem valid, and of point. For our own sake as well, and for the faith placed in our clumsy keeping.

.   .   .

In any case, Paul's departure from the synagogue could hardly be thought of as graceful, or conducive to further ecumenical niceties. He is stung; "They opposed him and resorted to abuse," reports Luke. He storms out of the premises, invoking a formula which comes down like a hammer blow. "Your blood be on your own hands."

The awful words bespeak finality, a curse on his adversaries. The imprecation is in use, we are given to understand, not between Jew and Jew, but believer and gentile. And therefore in this setting, all the more to be thought of as an ultimatum.

.   .   .

No hint of mutuality, especially of that mutuality we name a common hope, remains to be drawn on. Indeed, affairs at so early a stage in Christian history are here brought to an impasse. The centuries can only heap it higher and dig it deeper, as both sides hasten to reinforce their isolation and multiply recrimination against this wailing wall of awful beginnings.

.   .   .

That the departing anathema spoken by Paul is to be reverenced as the word of God cannot be doubted. That the same words commend themselves as an approved or sanctified model of Christian conduct vis-à-vis adversaries is much to be doubted.

The conclusion is of course an exercise in hindsight, perhaps even in the chastened wisdom which centuries of Christian wrongs against Jews have, despite all, distilled. Perhaps even, who knows, to the point of tears of repentance.

We Christians are indeed reluctant, even retarded learners.

. . .

Subsequently a vision, this time of the Lord himself, reassured Paul. He was "to have no fear," to "go on with your preaching and not be silenced. I am with you and no attack shall harm you, for I have many in this city who are my people."

We are in the realm of promise and reminder, both of which the tumult in the synagogue has served only to obfuscate.

The language, the epiphany of Jesus form an astonishing moment. Jewish testament and Christian hope (the hope also that a Christian testament, still nascent, is in unsteady formation, composed in the heat of the moment, in prison and other unlikely places, then orally passed on, eventually set to paper)—these are joined. Jesus, it is implied, is the God of the Jews. He takes to himself a language reserved for that God alone, in manifestations to Moses and other patriarchs. "I am with you," which is to say, the outcome of your enterprise is in God's hands, it is assured a good outcome, beyond malice or interference.

The vision, the presence of the Lord rather than an angelic or human emissary, is a hearkening back to the scene on the Damascus road, and Paul's conversion. There too the Lord had appeared and spoken in person. Thus the present vision marks, as though with God's own finger, another moment, a *kairos*. As in his conversion, so now; something unprecedented is in the air, portending, dark as to detail, a movement of the Spirit only minimally clarified, as though by a finger of lightning.

Whereupon (as in most lives) the dark descends once more, the world's closure, the open sea, open road, vocation, faith, the long trek.

Meantime, there is a respite; Paul settles in at Corinth for well over a year....

SIXTEEN

To Caesarea and Antioch.
Of spirits holy and unholy.
Of the curious Ephesian
"economy of images."

Then Paul sets sail once more...

He arrives at Ephesus, to encounter a strange scene, a kind of warp in time. A certain Apollos is glowingly praised by Luke as "an eloquent man, powerful in his use of the scriptures," more, as one "instructed in the way of the Lord and full of spiritual fervor. In his discourse he taught accurately the facts about Jesus...." And yet, and yet. Closer examination by Paul leads to a startling discovery: this man of parts is by no means a completely fashioned Christian; he knows only the baptism of John.

Thus Paul comes on something unprecedented: a Christian in formation, incomplete in his knowledge of Jesus and initiation in the Way. Yet this neophyte is wonderfully skilled in confuting the adversaries who so exercise, and at times squander, the best efforts of Paul. And even reduce him to spleen and exasperation.

"Apollos powerfully confuted the Jews in public." Here is a man cut to Paul's own measure!

More, there are others, disciples of Apollos, equally incomplete in Christian formation. When asked whether they have received the Spirit, they answer simply, "No, we were not even told that there is a Holy Spirit." They have received only John's baptism, they explain; their catechesis is stalled at that point.

Christians at the verge. Paul hastens to beckon them further; they are baptized in the name of Jesus; immediately they speak in tongues and prophesy. The Spirit and the gifts of the Spirit are thus declared common to the Christian community.

. . .

Luke adds by the way, as though to close the episode, a subtle afterthought, "There were in all, about a dozen of these men."

Are we meant to note here a reminder of the spiritual status of the twelve before Pentecost—and also a hint of our own condition, our times, the implication being that the "dozen" are here enacting the pre-pentecostal condition of the original twelve, with respect to the Holy Spirit, as well as our own unfinished Christianity? The notion is intriguing.

Pentecost is never done with. We too are in the status of the twelve who waited in prayer.

. . .

Life went on. To their chagrin (and, by implication, to ours), a further discovery awaited; the disciples were still, for all the miraculous event that had claimed them, radically incomplete humans. Less incomplete than before, to be sure; but only the morrow would reveal the next step on that chancy road. In the meantime (all life in this sense reveals itself as a "meantime"), they must await at prayer a new descent of the Spirit, a new access of understanding.

Peter's napkin, Paul's unhorsing, the power of healing that inexplicably flows through them, the contrary (and yet complementary) rhythms of going forth and return, chance taking on sea and road, reflection and revaluation!

Of the human there is no final version in this world.

A continuing Pentecost; no other way, no better way. All said, all done, no final way.

.   .   .

ACTS 19: 8-17

Paul's teaching, like that of Peter, is accompanied by miracles of healing. Renewal of spirit through the word of truth is shown forth in the healing of bodies. The consonance is at times astonishing; to be healed by Paul, we are told, the afflicted are not required to have immediate access to the wonder worker. It is enough "when handkerchiefs and scarves which had been in contact with his skin are carried to the sick."

.   .   .

(Such miraculous accounts put quite out of joint the olfactory equipment of commentators. One is variously bemused and astonished to note the scandal that gathers, the fulminations that accumulate, around Luke's narration concerning the healing power of the apostles. From one of these "experts" alone, the following *florilegium* is culled: "primitive and crude beliefs in mana," "magical beliefs in a Christianized form," "crude ways," "conditioned by primitive categories of thought," "pagan ways of thinking." Bedizened with such "scholarship," what need has the church of enemies?)

.   .   .

For some two years, the wondrous restoration of spirits and, one presumes, of bodies continues. "The whole population of the province of Asia, both Jew and gentiles, heard the word of the Lord."

.   .   .

Yet inevitably, the power of the apostles has its rivals; one person's magic is another's mystery. We have here a conflict concerning ownership of a name, a power. Who is to own the "power" implied in the name of a godly Being, a power released by invocation? (The Name, as we have learned, is both benign and dangerous. Public, confident Naming of the Name, early on in *Acts*, is shown to heal and restore. The same Name sends ripples of official anger through the minions of empire, and lands the invoking apostles in jail.)

.   .   .

Here we have a contest reminiscent of earlier ones recounted in the Jewish testament. Then, the prophet of Yahweh must contend in public for the fealty of the people, against the prophets of Baal. With this interesting variation in the present fray, Paul is not so much as mentioned as a contender.

It is the demons themselves, as Luke assures us, who in a way both ludicrous and violent, settle scores and vindicate the apostle. The scene of the contest is chaotic, humiliating to Paul's challengers. An exorcism that was to bring relief to the possessed man ends in an utter rout of the would-be healers.

By no means relieved of his disruptive (and disreputable) spirit, the afflicted man calls out, "Jesus I recognize and Paul too; but who are you?" It is not the first time we have heard the demons give evidence of "knowing" the Lord in a preternatural way. The worth of such knowledge is never left in doubt in Luke's Gospel; it meets only the scorn and rejection of Jesus. Such fealty, surrounded as it is with an aura of fear, wickedness, covert dread of life, avails nothing; as James reminds us laconically, it is "a faith without works."

The demons cannot do the works of God; neither can their votaries. Nor does a more or less magical incantation of the name of Jesus avail to work the wonders that follow on true faith. The demons, themselves without faith, recognize and make sport of all mere imitations of faith.

The outcome is dramatic and shocking, not to say hilarious. The pitiable man, no whit freed from his condition, rushes against the hapless magic men, batters then unmercifully, strips them to the pelt and sends them charging pell-mell out of doors.

And shortly, the word is out. Even for a cosmopolitan center like Ephesus, where an economy of magic, potions, astrology, and so on flourishes, this is a notorious event, a contention among giants. And Paul has prevailed.

.   .   .

ACTS 19: 18-20

On the heels of this, comes a no less dramatic episode in the same city.

What was from time immemorial a web of conduct quite taken for granted, woven in the common weal, is shortly revealed as something utterly other: sin, false worship, idolatry. A crucial distinction is thunderously announced by Paul: mystery differs from magic, true God from false.

Nothing of the life had been heard in the culture. The pantheon, like a magical web, close woven, radiated outward, formed in effect an elaborate social compact; economy, religion, family and, we may be sure, political realities, all held firm.

But now, something else. The Ephesians hear a disruptive thunder in their sky. No gods, one God! They shortly learn of sin, their sin, and its complex social ramifications. Nor are pagans alone affected. In the syncretic atmosphere, where any and all deities are welcome, we learn a curious fact: the dismayed, would-be exorcists of the episode, we are told, are Jews.

. . .

Then the turnaround. What might be thought of as a highly inflammable wave of reform sweeps through the city. Conversions by the score; and among many of the newly converted, a mood of revulsion against practices newly judged abominable. An enormous public book burning ensues. The value of the tomes, Luke declares, equals the daily wage of some 50,000 workmen.

Thus is the past symbolically sent up in smoke. The destruction signals a new start. The bonfire allows another sort of volume to get under way; the action of the fervent converts is incorporated in the *Acts of the Apostles*.

. . .

ACTS 19: 21 - 20: 5

For every action, a reaction of similar, or greater force. We are referring to a kind of physics of human behavior. It appears impossible on the face of it that events of public notoriety, threatening to the silver standard of the Ephesian economy, should go unchallenged. Events coalesce, as so often occurs, around the twin temples, religion and money.

The silversmiths, craftsmen and those of allied trades, are the first to feel the seismic force rumbling underfoot. A certain Demetrius emerges to articulate their grievance. He summons the venom and honey of a tried demagogue. Two issues are burning on the air; he will play indignantly upon each, and in proper order of import.

The first, to be sure, is money. The images of the goddess are after all, of silver; and silver is hardly to be reckoned base clay. Nor is its diversion or melt-down into other, less sacred forms of coinage, passing through other hands than the craftsmen, to be lightly suffered.

The second theme is religion; the goddess, one might conclude from the homily of Demetrius, has in her city the status of a sanctified star. A north star: from her, the city takes its soundings, its place of honor in the world. She, being immortal, is not to be unseated by the thunders of a mortal gyrovague. In face of the challenge posed by Paul, her devotees must, of religious passion, valor, jealousy, arise and vindicate.

The theme of religion, once brought to the fore by Demetrius, is rather nervously and quickly put to one side. Indeed one gains the impression that the religion appealed to is of a rather peculiar form. To the inflamed Demetrian mind, nothing could be conceived of so pure, nothing so endangered as the devotion awakened and sustained by the images.

Nothing, as Paul to the contrary insists, is so impure, so mixed, so rendered base, plunged as it is in the furnace of the economy and melded there; one product, one idol, one consumer item. Business as a form of religion, the undeniable religious aura of business, the profane elevated to the sacramental.

.   .   .

194 Daniel Berrigan, S.J.

It would be difficult to ignore regarding the same subject, the evidence of tradition and one's own experience, a melding of note in its own right. To wit, the capacity for greed is as deeply implanted in the human psyche as the capacity for religion. The two are polarities, dangerous opposites which in their pure form, are advisedly kept separate.

Joined on occasion, fused by a given culture into a weird amalgam of greedy religion—a muddle of inflamed ecstasy erupts, part fury, part cupidity, as in the farrago of Demetrius.

Nothing, after a time, is clear; and the puddle of unclarity, as we read, flows distressingly abroad. A shouting match erupts in the Ephesian theater and continues incoherently for some hours. "The assembly," as Luke notes, "was in an uproar"; he adds dryly, "and most of them did not know what they had come for."

.   .   .

What the new faith and its chief sponsor must contend with, in the ancient "givens" of human nature! (And the proposition admits reversal as well.) The Ephesian rampage is to be repeated again and again in other settings, Paul and his companions setting their world on its civilized ear. The word of the cross is to the Greeks plain nonsense; it is the word of the drachma that makes sense.

.   .   .

And Luke who recorded the life and works of Jesus, once again sets quill to scroll. Does he have a sense of *déjà vu*? These giants, Peter and Paul and friends, whirl in a troubled orbit, even as the greater One before them. Contention, voyaging, the word of God making large trouble in the world, the world exacting revenge. There is no escaping the terrifying gravity and grace of this Way: the Triune Center, then the wide and wild swing of life.

. . .

At first greed and mystery in conflict, then money and religion at peace. Thus the history of religion. (Not thus the history of faith.) In the beginning was a kind of awful purity; it was like the purity of the first week of creation. The images of the goddess shone with an awful purity in the dark shrines. Their promise was infinite; heaven on earth. To their possessors and votaries, they smiled the shadow of a smile, like the ancestress of La Gioconda; they embodied the prosperity they promised.

Were the images of considerable net value? They had heft in the hand and calculable value in the scales. They must therefore be defended; it was all quite simple: defended, not on behalf of the honor of the goddess or the image alone or even primarily, as Demetrius would have it, for worth, for income, for cash flow.

. . .

This is our history also; in the beginning was purity. The silver images were an abomination before the gaze of Christians. They must be disposed of.

But then religion replaced faith (invariably at the beckoning of the empire). And the goddess was not content with her exile. Awfully and artfully, she repossessed her shrines. Idolatrous images reappeared, in another form. Something known as money moved swiftly into sanctuary and pulpit. (We remember that by now, religion played surrogate to faith.) The coin of the realm! It was sound tender, readily it passed from palm to palm, secular to sacred. And it bore the superscription and image of Caesar.

The move signaled a kind of peace, a mutual aid pact. Why indeed should the church-empire conflict, which in the beginning had been regarded as evangelically inevitable? Why not resolve it? Why not celebrate interests that were, all said and suffered, mutual?

.   .   .

The open door of a tomb closed once more. The hinges moved smoothly, soundlessly in their sockets. Very few heard. The resurrection was bought off.

.   .   .

In the original event at Ephesus, according to Luke's telling, the tempest whirling around the images and their devotees remains unresolved. The non-resolution is of great import, and offers eventual likelihood of a truly evangelical ending. Which is to say, no church-state pact is signed. In pagan shrines, Luke implies, the images of the goddess stand in place, continue to stretch out their palms with promise and plenty. But only there; they do not stand in the Christian place, nor in Christian hearts.

.   .   .

Or so it is said. But perhaps an analogy is in order, a contemporary version of the original Story of the Conflictive Shrines. To wit:

"Now in those latter times, the Christian movement gave rise to a serious disturbance.

"There were thousands of scientists busy in the land; with the collusion of politicians and the military, they were engaged in turning out countless and varied images of Mars, the god of war. The deity was pictured according to every violent whim; in one, he gloried in the defeat of an enemy underfoot, in another he raised a spear tipped with lightning, impaling an enemy. There was an image for every citizen's mood.

"This image industry bore in fact the main burden of the economy. It provided lucrative jobs for millions of workers, from the most skilled to the least. It also kept stirring the citizens to a bellicose mood, favorable both to the military and the industrial complex.

"But the Christians objected. Not only did they refuse to work in the mills of Mars, they picketed and sat in and at times, even dared perform acts of sabotage against the images, pouring their blood over them, casting them to ground.

"The matter became more and more serious. The president was apprised. He summoned a meeting of scientists, generals and labor union leaders. 'Gentlemen,' he began gravely, 'you know as well as I, that our high standard of living depends on the unimpeded progress of the Martian industries. You see moreover, how certain religious fanatics are making capital of their perverse teaching and thus unsettling our people's sense of the common weal, even here in the nation's capital. They go so far as to teach that these revered images of Mars are idolatrous!

" 'Make no mistake, there is manifest danger for us here. It is not only that a vast and complicated industry risks being discredited. We must envision also the closing down of an enormous network of factories, furnaces, wholesale and retail outlets. More, these workplace-sanctuaries of decent, main-line Christians will shortly cease to command universal respect. What will become of us then, what of our religion, our sound family values, our children's future?'

"Now when his audience heard these words, they broke into an unaccustomed uproar; they began to shout a spontaneous pledge of allegiance: 'Great and loyal and worthy of all support is our work, great are the factories, laboratories, bunkers and bases of Mars. It is through these that our country flourishes, unparalleled in the world!' "

.   .   .

Paul departed Ephesus, his point made. The point being a strange one at first blush; non-resolution, non-assimilation. He moves on, subsequent to what he undoubtedly considers a truthful witness.

In the city, meantime, the Romans move swiftly to restore order. Order is indeed their specialty (Roman law being one thing, Roman justice another. As Paul will discover.)

And this, the Roman speed and obsession with political order is quite normal, and within the ambit of imperial authority. Their official, the town clerk, makes this quite clear. The Romans have no interest in a pagan-Christian imbroglio. With regard to the existence and multiplying of religious images, they are officially neutral.

What is of surpassing interest is the clarity of the attendant issues, unresolved though they be. The contestation is not, as the Romans would have it, between pagans and Christians, but between Rome and the Way. The empire has not yet won over the church, nor has the church, in Paul, become a succubus of empire.

.   .   .

We have here a precious occasion and moment; to take breath, to take soundings. No better occasion to ask ourselves the question that means everything: who are these Christians, ourselves, vis-à-vis the principalities?

SEVENTEEN

Of the child who fell asleep,
and the wondrous outcome of this.
Also of farewells and fresh starts.

"We" once more; Luke our scribe has joined again in the journey and its events.

The first of which is charmingly unusual—and just as charmingly usual.

That someone be raised from the dead is one of the noble, even repetitious occurrences of our story, especially as it touches on Peter and Paul. And Luke's aplomb and good humor make for a lovely tale.

We are in Troas, at the home of a Christian. A crowd fills the room; it is the evening of weekly worship. The lamps are lit, the twilight air of the room is heavy with the odor of burning oil. A child has taken his place at a window sill, half out of earshot, in the way of a child, curious and detached at once.

The preacher has his way too. His sermon we may imagine, rolls on, unrolls long as a major letter, and as detailed. There is ample reason for the preacher's lingering over chapter and verse, verse and chapter of God's word. Paul after all is about to depart, and the journey and its outcome are chancy.

In any case, large portions of the message, mingling with the odor of the lamps, form a heavy soporific. The boy's attention wavers; then (surely not the first or the last to be wafted into morphic repose by theological droning),—the child nods off.

Then to the horror of all present, plunges headlong, some three stories to the ground. He is picked up dead.

And that, in the ordinary way, would be the end of the matter, the episode concluding in communal grief, a service and burial.

But we are in no ordinary way. Paul, man of the resurrection, "went down, threw himself upon the child, and clasped him in his arms. 'Do not distress yourselves,' he said. 'The child is alive.' "

Which, as matter of fact, he suddenly, inexplicably was.

.   .   .

Death, intervention, then life! We have met with these before, and been astounded, not merely at the stories, but at the level calm of their telling. As though it were the most natural thing in the world (natural that is, to the healer) that this or that one die, under whatever circumstance, then (equally natural) that the power of Jesus be invoked, and the corpse stand again. And this occurring in our world, no other.

.   .   .

The healer, whether named Jesus or Peter or Paul, will bear watching. There is a power at command which is literally unfathomable. We have no words for it; we can only approach it with awe. But this at least can be said. In the first place, Peter and Paul invoke a power not their own; their confession of faith is a great disclaimer: "In the name of Jesus."

By way of clue to their resource, we know something of these two; each in his own way has undergone death, and come through. Henceforth, hands, head and heart, he is a channel of life through whom the power of Jesus may work its abundance.

And what is to be said of Jesus, the fountainhead of this life-over-death power we witness in *Acts*? What He gives is what He is: "I am the Life." A declaration implying nothing static, automatic, magical, manipulative. The life He offers is His own, "given for you." In the first instance (and this is valid in quite another way for Peter and Paul), He raises others from death because He, "being Divine," as Paul writes, has first undergone death. What He offers is his own life, given; then, through others, given and given again.

. . .

The onlookers of such wonders are ourselves; we long even to be the witnesses. But we are by no means marked by the assurance and calm of the protagonists. We are uncertain as to the meaning of these episodes; are they "historical", are they mere analogies, pious stories that never touch earth?

There is reason for our dismay, even our distemper (including that of the commentators). Long before the miracles we read of, we have ceded our human outcome, more or less explicitly, to death. This is an agreement old as Genesis. In virtue of it we are granted entrance into the world; we shall leave it (leave it to others, who themselves stand under the same burden and law), at the behest and raised finger of death.

Thus our shock and grief, when the terms of the covenant we have made, or was made by ancestors in our name, come due. But these emotions are muted as, shortly or after long years of mourning, time's reality comes home; birth and death meet on a middle emotional ground: the joy of one stanches the tears of the other.

. . .

Commonly we speak of "nature's course." The presumption is that the aged alone will die, that all humans will attain a quasi-patriarchal term. Under this assumption we go about the business of living, some in assurance that in their life's task, means and ends are in close embrace; others with a shrug dismissive of the whole affair.

. . .

Did the agreement hold firm, were nature respected in this matter of longevity, it could be conceded that in the world all goes, if not well, at least according to agreement. Life was proving, if stern and exacting in the matter of dues, at least sensible and consistent—and sometimes even generous.

The pact that welcomes us into the world and beckons us out of the world touches on the death of the aged only; or so we think. The others, children, youths, young brides and husbands, infants, these are safe. Or so we think.

. . .

Then the arrangement is violated, brutally, summarily. Nodding off for a moment, a child plunges from a window downward to its death. We have a parable before us, an all-but-unbearable sign. Innocence, life hardly under way and snuffed out, dumb unreasonable fate, the thread cut before it is fairly spun. The story of one child is the story of all those who die out of due time, those who plain reason tells us should not die, whom mischance cuts off, or murder or disease, all who are victimized and tortured and made to disappear, day after day in a world whose most persuasive image is that of a vast madhouse.

.   .   .

Like a hundredweight the absurdity, the hideous unfairness, fall—on us, crushing, suffocating. Our suppositions, our firm place in time and this world are suddenly shaken. We are jarred out of sensible orbit. Does calm reason govern things, does a center hold, or our pact with the universe? Are children safe, and only the aged beckoned away (and they gently, and with muted tears)?

.   .   .

In our Gospel we read of no healing intervention touching on the death of the aged. The fact might prove self-explanatory, this choosiness of the healers, their skill favoring only the young with a coruscating moment of resurrection. All fair, we think, all according to agreement. Life in this world is due the young, or why be born at all? A span, a term, an achievement, one's feet upon a Himalaya from which to shout a word of conquest. All this is due.

Thus we think, and thus Jesus and Luke and Peter and Paul by inference agree. Violent death, accidental death, where it presumes to lay claim on the young, is interfered with. Thus the daughter of Jairus and the widow's son of Naim and Lazarus and this unnamed child (and youthful Jesus raised by the Father's powers)—all agree. And shout their Alleluia!

.   .   .

ACTS 20: 18-36

So Paul departs Ephesus as though for the last time, as though no return were probable. This is the note of his farewell: poignancy, and then what assurance!

We have had farewell speeches, notably the lengthy one recorded by John, spoken on the last night of the life of Jesus. That one, by way of contrast, dwelt heavily and personally on the theme of departure, the gift of the Spirit, the need of unity among the disciples. Whatever was said in a personal vein was referred in a mysterious way to His sense of dwelling with God, beyond the terror and vicissitudes of life and imminent death. A transcending farewell, in sum, in which death and tragedy were muted in favor of an almost buddhist summoning of "the beyond, the within."

.   .   .

Jesus, and now Paul, each saying his farewell; a revelation of the character of each.

In Paul's valedictory, the confessional note sounds again and again: "You know how I..." in sum, acted honorably among you, down to least detail, earning my living, refusing to make the gospel a burden to yourselves.

And nothing, not a whit to reprove himself for, whether in conduct or motive. It is as though he were planting himself even then, by main force of eloquence and works, centrally in our history, our scripture; making certain his place in the canon, presenting himself as apostle, founder, *magister,* the one who penetrates the inner life of the Holy One, the *mysterion* of God in Christ.

And all this was accomplished, as he insists, in the teeth of great obstacles. He summons up the all but incantatory phrase, "amid the sorrows and trials that befell me through the intrigues of the Jews."

Confessional, self-exonerating. "No one's fate can be laid at my door."

And one wonders what events preceded, what strengths of his had threatened or perhaps even crushed lesser spirits. Else why should so tormented a subject arise at all?

And then, a breathtaking grasp and claim on—lowliness of spirit. "Serving the Lord in all humility...I have kept back nothing, I have disclosed to you the whole purpose of God."

The whole purpose? of God? We are hard put to think, in our day or his, of any personage, prophet, apostle, of whom or by whom such a claim might make sense. Or perhaps we are in the realm of Attic rhetoric, wherein a large statement seizes attention—in order that a smaller truth (small as a grain of salt, and as pungent) might win the nod.

And finally, he looks to the future, and is by no means reassured. After me, the deluge? He envisions "savage wolves, coming in among you...not sparing the flock." Worse: "Even from your own number, men...who will distort the truth...."

Come now, is there to be no trust in a new leadership, in the resources of the community? Such a nagging sense of minority status, he and they—but they more than he, and the flock all the more assailed and under attack for his absence.

More tears, and farewell.

.   .   .

The striking difference in tone on the two farewells. The edginess, brusqueness of Paul. He ranges about the world in a high noon of light and darkness, no nuance or penumbra. Little disposition to attend to the minor meanings that so often determine the majors. (Those minors that might to his thinking as easily distort or diffuse the Great Questions.)

He can never stand content in a predawn or twilight of the mind, those nether, less defined hours of near light and near dark. They deceive; they offer only hints and starts and vague outlines. He thirsts for the maximum, the hour of pleroma. His tone is of high noon, the Christian hour. He takes his stand there, in blinding light and heat. It is then that the character of truth, and of the truthteller, stand for all to see. He and all other claimants of truth must stand, take their stand, be judged in that fierce, vertical flame.

The style is the man.

. . .

His style, and then our own, and the difference. We thirst for complexity as he for simplicity—the arrow whose terrible innocence knows only the target.

Our world is alike, despite the centuries that intervene. That world, his and ours, demands a close, responsible look. But the report from even the shrewdest eye, we conclude, had best be a tentative one. Our *compañeros* on earth near and far, are so mixed a multitude, clamorous with their claim, their self-interest, their religious passion. So was Paul's world mixed, Jew and gentile, pagan and monotheist.

But we differ greatly from him in the burden we carry. What we have had to learn, and absorb, and swallow with dry gullets is the bitter draught of history. Of Christian history; of crime, war, pogroms, the cross subservient to the flag, the flag-draped cross, inquisitors, forced conversions, crusades, all. To this our day, and its pale double-dealing Christian purveyors of nuclear terror and domestic misery.

. . .

Innocence in the beginning was no art, no achievement; it was a simple eye resting on history in the making. The right was clear, so the evil. One had no part in the evil; one was ineluctably sure of standing elsewhere in the world.

Innocence today? It is an all but lost art; its recovery is an achievement beyond praise, rare.

. . .

Paul was an innocent, in this sense. He was starting over, plowing a virgin field. He hefted, at least by comparison with ourselves, a small burden; only his personal history to unlearn and renounce.

For this he comes across in Luke's portrait as an innocent, a newborn giant among lesser giants; and his adversaries as a race of pygmies. In *Acts*, we are given no other measure, whether from himself (all that fierce swagger of faith, those dogmatic squads on parade!) or from Luke's steady pen.

. . .

And we wonder: was Paul never afflicted with doubt, second thoughts? Was the world's malice held so steadily at arm's length as never to touch or pierce?

Not true. It is not to Luke's purpose to dwell upon the inner life of the giant. *Acts* is a moving, roiling map of purpose and vital beginnings. It is like the uncapping of a volcano, the flow of lava altering the landscape.

The map must be redrawn on the house, as Paul and his companions enter a region, confront the principalities, and move on.

We turn elsewhere for a glimpse of Paul's inner life. And what we learn! What fierce shock leaps from the page as we open the text of his letters to the churches. Superman? He is assailed with dread. What will be his reception among his own, what his next move?

He writes to the Corinthians: "I came among you with great fear and trepidation." And later in the same letter, a very torrent of sorrowful rhetoric, as he compares with incomparable art his sorry estate with theirs. "We are fools for Christ's sake, while you are sensible Christians! We are weak, you are powerful! You are honored, we are in disgrace!"

. . .

Does Luke offer us a superman of the spirit? At least Paul, to his credit and our relief, does not. "To this day we go hungry and thirsty and in rags. We are beaten, we wander from place to place, we wear ourselves out earning a living with our own hands. People curse us and we bless...."

It is the voice of a new age, convinced in a complex way that it is the last age. But the one who speaks for the new age, and moves against the old, the "crooked time," feeling the pull of one and the push of the other—this is no armored knight. We hear him speak of himself, a vulnerable human, burdened with our inner divisions and perplexities. "The good which I want to do, I fail to do; what I do is the wrong which is against my will...."

And yet, testing himself and others, irrefutable in mind, so convinced of his belief that he escapes obsession only by gen-

erosity of intellect, a breadth of a compassion that finally bends
and bows, like a great millennial tree grown tender in its fronds.

World shaker, yes, but pastor first of all.

.   .   .

And what of the centuries since Paul, the years whose tide
beats up and against our own lifetime? How shall we withstand
them or answer for them? We are all but swept away in a relentless current, an undertow, a faithless persuasion. Things will
never be different, evil is in command!

It is not that we carry the guilt of our ancestry; if we know
our texts, we spurn that old, crippling malaise. Ours is a simple
matter of accepting a history which, like it or not, runs in our
bloodline. The blood is a merciless teacher; the blood of the innocent cries out its instruction. This is the evil even goodness
can come to. Humanity is alight with grandeur and heroism, but
also dark with murder. Take heed of it.

Such an understanding, of standing not at the beginning, but
far along the way of the centuries—such must inevitably affect
our thought, imagination, language, the very fabric of our faith.
Our creed today, for all its ancient certitudes, is only somewhat
forthright, only now and then assured. Before we utter a word,
we look backward and forward, to right and left. Menacing
shadows lurk around. We take in account, or try to, a history of
victim and victimizer, ignorance and obsession, fraudulence and
depravity; and then the saints and martyrs, each and all created
by versions of our faith.

.   .   .

The sensibility of our credo, like it or not, is in stark contrast
with Paul's; ours carries a weight of "perhaps." There is so

much we cannot, in good faith, declare forthrightly. We make do, we stutter, we leave our clumsy, half-disclosed fealty in the hands of Mercy.

Let it be said direct: we cringe from the Pauline "cutting edge" as Luke sharpens it, thrusts it at us. We have seen what phrases like "the intrigue of the Jews" lead to. Whether in the fauna of creation or the human family, we know of no "savage wolves." We cannot allow ourselves the luxury of an implacable belief, eye and tongue inflamed against others.

.   .   .

Like it or not, our times, their monstrous defaulting on the human, as well as the crimes of Christian history, commend a subtler, more hesitant approach to the faith. Which is to say by implication, also toward one another: Christian to Jew, Christian to all. Something simple, from the heart; I believe in You, I trust You.

And with regard to you, brother and sister of other faiths, I refuse to make of our differences an inflammatory matter. I refuse debate, provocation, pride of place. I shall magnify, learn from, celebrate, admire our likeness, shall make light of other matters. For my credo moves in two directions, to you and to You.

.   .   .

Such formulation takes in account our weakness. And now and again, our sorry strength—which we rarely dare recognize as such, or take slight satisfaction in. In us the Pauline fire is subdued; it lies in sleepy coals.

Perhaps we see in Pascal the first of those who came upon the failing fires, poked them gently to life with his "wager." It were better, he wrote, to believe than not, since if we lose (in the hypothesis of there being no God, and we laying our bet wrong)—why then we have lost nothing.

And if God exists? Then, laying the wager upon the Existent One, we have won God!

.   .   .

ACTS 20: 36 - ACTS 21: 2

A tenderness gently and persistently flowed in the curmudgeonly public man; Paul was so beloved! "There were loud cries of sorrow from them all," Luke writes of the farewell scene at Ephesus. "They folded Paul in their arms and kissed him. What distressed them most was his saying they would never see his face again."

He had made much in his summary farewell of his life in their midst. To him, that life was his best and chief apologia. In nothing of the crude and common tasks of living had he put himself above them. His was no dandyism of spirit; his place in the community assigned him hard work at their side and plain provender at a common table. His distinction, the greatness of his spirit, arose from this understanding and conduct; he was their brother. Flesh and bone he was one with them, a communality of grief and hope.

.   .   .

If he commanded a language by turns angelic and rampageous, if in his pronouncements he was apt to set loose Mosaic thunder, as well as to bring to wintry spirits a green hint of springtime, if at times he took to himself the dangerous role of

Ordinator of human fate, and on other occasions wept for very weakness and default—why these were the wild oppositions that met in him, made of him the curator, interpreter, oracle, the *nonpareil* of the centuries we name Christian.

. . .

Those who assembled in tears to say their farewell by the strand beheld one shortly to depart from them. He had chosen with all his leonine heart to stand with their humble estate. That was the image that ever so slowly receded on the watery horizon, mingling their tears and the salt sea; the workman who need not be ashamed, the friend, the reprover, the unquenched tongue and spirit.

. . .

The image and then the after image. Ours is the latter: it is burned in the brain of the ages. His outline hovers there on the shore, prepossessing, ominous, a stigma, a brand on the soul. We will never have done with him. He had dared utter, and the church dared accept, such words concerning Christ as no other conceived or spoke. "He poured Himself out, taking the form of a slave; therefore has God exalted Him." And again, "Jesus is the Yes of God." And again, "In Him everything in heaven or on earth was created, not only things visible but also the invisible orders of thrones, sovereignties, authorities and powers; the whole universe has been created through Him and for Him." And yet again, "God has made known to us a secret purpose, in accord with the plan determined before hand in Christ; that the universe, everything in heaven and on earth, might be brought into unity in Christ."

. . .

Astonishing, those utterances—conceived in anguish, in circumstances foreign or hostile to faith, in prison, the threat of the sword overshadowing him. His tempestuous spirit received, held, channeled the wisdom of the Spirit, sent it flowing in our direction.

. . .

Perhaps his greatest tribute: to this day Paul is detested and loved with an intensity and perdurance reserved to no other, save only his Master.

EIGHTEEN

Concerning vocation and friendship,
and the anguish attendant thereto.

Not often is the Spirit ignored or contravened in *Acts;* perhaps only this once. And on the occasion, it is the disciples who gain an inkling of imminent danger and immediately bruit it about. Is the word of the Spirit given for their strengthening rather than his warning, since he is already aware of the perils ahead, and is determined (also "in the Spirit") to ignore them?

"Do not risk the journey to Jerusalem," is the locution they hear, and transmit, with large misgivings. And he proceeds anyway.

Whose spirit speaks, mine or yours? Are the spirits one, or many? If one, why the disagreement; and if many, whose is to prevail, and on what grounds? We are not told. Something is implied; the Spirit who impels Paul is so strong a wind in his sails, so great a light in the encroaching darkness, that he must follow, follow.

The outcome is simply presumed here; in Luke's account, and as though endorsing the decision in his own person, the decision is beyond discussion or apologia. None is offered. "When our time ashore was ended, we left and continued our journey."

.   .   .

A more portentous event by far awaits the travelers after they put ashore at Caesarea. They are made welcome at the home of Philip the deacon. Luke mentions as though in passing the gifts of a truly remarkable family; the four daughters of the household are prophets. Such are the living caryatids who uphold the house, whose gaze penetrates events far and near, times near and far.

Shall we call them daughters of Pentecost? In any case their gaze, as ancient testaments make clear, is far from stony; these daughters are hardly to be thought of as mere statuary, however apt in bearing the weight of the new faith. Though it is implied here that on the arrival of their distinguished guest, the maiden seers are silent as stone.

(We are not told why they say nothing, why the warning of the Spirit is conveyed through someone else; still this reticence of Luke comes as no surprise. Indeed the book is filled with such lacunae, to a point that surpasses, and yet entices, all surprise. Of what good is a story, however venerated, that is void of sharp turns and catapults? In the life of faith, Luke implies, surprises abound. The women are silent.)

What a household! Already it includes Paul, and the daughters who hold the home free from the sheer gravity and tug of semblances. And Philip the father of such daughters, whose main gift, we are told, is service of the poor; and who is here called "the evangelist" in tribute to his aptness for the truth.

As if these were not enough, and more. As if the house were not already filled with the whispers of spirit! To the door came yet another visionary, a certain Agabus; he is referred to elsewhere in *Acts* as one who saw in his mind the coming of the terrible famine. At that time his clairvoyance enabled the generous to collect alms and so avert the worst of the catastrophe.

No one could claim that Paul was not forewarned!

We have then for a household the silent daughters, Philip keeping his counsel, Paul to all intents, laconic and quotidian. And Agabus, no stranger to the drama of the situation, determines to dramatize it.

. . .

It is nothing new, this tactic of bringing a symbol to bear, when a situation is literally beyond words. You must like Jeremiah break a vessel and hold the shards aloft, if people are to understand the monstrous breaking and scattering of the tribe. You must summon friends, then break bread and pour wine and repeat ancient words, if you are to understand the breaking of bones, the spilling of blood—the bones and blood of the Lamb and the martyrs. And so on.

So here. The act is spontaneous, of the moment. It took the household quite by surprise. Abacus too it took by surprise. Words failed him, sorrow stopped his mouth. We picture the host, the daughters, Paul at prayer, all reduced to the silence that falls when a mood of foreboding darkens the air. Suddenly Agabus seizes Paul's long cloth girdle, binds it about his own hands and feet. Then he speaks: "These are the words of the Holy Spirit...." Thus Paul will be bound, delivered over.

. . .

Be it noted that the oracle of the Spirit by no means forbids Paul to undertake the dangerous passage to Jerusalem. What is to be shall be. The word is rather a kind of account taking: let all, especially the protagonist of the contest, know what lies ahead. As well as those who, in community with him, in prospect of his suffering, see their faith infused with dismay and sorrow.

Let him know, let them know. Let them together wrestle with the prospect. If he goes, he is beyond doubt to be lost to them; the Spirit has spoken.

.   .   .

And if he does not go to Jerusalem? But not going is unthinkable. The Spirit has spoken, we presume, to him also: God. The message to Agabus speaks simply of an outcome, under a certain hypothesis: if he goes, this will transpire.

In Paul's mind the "if" is already canceled. For him a wind blows strong and irresistible, in one direction only.

(What word was spoken by the Spirit to Paul, even whether such a word was granted him—of this we are told nothing. If we can judge, considering the set of his face and the purposeful words he utters, the word has taken another form. The imperative: Go.)

.   .   .

In San Salvador on the seventeenth of November, 1989, as is known around the world, six Jesuit priests, together with a domestic and her daughter, were dragged from their beds and murdered. The event was hardly unforeseen or even unchosen by the priests.

For at least a decade, the space of the horrendous civil war, they had dwelt under the livid threat that at length broke through their doors and exacted their blood. At one point several years ago, an ultimatum was issued against them: thirty days to leave the country, or be killed. They chose to remain and take their chances. The word of the Spirit, one concludes, was: Remain.

Instead of leaving the country, the Jesuits sent a modest appeal to their brothers around the world. Please be apprised of our predicament. Please come, if possible, to El Salvador. International attention is our only hope. A slight interference, the presence of outsiders, might, just might, delay discharge of guns already cocked and aimed.

Grief impels these lines. It was at that point, some four years before their deaths, that another New York Jesuit and I resolved to go. In the course of our visit we met the six who were subsequently murdered. It occurred to me at the time, that it might be useful to their survival to publish a small account of the journey, of the friendships we formed, of the dangers and complications of life in that tormented country. I did so. But nothing we could do turned the guns aside, as we were to learn to our horror and grief.

.   .   .

The reality of the Jesuits' prospect required neither drama nor dramaturge. Day after day, year after year, as the guns resounded to and fro like mad metronomes, the mortal danger wherein the priests stood, what form the end might take, could hardly have been made more vivid to them. Certainly not by us, their unclairvoyant visitors from *el Norte*.

The priests lived with death. They had no need of a drama, a play within their play. Why should someone seize the cincture of one among them, bind himself over, and so declare their plight? The Spirit, one might conclude, had spoken to them; a circuit of doom and glory bound them, each to each. One in life and work and consequences; remain.

.   .   .

After the murders, many of us have been arrested, in attempts to call those responsible to an accounting. And since little likelihood exists of a just outcome in their case, we concentrate on a single outcry: stop the murder of the innocent!

Jesuits who attended the funeral of the priests in San Salvador, brought to our country a portion of blood soaked earth, and in procession, bore the emblem to the White House. There, they anointed the pillars. There could hardly be a clearer assigning of responsibility.

. . .

Agabus has declared through the symbolic binding, certain boundaries of knowledge, of the form of Paul's future. The prospective binding of the apostle could only signify the drastic curtailing, if not the end of his extraordinary mission.

The response of his community to this dire likelihood is a spontaneous outcry; it is beyond bearing that Paul be taken prisoner, yet again! Friends are appalled; they beg him to remain free, while he is yet able, from bonds whose very prospect is a throttling of hope.

And he will not. He will counter their dread by introducing a larger, more awful threat, and embracing that. "Why those tears, why try to weaken my resolution? I am ready not only to be bound, but to die in Jerusalem for the name of the Lord Jesus."

. . .

What friend willingly consents in mind to the suffering of a friend, no matter the nobility of the cause? The office of friendship, we think, is to act as a counter to heroism, to bank its intemperate fires. In discharging that office with all one's might, as the heart drums insistently, the friend acts all the more nobly. The friend protests, weakens, warns, declares null and void, the hot will of the one who runs to death. "Let this cross be far from you!"

. . .

The outburst of Peter in face of the announcement of Jesus—so heartfelt and altruistic, so right (and so wrong), so in accord with the heart's deep welling (so weakening and delaying of what must be)—is coldly received by the Master, is perceived only as an assault on invincible will. And is rejected in tones brusque, final, scandalous: Stand aside, Satan.

Thus the friend, protesting, impeding, standing athwart, is locked in combat with the beloved one. "Simon, son of John, do you love Me?" Friendship, and then vocation. Which is to prevail? How shall a sedulous friend resolve the dilemma? How stand with the other, and still pay respect to the friend's vocation?

The solution, such as it is, is hardly a relief. It illustrates the awesome and perilous nature of the good things in question: vocation, friendship. When they clash, one good becomes the enemy of another. The outcome can only be a multiplying of sorrow. Cost what it may, the first bows before the determination of a friend—that he go where he must go, where he is quite literally and beforehand "bound." And then, the new agreement is sealed, in blood. It is the blood of an all-but-unimaginable pact.

In order to conclude the pact, the friend must summon to imagination, then together with his friend, leap the void that lies between friendship and vocation. It is quite simple and final. He joins his friend in death. "In very truth I tell you...when you are old, you will stretch out your arms and a stranger will bind you fast and bring you where you have no wish to go."

. . .

They all came to this, those of the early fellowship. One, their Friend, preceded them. The others were slow, but eventually grew hardy in purpose. Their Christianity was a fellowship of death and of the overcoming of death.

. . .

"So, as Paul would not be dissuaded, we gave in and said, 'the Lord's will be done.' "

Now we have something more than friendship, as the world would understand it. We have a community standing in farewell on the verge of the unknown, not in farewell, but in an accompanying spirit. The wind in Paul's sails bears them along like a great moving hand; all undertake in spirit the same errand, the journey toward Jerusalem. Friend and friends, they are bound over. They bend to Paul's will and prospect, "to die in Jerusalem for the name of the Lord Jesus."

The members are well advised not to doubt the worst, to embrace the darkness of their own foreboding. The Spirit that impels Paul is a Spirit that suggests: You will go in the same direction; the danger follows the faith, as a sail the wind.

And this for Paul's sake, that he not go alone on his dolorous way. And for their own also. The journey is theirs, and the binding over; and eventually, in likely prospect, the martyrdom as well.

NINETEEN

An aside: of martyrs and martyrdom,
ideology and faith.
Concerning ourselves, finally.

The martyrs test the church.

The church knows itself, which is to say, knows its own voyage, has mapped the path by water or by land toward Jerusalem; has also calculated to a nicety the consequence of the journey. But this, it must be said, only insofar as it knows, embraces, honors, exonerates its own martyrs.

This attitude and activity in regard to our own can only be called crucial. It implies at the same time that the church rejects the ideology which the state invariably, for its own perverse delight, and to cover its crimes, attaches to the believers whom it marks for destruction. This is an insulting tag attached to a noble corpse: "ideologue" or "troublesome priest" or "disturber of public order."

Thus the sequence: the state executes the martyrs, then denigrates their death behind a meticulous (or foolish) scrim of duplicity and doubt.

.   .   .

It was thus in the case of Jesus; he must not only die, Roman law must be vindicated in his death (and He be dishonored, his memory smirched) by charges of subversion, threats of destruction of the Temple, endangerment of law and order.

In His death we have something more shameful even. The state can be counted on for depraved conduct. But here we have a classic instance of religion abandoning the Martyr, joining the vile, secular chorus of dishonor.

Worse and worse; supplying out of its own foxy canons a philistine logic to conceal its implication in the crime: "One of them, Caiaphas, who was high priest that year, said, 'You have no grasp at all of the situation; you do not realize this; it is more to your interest that one man should die for the people, than that the whole nation should be destroyed.' "

. . .

The church can react only with scorn. Martyrdom is included in the church's catechesis; the church knows why martyrs die, and says so. More, the church makes it clear that in certain circumstances, such violent death is the only honorable witness and outcome.

Then, their death accomplished, her task continues. She raises them to the altar for holy emulation. They are now inscribed in the calendar of saints. Her supreme act of worship proceeds under their invocation. For they are, after Christ and Mary, her chief glory. She knows it, and (at least sometimes) says it boldly, defending the martyrs against all comers.

. . .

The defense is risky. Honor of the martyrs places the large community at risk. Often guns again are lowered, the terror is renewed, others are placed in danger. The mere declaration of how and why the martyrs perished, heightens the immemorial struggle between the church and the worldly powers—a struggle in which the martyrs were forerunners. It is in this sense that the whole church is called to martyrdom: to understand and vindicate the nobility of the noble dead.

.   .   .

In San Salvador, as elsewhere, noble tongues are silenced. But the truth must continue to be spoken; the truth of their death, the cruelty and injustice of it, the precious connection between their death and the integrity of the Gospel. This is judgment; the heavy tolling, not of a passing bell, but a presentiment of the last day itself. The bell tolls for the defeat here and now of the violent victors, for the triumph of the victims.

.   .   .

The martyrs, all said, stand surrogate for Christ and the church. Their crime is their firm withstanding, on behalf of an irresistible word of love. In this they have spoken for the whole body of Christ. Then, their death accomplished, the community takes up the task; not to justify the innocent death, nor to seek justice (a case improbable of success at best, since the unjust and violent sit also in the courts).

The task is otherwise: to confront the powers with judgment, a call to repentance. Even murderers, and the powers which impel them, must be salvaged, those who are furthest from the saving truth, from the mercy and compassion they have gunned down.

.   .   .

The consonance between church and martyr: the martyr standing witness for the church, the church vindicating and honoring the martyr.

An ordination photo of the murdered Father Ellacuria shows him prostrate on the sanctuary floor while the litany of saints is chanted.

A photo dated Thursday, November 16, 1989, shows him murdered outside the Jesuit house. His body is prostrate, face down. It is exactly the position of his ordination rite.

· · ·

The church, from time to time (and wondrously in our own time) earns the name: church of martyrs. The title signifies the living consonance between the witness of those who die, and those who survive. Both speak up, both pay dear; some in blood, some in the bearing of infamy and danger.

· · ·

This continuing burden of truthtelling is, it would seem (and here one speaks with trepidation), mainly a matter laid upon the local church. The situation could hardly be called ideal. When the highest authorities of the church refuse to vindicate our martyrs, and thus refuse to confront the powers clearly and unequivocally, only the local community can supply for the moral deficit.

The situation implies a kind of vexed and sorrowful logic. A given community has nourished the faith of the martyr with word and sacrament. A spiritual ampelopsis has joined the holy one to the body of Christ. It seems only fitting (though regrettable as well) that after death, both the good repute of the martyr and the continuing witness against the powers, should lie in the hands of those (invariably the poor) who survive and mourn. Let the great be silent, or mouth platitudes, or scavenge absurd political innuendo—it is the humble who know, who speak; their tears are eloquent.

In the great world, and the great worldly church, other concerns are in the air. The blood and torment are distant; they are carried on the airwaves and tubes, a phenomenon known fatuously as "international news." There, the images of the dead are seized, distorted, manipulated, shuffled about. Hours or days before, a phalanx of thugs did their worst. Now the dead are victimized once more, they become another "news" account, granted three or four minutes of spurious immortality. Their witness is submerged amid the waste of zany, frivolous, scandalous, violent "news bytes." So what else, so to speak, is new?

. . .

But secular ideologies and special interests are not restricted to the mass media. Add to the above the political and economic interests of ecclesiastical headquarters. Suppose for a moment (one need not suppose!), that those who died, perished for speaking on behalf of the inarticulate and powerless. Their death occurred in a minor, indeed inconsiderable land, worlds distant from the highly "developed" church and its ties with the "developed" superstates.

The situation does not invite moral clarity. Too much at stake at headquarters, too much of the past remains unacknowledged, unrepented. Proclaim the martyrs, commend them to the faithful? In the case of Jagerstaetter, the Austrian peasant who perished under Hitler, declaration of official sainthood would open the malodorous question of the collaboration with the Nazis, of almost the entire Austrian church.

Too hot to handle! So the matter must be gotten around. A conclusion is reached in exalted circles that the murdered Christians simply do not qualify. They defended no recondite or required "dogma." They died neither for the integrity of say, the doctrine of the Eucharist, the virginity of Mary, the bodily resurrection of Christ. A mutter is heard from influential lips. The victims died in a politically volatile situation; it is reported that they took sides, that they were defenders not of the faith, but of one ideology or another.

It could be conceded perhaps that they died for the sake of the powerless and poor; but this hardly suffices to grant the entitlement. So it is thought and said. Or is not said; but the silence wears a frown of thunder.

.   .   .

Let us be clear as might be. Innumerable sisters and brothers have died in our lifetime "for the sake of the powerless and poor." Let us think in consequence of this, of a scriptural teaching baptized again and again in a sea of blood. A teaching, let it be added, generally neglected in high ecclesiastical circles: the teaching of the Body of Christ.

Paul writes of the mutuality and integrity of all members of the body, the consonance of the lowliest with most honored, "so that there might be no division in the body, but that all its parts might feel concern for one another. If one part suffers, all suffer together; if one flourishes, all rejoice together."

.   .   .

Bishops and others, we beg you, take notice. This passion for the integrity of the body, this rejection of the rejection of the lowly. Behold the Scripture on behalf of which a host of martyrs in your lifetime and mine have staked their lives.

.   .   .

In face of the ambivalent speech (and the even more ambivalent silence) of authorities, the harmless pieties, the intertwining of profane and church interests, are we not justified in insisting that the authorities of the church speak clearly, passionately, in defense of our martyrs? That they clarify issues of faithful, political witness, that their words resound with the same truth that at a crack of gunfire, turned mortal bodies to pentecostal flame?

.   .   .

This is unpleasant, and to the mind of many unfortunate. All said, it is simply true; faith is a political matter, inevitably. So is martyrdom, in most cases. The task is to separate out in mind and heart, the political content of a given death (one's dying for the poor, who themselves are joined to political parties of revolution, the "church of the poor"—thus taking sides, and inevitably)—to separate this political implication from another lurking issue; that of ideology, high and low, ecclesiastical or secular, the itch and appetite of special interests and hankerings; above all, the appetite for power, control, secrecy, non-accountability.

.   .   .

Thus the death of the martyrs urges a scrutiny of conscience on the part of all. This includes a self-scrutiny of authority, of its ideology and behavior. Especially an ideology which inhibits the truth concerning the murder of our sons and daughters, the "honor and dishonor" of their deaths.

Let us for Christ's sake hear loud and clear, and let the assassins hear, and the faceless politicos and oligarchs hear, why our martyrs stood where they did ("the standpoint is the view-point"), why in consequence they, whether known or anony-mous, were eliminated. Let us hear praise of the martyrs; let us hear an unambiguous call to the faithful: the holy dead must be emulated.

TWENTY

In which Paul travels to Jerusalem
and is arrested.
Also of the curious phenomenon
known as Roman justice.

For Paul, to be sure, trouble is in store. That menacing prospect, always nearing, always at hand: prison, threat of death, thunder on the left, oracles he could well do without!

He is in bonds indeed, and menaced by the crowds, to whom he appears as an arrogant interloper, disregarding of the law, a renegade Pharisee and worse. And in the midst of such travail, during a night in prison, yet another vision of Jesus is granted him. The word is one of ambiguous comfort. "Keep up your courage! You have affirmed Me in Jerusalem, and you must do the same in Rome."

.   .   .

Paul is at the beginning of an interminable legal wrangle concerning his fate. For the remaining chapters of *Acts*, Luke will have only this to relate: Paul's meandering, oft-delayed journey from Jerusalem to Rome, in shackles. All along the way he will be shunted from pillar to post at the behest of various bureaucrats. Each of these worthies, highly placed and low, has a weather eye alert to his own career; each is canny in the way of his kind, lest he be burned by an inept disposition of this extremely hot case. Such were (and are) the fetching ways of empire.

Paul thus represents a classic case of the imperial dilemma, of which we have heard much before in *Acts*. Indeed it seems as though the coming of the Spirit has introduced the dilemma into the world. A violent system, in contention with the truth, cannot budge, cannot alter its ways, cannot finally make up its mind. Either prison must be decreed for the conscientious malefactors, and a concomitant and most unwelcome public impact be borne. Or the prisoner must be released in full knowledge on both sides that the conscientious crimes will go on.

.   .   .

The ways of empire continue. The case of the first Plowshares drones on for a decade; they too have known a journey of sorts toward Rome.

What is to be done with these troublesome Christians? Many a judge and prosecutor has etched deep wrinkles in canny foreheads over the dilemma. If we let them go... If we jail them...

The dilemma be it noted, is theirs, not ours. This would seem biblically significant.

.   .   .

What to do? On the horn of this dilemma many a sound civil servant has hung, sicklied o'er at the unpalatable prospects.

In midst of it all, we note that Paul possesses his soul in peace. He rides with the confused riptide, knowing that he neither set it in furious motion, nor is overly concerned about a just outcome.

.   .   .

The literary method of Luke is of more than passing interest here. Why, one asks, such a detailed account of the desultory itinerarium, geographically and juridically, of Roman justice, as it attempts in fits and starts to dispose of its famous prisoner? The clue, one would think, lies in the community for whose sake Luke writes. They are a people beset by the same empire which lays such a heavy and ambiguous claim on Paul.

.   .   .

For the sake of his community Luke is peeling away the myth of empire, specifically in its assumption of civilized behavior, integrity, justice, efficiency. Are the Lucan Christians overawed by the pretensions of the mighty? Let us then see in some detail, their conduct in Paul's progress toward Roman justice.

Their attitude toward the prisoner is ambivalent. Every official in Paul's path would seem to lust after a glimpse of this prisoner. He bears an aura of truth and integrity; he is fearful and irresistible at once. So they come successively on stage, to question, to debate, to listen. And in short order they are reduced by their prisoner to the status of minor players. They are shown up, either through their own words, or through Luke's comment; bribe-takers, bumblers, evasive, kowtowing, double-dealing. On a human scale, they are constantly eclipsed by the moral rectitude, eloquence, and acuity of their captive, a titan in chains.

.   .   .

Delivered over, Paul begins his interminable, Kafkaesque journey. He is posted first from Jerusalem to Caesarea. A letter addressed to the Roman governor is sent with him, explaining the case and in effect, passing the embarrassment along. (The letter is uncannily reminiscent of the no-charge decree of Pilate against Jesus, also reported by Luke: "I find no case for this man to answer." Surely a peculiar instance of Roman justice, since the declaration of innocence is shortly followed by capital punishment.)

Thus Claudius to Felix: "...there was no charge against [Paul] which merited either death or imprisonment." The illogic continues: "I am sending him to you without delay." No charge is brought down; the prisoner remains nonetheless in custody.

TWENTY-ONE

Of Felix, Festus, Agrippa,
Judges who shall be judged.
Of the pathology of power.

ACTS 24 - 25: 23

Luke pauses unaccustomedly over the character and conduct of Felix. A lower case Pilate? In this decaying minor monument of empire, tergiversation is raised to the level of high art. The statuary strikes a heroic pose; there is only one defect, it cannot budge from place.

In the case against Paul, the delay stretched out for two years, a negligent bureaucratic yawn. Dalliance nicely substitutes for untimely, unwelcome decision. We are in the presence, one after another, of very *magistri* in the arts of survival, skills conned one would think from an ancient imperial handbook, perhaps older than the Bible itself. Indeed, many of the ploys of Felix and his ilk are embedded in the Bible itself; cf. the *Book of Kings*.

. . .

The time of no decision is not entirely wasted by Felix. Desultory as he is, the official knows that he has on his hands a rare and intelligent specimen. Were there long, official hours to get through in his lonely outpost, few diversion at hand? A whiff of distaste rises from Luke's page; luxury, boredom.

And yet Felix is accounted no fool. Paul, detained under house arrest, is summoned before him.

What does the Roman anticipate from his prisoner? This official named in irony Felix, the "happy," "fortunate" one, this shadow of Pilate, an echo of a world-weary whimper: "What is truth?" Felix, Luke assures us, is "well-informed of the Way." It is his business to be so informed, as it is to be posted on the weather, or the condition of highways, or the imperial bank rates. Everything is important, and nothing; everything is—information, facts, grist for the crepitating mill. Nothing, let nothing touch the heart or stir the millpond of routine.

.   .   .

There exists a cast of mind, often connected with a measure of secular power, that has seen everything and learned nothing, taken nothing to heart, grasped no truth for its own. The world and its inhabitants are no more than a populated, abstract chess board; movers and shakers shuffle people about, hither and yon, pieces in the game.

Is Paul to be accounted a chess piece in the hands of the Romans? Hardly. For the first time the apostle stands eye to eye with his captor and adversary. For a space, the champion of the Old Way of ruthless principality and power confronts the giant of the New. An old way is collapsing; a new one emerging. More to the point, in Paul the new Way is offering hope, a handhold to the hopeless old.

No taker. Felix brushes the proffer aside, as of no interest. It holds not even such interest as might awaken wrath or joy or a resolve to finish off the affair, to vindicate or punish Paul; nothing.

.   .   .

Thus goes a certain kind of history. Men radically incapacitated with regard to the truth, bestride the world, whether by inadvertence or choice wreak their havoc, smile a feral smile, brush aside impeding or combating ideas. Ideas such as the one embodied before Felix; the most improbable one of all, faith in a recently executed criminal in a remote Near East colony, "faith in Christ Jesus." Hot coals have touched the Roman's flesh; but the flesh is cold, a corpse.

.   .   .

What might it entail, were Felix to believe? Other Romans, a multitude of them, one day will profess a far different fealty, will bow before the Jew Jesus. Such converts will usually be required to die for their beliefs, illustrating in blood the incompatibility of empire and faith. And when on an awful hour, an emperor will make his confession of faith, and still remain firm on his throne, neither his spiritual estate nor that of the church will be notably improved.

.   .   .

As to routine, perhaps the prisoner has some amelioration to offer; let us see. Paul and Felix are *vis-à-vis*, no audience is present. Felix bids Paul speak, anticipating—a diversion, an account of far-away peoples, the travelogue of a distinguished gyrovague, a Marco Polo of preachments?

More than Felix bargained for. A homily is discharged at him, straight as a launched arrow. Paul speaks "of faith in Christ Jesus; [then] the discourse turns to matters of justice, self-control and the coming judgment."

To say no more, we (and Felix) are beyond our depth in the presence of a scrutinizer of hearts, practitioner of a skill of which the empire and its nabobs have no recognized need.

Concerning a subject like "faith," Felix can have no quarrel. A casual Roman agreement is in force, the mind of empire is broad as its borders. Let a thousand religions bloom! and as many charlatans, to the honor of as many gods! An ininerant guru might indeed freely ply his trade, discourse windily concerning his favorite deities, to no discernible ruffling of Roman order.

. . .

Thus the prisoner could ambition entertaining his captor for a vagrant hour, and perhaps win favor in so doing.

But then, but then—whence those successive bolts of lightning—"justice, self-control, judgment"—Felix loses his Roman cool. Like his mentor Pilate, who incontinently fled from wisdom, Felix grows alarmed; the truth has beckoned, a ghostly finger, and imperious.

. . .

The old way is its own impediment and scandal; it cannot remain itself and welcome the New. Jesus had implied as much. "In the world they lord it over one another." Has the imperial way ever been put so simply, so devastatingly? That way, the way of the jackboot, the gibbet, the kangaroo court, the interrogation center, the misery and the surfeit, the booty and slaves, the stupefied populace and the purring throne, the bread and circuses, the oligarchs and the landless, the world markets and world wars—if that way is to arrive at the truth, it must renounce, like the clatter of dropped swords upon a pavement, all the habiliments of illegitimate power.

It is simple as that. The two ways, the one lording it over, the other communitarian and compassionate, are radically incompatible, cannot coexist, whether in a Felix or in his empire. Say welcome to one; say farewell to the other.

Felix ends the interview; the abrupt closure reads like his epitaph: "Enough for now; when I find it convenient, I will send for you again."

His life is shot through with covert corruption; he stands nonetheless with confidence and adroitly within the law. "He had hopes of a bribe from Paul, so he sent for him frequently and talked with him." We are left to imagine the sorry outcome of this, greed in combat with the truth; between the lines Luke has devastatingly probed the imperial use (which is to say, the misuse) of power.

.   .   .

The governor will grant his distinguished prisoner much, a tolerable form of house arrest, frequent and presumably respectful dialogue (that beloved code of authority, signifying not much). Felix will grant everything but—justice. Two years pass, and Paul remains uncharged, untried, unsentenced. No bribe has been passed; Felix swings like a weathervane in the world's saucy weathers; he has many constituencies to please. There are grave impediments against a just outcome.

Two years prior, at a preliminary hearing, Paul had addressed the governor: "Knowing as I do that for many years you have administered justice to this nation, I make my defense with confidence."

Two years; long enough, one thinks, to shatter confidence of the most heroic cast. Paul, Roman citizen, is granted everything by the Romans except—justice.

.   .   .

Felix's term ends; he is succeeded by a certain Festus. But the change of authorities in no way implies a change of tactic; the new governor's method is as otiose as the old. Time, it is presumed, will resolve things, especially those matters whose present resolution is—untimely.

And now another worthy, a king, Agrippa by name, enters the scene; what a close harrowing of Paul! Every sector of society is to review, for its own inviolate interests, the "case of Saul, Jew, Roman citizen, presently a follower of the Way, and known as Paul."

The implication is manifold. Paul's preaching has touched official nerves throughout the empire, Jewish, Roman, financial, religious—and perhaps above all, political.

.   .   .

His preaching has seemed a simple, even harmless matter, as modern sensibility would purvey the Jesus event. And yet, and yet. Once, a preacher set quaking the great theophanies of empire, he loosed on the air the aura of an unmentionable Name and Event. Through Paul the modest, even tragic Nazarene, presumably once and for all disposed of, threatens to rend the seamless robe of empire! No wonder the delays, the successive, increasingly fruitless consultations, the toadying and bowing and scraping, the passing of Paul from one eminence to another.

What disposition is to be made of the intemperate teller of this unlikely tale—the dead man, the invocation of whose name suffices to make the halt and lame stand sturdy, the very dead walk again?

. . .

ACTS 25: 23 - 26: 32

Luke's account of the slowly unfolding legal charade is quite straightforward, and for that, is all the more telling. Much by way of moral implication is left to the reader. All these legitimacies, claiming the body, the custody; all those tragicomical assemblies, eminences, courtrooms, crowds!

And now perforce, a Jewish king enters the story. It is as though this oxymoronic figurehead, signifying an embrace between emperor and collaborator, were entirely normal, to be taken for granted. Hail little Caesar!

The king and his sister "came in full state and entered the audience chamber, accompanied by high-ranking officials and prominent citizens." The episode might well be entitled "Paul in Wonderland." Is the defendant weary of an interminable charade? He is; and yet he launches again into his story.

. . .

Once again Luke thrusts Paul and his conversion tale to the forefront. The church can never have done with him, with that story which will have no end, as long as time tolls—the conversion and its consequence. For in a sense, the story of such a one is the story of all. Paul is the living icon and voice of the body of Christ, moving through time.

There is really, all said, but one story. It has been told before
in *Acts,* it belonged to Peter and John and a few others. Be
healed and heal, speak the truth boldly, confront the powers.

According to Luke, Jesus had put the matter direct, by way
of self-understanding and vision of the future. What He had undergone in the world, all would undergo in turn. It was a sorrowful law of grace in bondage to the iron phalanx of the powers; "...they will seize and persecute you. You will be handed
over to councils and put in prison; you will be haled before
kings and governors for your fidelity to me.... Some of you will
be put to death...."

.   .   .

Lifelong, Paul keeps a vivid sense of his own "before" and
"after." The horror and the hope, who he was, who he became.
The tale was (and is) both fascinating and unacceptable. Pagans
or Jews, they listen rapt; and they turn away. When he speaks of
his renegade self prior to the Damascus lightning bolt, he dares
a rhetoric of harsh solace; he places himself at their side. He is
one of them, nay worse than they, the Roman bureaucrat con-
sumed with boredom, the renegade Jewish "king."

Dispassionately recounting his crimes, Paul inserts the blade
in them also, opens their wounds. "...I sent many of God's
people to prison, and when they were condemned to death, my
vote was cast against them.... I tried by repeated punishment to
make them commit blasphemy; indeed my fury rose to such a
pitch that I extended my persecution to foreign cities."

A lightning bolt cast him to ground. They too see for a
blinding moment, and are rendered all the more blind for that.

TWENTY-TWO

Paul and Roman law.
Of power and powerlessness,
and the empery of death broken.

ACTS 24 - 25 - 26

Paul concludes his speech before Felix, repeating almost verbatim his previous words before the Sanhedrin: "The issue in my trial before you today is the resurrection of the dead."

Then before Agrippa, the same all but obsessive theme: "The messiah would suffer, and that, as first to rise from the dead, He would announce the dawn to both Jew and gentile...."

So Paul concludes his apologia, on a note that will reverberate in the air of the centuries. It is a strangely resonant, even calamitous note in the ears of the principalities: resurrection. Death the loser, death the pretender, death no dominion, imperial death downed once for all.

Take it or leave, Festus and Agrippa, officials and potentates. You have lost the initiative, your bound man is free, your ordinances avail nothing, your pomps are but the "rag and bone shop of the heart." Your time is foreshortened. You dwell in darkness, even as you fear the light that reveals your works. Notwithstanding, you are helpless to hinder the dawn.

. . .

Festus, that self-contained Roman ramrod, is unaccustomedly aroused by Paul's words; he shouts aloud, quite beside himself. "Paul, you are raving, too much study is driving you mad."

We are bewildered by his outburst; another Lucan surprise. Can it be that in Festus, the squared blocks of Rome are cracking like an egg of Easter? What power is bespoken here by this world-embracing, world-forsaking Magian of words and works? What hint of momentous change, loss, beckoning, what lightning plays havoc around the thrones? What if the prisoner were proven, in a sane, four-square Roman world, madly right?

What if the dead man walked? what if (but it is manifestly unthinkable) the colossi were tottering where they stood?

.   .   .

This is a moment when (under fierce duress, whether of truth or fantasy) the mind reels and spins, all but loses its moorings. Whatever the subject (whether truthful or fantastic is not known)—it simply lies beyond the mind's capacity. It were best considered a kind of taboo, left unspoken, unexamined, unto itself. Any other way lies madness. Madness in the hearer to match the ecstasy of the seer.

Thus Paul's bearing, his assurance, above all the *Mysterium Tremendum* he insists on airing: these drive the self-contained Roman to the brink.

"Humankind cannot bear very much reality." The relentless Pauline rhetoric is like a scissors of fate; it cuts the moorings, the trireme plunges outward on a riptide, tormented, uncontrollable.

The world of Festus has turned to wild water. He shouts aloud. And on Paul's part, what response can avail against the charge of madness? Granted that it were true, of what point a riposte?

Indeed in such a world as Festus and his masters rule, who is to be accounted sane and who mad, the governor or his prisoner?

.   .   .

In the world of Festus and his prisoner, or of American judges and Plowshares prisoners, of the learned goblins of nuclear witchcraft and the endangered peoples—in such a world, who is to be accounted sane, and who mad?

.   .   .

Festus were well-advised to beat a retreat.

But Paul is not finished. He turns to the Jewish pretender: "King Agrippa, do you believe the prophets?" And then, with sublime insouciance, as though it were possible to draw forth the best from the worst: "I know you do."

Paul knows nothing of the sort. His blade is pinking the adversary; it is his old delight in dilemmas. Let the Jewish collaborator, he of the house of the murderer of John Baptist and the tormentor of Jesus, let him but admit to belief in the prophets, and he must in simple logic admit to faith in Messiah Jesus. Which cannot be, or the very stars are grown foolish.

On the other hand, let him deny faith in his own tradition, what will Jewish ears make of that?

Progeny of Herod, that infected bloodline, could hardly be thought apt to bear the burden of truth. Frivolity therefore; it were best to lighten a moment that threatens to fall like a hundredweight. Agrippa: "Then with a little more persuasion you would make a Christian of me?"

It is as though an ape on his shoulder had taken speech to itself; it would contrive a like chatter. We must at all costs make great matters Lilliputian; then we shall be safe in our houses.

Sublime, solemn, the response of Paul. "I wish to God that not only you but all those who hear me today, might become what I am—apart from these chains!"

. . .

Could they utter a like wish, those who forge the chains? Could they rise to this; envy of Paul and his chains, his future ominously uncertain, bound over to judgment as he is? Paul has once more reversed the situation; he holds his captors captive: in his dignity, in the verve and play of his rhetoric, most of all in his bearing, valorous, free of cant and pretense and the trappings of moral emptiness. The old way claims the New for its prey; and on the moment, the New emerges victorious.

That onerous "appeal to Caesar" he had launched! Was Paul contriving a test case centering on himself, a case that might eventually issue in Roman toleration for the new faith? A surmise is all one can muster. What is certain is that the labyrinth of Roman law holds him in grasp. The hold will remain firm through the end of our tale. Paul, uncharged, unconvicted, for all we can gather of Luke, is a prisoner for life.

. . .

There are worse fates, one reflects ruefully. Is the long travail of Paul at the hands of the Romans the source of his scorching diatribe against the law in his letter to the Christians at Rome?

. . .

The law, the law! Some of us know at first hand, something of that relentless, irrational claim. For a decade now, the Plowshares Eight have been in the toils of American law. Appeal, upon appeal, shunted this way and that, a Jarndyce vs. Jarndyce nightmare, an exercise in timelessness and triviality.

And early one morning recently, two federal marshals at the door, a dawn voyage across Manhattan under guard, hours in a holding cell, then another absurd moment; a hearing before a magistrate. Charge: refusing to travel across the continent for a hearing before yet another magistrate. And all this fuss and expense of time, money, gasoline, marshals, light and heat, pomp and solemnity, funereal faces and laughable "crimes."

The crime: in this instance, arrest at a federal building for protesting American collusion in the murder of the Salvadoran Jesuits. I am pursued with metronomic vigor; there is hardly a word of the pursuit (let alone the capture) of the murderers.

．　．　．

The truth will out, in a strangely befitting reversal of roles. A universal respect is granted this prisoner, on land, and shortly thereafter at sea. Would Luke have him attain in our eyes a kind of olympian pre-eminence, centurions and sea captains yielding before his counsel?

The turn of events is wonderfully restoring to the community of Luke. Rome may do its damnedest, but no worldly power, not even the mightiest, will prevail over the gospel and its tellers.

Indeed (then, now) the worst turns to the best. The tyrant succeeds only in creating martyrs. In so doing, he strengthens the community he would crush.

TWENTY-THREE

An interrupted, all but ruinous voyage.
Despite all, a beneficent outcome.

ACTS 27: 1-44

The sea passage from Palestine to Rome attains a larger meaning. The vessel, populated by a motley contingent of soldiers, merchants, guards and the small knot of believers, is hardly in open sea before it is discovered to be disaster bound. The skills of those responsible for a prosperous passage bend to vigorous action, and seem for a time to prevail. All in vain!

Indeed in normal times and seasons those in command of the vessel would be judged able to bring crew, passengers, and cargo safely to port. Alas, the season is far from "normal." A wintry sky looms above, heavy with discontent. A storm arises, its fury threatens to swamp them. Despair settles on every face.

On every face save one, so we are told. It is the prisoner who inexplicably issues commands, wrests a modicum of hope from all but certain disaster.

.   .   .

Paul, we are told, shouts his orders above the winds, even intervenes in a threatened mutiny. And then, on the unsteady deck, the prisoner performs an act that seems at once strangely inappropriate to a dire hour, and dearly familiar. He summons an ancient symbol, and a new.

" 'For fourteen days...you have been in suspense, going hungry, eating nothing. Let me persuade you to take food.... Your safety is not in doubt.' With these words he took some bread, gave thanks to God in front of them all....."

No magic here; the storm rages on. Yet the taking of food at such a moment becomes a spontaneous, sacramental, all but surreal sign. The slavish panic subsides. Bread is broken, more heartening to body and spirit than any mere word of reassurance.

.   .   .

The Paul who was symbolically bound by the prophet Agabus, and then by Roman law was seized and bound more straitly by far—he stands free of heart, unbound in soul. Who can summon for us a symbol that saves?

On the endangered ship there ensues a strange renewal of resources, strength, even hope. In the tiny action betokening a willed normalcy, calm is regained.

Paul knows one thing, and it suffices. He is bound for Rome, and his appeal. He stands assured; beyond all mischance, he will arrive there. Nothing in nature or human malice will avail to miscarry the outcome.

And if his companions on board are buffeted and all but sunken—nevertheless, they too are included in the apparently deaf and dumb Providence of the wild hour.

Paul's visionary bones are unshaken. Those aboard stand under the dark wing of a Providence that despite all, has heard and spoken. "Last night there stood by me an angel of the God whose I am and whom I worship. 'Do not be afraid, Paul,' it was said. 'It is ordained that you shall appear before Caesar.

And be assured, God has granted you the lives of all who are sailing with you.'"

.   .   .

It is a good story, we say to ourselves. Paul drinks danger like a bracing wine; his soul is resonant with the winds of Spirit, confident as to outcome.

Outcome? What prospect keeps him like a Flying Dutchman, speeding toward Rome? Why this passion for safe arrival, when the event (as he must know) can spell no amelioration of his fortunes, but only misfortune multiplied? What is this hope of his, for justice in this world? Does he dream perchance that Caesar's conscience surpasses that of his colonial lackeys?

.   .   .

Luke, it would seem, is as detached as Paul; better, he takes to himself the detached mind and heart of the hero. Whatever the event portending, we are in better hands than Caesar's.

.   .   .

Thus, to no satisfaction on our part, we turn the final page of *Acts*. And (perhaps by instruction of Paul?) we are simply granted no resolution, no outcome. Did Luke know only as much as he sets down, or was he perhaps, conscious of the predicament of his community, anxious to publish his notes quickly, unwilling to delay until a judicial resolution of Paul's case?

The speculation would seem idle. Let us take Luke at face value, his talent and intent. To end the saga with Paul still bound and very much alive, is in itself a metaphor of note. We do ill to ignore it, that blank page.

.   .   .

A phase has ended, another begun. Only once more will we hear direct speech from Paul; he has become *le grand silencieux*. His captive state is his only apologia.

.   .   .

It is difficult not to read a heroic intent in these last chapters. On land, in public and private, Paul's weakness is inexplicably made strong. In contention and setback, his moral nobility ignored, his rights scorned and outright denied, he stands there for the church's sake.

.   .   .

Then comes the passage at sea. Skilled as Paul is in confounding adversaries, he is less potent in dominion over nature. The seas are not stilled; the craft is wrecked and eventually breaks up under the appalled eyes of the survivors. And no life is lost, as the prescient spirits foretold.

Thus a dramatic emblem is set in place, crises are implied and their (at least partial) resolution. A pattern is strongly suggested in the horrendous voyage, for the sake of Luke's community, for the communities of the future.

The life of faith is anything but a serene passage. Thus it has been from the start, thus it will be. "In the world you will suffer, but have confidence, I have overcome the world."

.   .   .

According to Luke's Gospel, the shadow of death, slowly then quickly gathering, lay heavy on the heart of Christ. The prospect was at once horrifying, inevitable—and matter for rejoicing.

The *agon* of the Master is done with. Now the disciples walk a like, bloodshot track, the "Way" of the believing clan. It cannot be otherwise. Oh would that it were otherwise! is the plaint of His heart and theirs.

.   .   .

No fidelity in a vacuum, no Jesus apart from Herod, Pilate, the conniving high priests. No greatness of Paul apart from the machinations of tyrants great and small, but finally, puny: a Felix, a Caesar. The faith is a story of crisis, tragedy, the rise and fall of a hero. It cannot be otherwise. Creation has fallen from grace; the scythe of death cuts a wide swath, wide as existence.

.   .   .

Luke would isolate something of the above, what one might think of as a metaphysic of the faith. *Acts* is the story, all told, of two heroic figures, Peter and Paul. They bestride the world; they speak the word entrusted to them, are finally seized and murdered. And despite all, in a logic beyond all logic, they are *presente,* living, resurrected. They have become "My two witnesses...the two olive trees, the two lamps...in the presence of the Lord of earth." (Rev. 11:4)

They stand there, alight; stand there, rooted.

.   .   .

Thus goes the tale of our beginnings, a story of heroes: for our sake, for emulation and intercession. Our ancestors include heroes, saints, martyrs. A high calling: terrifying, enlivening.

.   .   .

"In this way all came safe and sound to land." Conrad, Melville, and much earlier, Paul. We are in a company whose vocation is—accompaniment.

At sea a fearsome storm arises. Such are the times.

But we are not alone. Through dark time and benighted place we stand with friends, sisters and brothers. They are larger than life, larger by far than death. Through them we yield not.

.   .   .

Paul has come through, and not only he; all survive, we are told, though barely, like land creatures plunged out of their element. They stagger out of the surf onto the verge of the world.

.   .   .

What of the God of Paul, who on this occasion plucks every soul from the deep, a precious detritus—and on other occasions notorious to ourselves, saves few or none at all?

Truly, according to Luke and the earlier prophets, the hand of Providence is ambidextrous. In the right hand we imagine a ship is held in tender suspension from all disaster. Then from the left hand another ship is let fall; it plunges to sea bottom with all aboard. And we stand bewildered, uncertain what to make of it all, our times and Paul's; the wreck or safe passage of land and air and sea vessels, the salvaging (or utter loss) of crews and contingents.

. . .

We long for light on such dark matters; and light is not granted. It is simple as that. Faith is as simple as that, as comfortless and final.

For whatever comfort we can gain, scant to the point of vanishing, we fall back appalled to another story of Luke; the last lightless hours of God's son. Of those hours we are granted to know a great deal. Of comfort, as we learn, He knew little— little to the vanishing point.

. . .

The present writer, no Luke, confesses himself often at sea on such matters; and no calm sea at that. (Luke also, in some remotely similar sense, was at sea; the "I" breaks through once more as the fateful voyage of Paul is launched.)

. . .

At sea, at sea; and land, wherever it may be, a cruel mirage.

What is a Jesuit to make of the murder of his brothers, whose only crime was their standing by, speaking for the victims in an unutterably dark time? What to make of the death of two women, a mother and daughter whose only offense was their modest livelihood, serving the priests at table?

What to make of a heaven under which such crimes are consummated, their anonymous agents vanishing into the night? What make of a God under whom (God help us), or in despite of whom, and certainly in contempt of whom, such wickedness is wrought?

We think we know, and perhaps say we know—and we know precisely nothing.

This too is faith, this confession of ignorance in the teeth of such storms as all but pluck us from life.

· · ·

Christians are by confession, know-nothings. The admission is a kind of weakness and a kind of strength. The knees turn to water; the purpose stands firm nonetheless. And the admission, the ignorance, is as close to salvation as one is likely to attain in such a world, under such a God.

· · ·

Sweet murdered mother, sweet child, thank you. In the life you have won, others will serve you, you will sit like a queen and her daughter at the banquet of God.

Valiant Jesuits, my brothers, thank you. You stood where you were called, and fell where you must. May your prayer win, even for us, a measure of that virtue most rare in a world of gunmen and guns: steadfastness.

· · ·

ACTS 28: 1-15

Delivered safe from the sea and landed on Malta, together with his captors and compatriots, Paul shines.

There follows the curious episode of the viper in the firelight, as the exhausted voyagers are succored by people of the island. "By the viper's sting you will not be harmed." Such words, taken literally, are verified in the rudest circumstance, as Luke attests.

It is not only that this singular captive is himself immune from venom. He is also, from the day of his own healing, a healer. The passage at sea, the escape route narrow as a knothole, the chancy landing among superstitious strangers, none of this has dimmed his powers. He is invited to the home of the prefect of the island, Publius. The father of the host lies ill. Paul prays, lays hands on the patient and heals him. Inevitably the word gets abroad, and the sick of the island are borne to his side.

.   .   .

All this we are used to in happier times and places. Luke would drive the point home; ill fate or prosperous, in bonds or free, Paul pursues equably the work at hand. There is no tacking before this or that wind, no kowtowing to captors, no hindering the word. Indeed, the fairest freedom Paul knows is wrung from dire times.

His hands may be bound close; but the task of the free is to test the limits, perhaps even to succeed in enlarging them. The shackles are useless; Paul raises his hands, blesses and heals.

He has simply manumitted himself.

.   .   .

We sense the absurdity of the chains, the absurd fiction that hems him in. Who is free, who captive? It is as though the manacles were made of thin air.

Healer, prisoner; he is not the first to unite the irony. Nor the last.

.   .   .

The chanciness of that "Way," that "new life"! Constantly, as though it were an image of humanity breaking its chains, the "Way" opens a wide and wider circle of imagination's powers. What would the world look like, did the world know "the Way"? To discover the answer (and indeed "answer" is inadequate to the reality; the faith is no conundrum awaiting its sphinx)—Paul must be tumbled about the world, watery world and solid.

. . .

And what does he discover? "The Way" by no means points to an answer; the Way has its own validity, solidity, meaning. Step by step he must trudge on, unlearning, learning as he goes.

Or he takes passage and a watery wake opens. Then at long length dawn, land near and dear and yet unattained, "a kind of bay with a beach." It is all one. What he will discover as the mists clear, what peoples will approach or recoil from him, what unknown speech is spoken—this is the Way, the means, the end; wherever he pitches tent and breaks bread. And then, at the whim or good pleasure of his captors, where he passes on. Bound over.

. . .

It is by no means new to him, this captivity. He had held himself for years captive to the word. No question in his mind of status or enforced dignity or a lofty place in this or that community. We learn from his letters something constant, ominous, to the contrary; how vulnerable his person and teaching, what a penalty small minds exact of great, what petty bickerings mar the splendid (and all so fragile) surface of the heavenly vision.

Tumbled about the world. In no wise delicately or gently held in hand by Providence. Nothing of exceptional treatment, except for one remarkable circumstance—this episode at sea.

The outcome is in exact accord with his prediction. All come ashore safe and sound, the "two hundred seventy-six souls on that ship." Paul, that regent of the spirit, comes trailing his sodden rags, half-drowned, rolled landward like a tumbleweed. Danger on land, danger at sea.

That watery way, so near an image of death; there will be more to pay, and still more.

TWENTY-FOUR

Of Paul's arrival in Rome.
The book ended,
and yet never ending....

So against all chance, arrival at the imperial capital. And the hope arises for resolution of the onerous case. Paul, we are told, lingers in Rome "for two full years at his own expense," held in an undetermined sort of house arrest. He is still "bound," yet he stretches out his hand to friends, speaks freely with them, evangelizes, encourages.

And this in quite striking contrast to the last days of Jesus, as Luke records them.

Jesus dies on the page; we are told in some detail the why and how. Not on the last page, perhaps the second last.

We turn that page, and it flames up, self-combusting. The last page is pure glory.

.   .   .

Not so with Paul, at least with the Paul of Luke.

This is what we are left with: Paul dangling at the end of a truly bizarre "case." The book ends abruptly, he is never brought to trial. Yet in no wise is he put down or turned aside from his purpose.

.   .   .

Yet once more he quarrels with local Jews, and a meeting, held "dawn to dusk," ends badly. It is insufferable, all but insuperable with him, this peevishness of spirit. And yet he cannot contain himself; when "our people" will not yield (and yet we are told, "some were won over by his arguments"), he launches an Isaian thunderbolt. It is his last word on the page.

We end the book with that. And yet the outcome, we feel, is not set in adamant, is still negotiable. The conflict has not reached the awful millennial impasse of which we know much. One has the impression of a strong hope in the air; these fractious elder and younger brothers have by no means renounced one another, or despaired of eventual reconciling.

.   .   .

The book closes, our longing is intact. Then we raise our eyes from the text, overwhelmed, perhaps even in tears. That awful subsequent history, our own! Would that our bloodshot century, and so many before, had not canceled the possibility of another, far different ending!

.   .   .

Once upon a time…some other finale. Hope beats on; the story is not ended. Let us refuse to close the book, against our hope, against our grain, our ancestry—our future.

.   .   .

Let us speak of two brothers.

Of the older let it be said that today he is bewildered and torn; he has lost his hold upon the younger. In the eyes of the elder, his brother has abandoned the ancestral house, absconded with the inheritance, under foreign skies serves a strange god. So the first born mourns and casts himself about the world in witless and bootless anger.

As if this were all, this estrangement? If it were all, matters between them could be called, if not satisfactory, melancholy—and manageable. The world, after all, is ample enough and more to bear the estrangement of two brothers. Thus goes the theory (a bit neat when placed against the messy facts); they are free like those brothers of old, to choose each his territory, and settle down under vine and fig tree, to live free of violence—wrought against each other, or against third parties who chance to cross their turf.

Those third parties! There is the rub. Of which more later.

.   .   .

Meantime, the centuries since *Acts*.

Meantime: which is to say, interim, armed truce, nothing settled, no reconciliation in sight. And then, now and again, something infinitely worse.

The younger brother grows powerful, enlists the help of allies, moves against his elder. He simply cannot live at peace with this brother, whose face conjures up before his inflamed mind—what? Let us dare say it: the features of the holy One, the gestures, the intonation, the fidelity drenched in time and symbol, the panoplied memories of the tribe; ancestry and blood, the voices that beckon, the guardian spirits that vigil to right hand and left.

It is all too much to be borne; the younger erupts at times in a religious mania. His fevered dreams give him no rest; they are peopled with the faces he banishes by day. He reads the ancient scrolls, they torment him with a litany of the great ancestors; who begat whom, from the beginning to the advent of the holy One, and on and on—until he reaches his own name. It cannot be borne. What is he to do, trailing as he does an umbilical he cannot cut, even in nightmare? He grasps a sword, he will sever it by day.

. . .

In the past, when the mania took hold, it were advisable that the elder brother go in hiding. He has done so again and again. He knows when the mood may strike, when the moon is blood-shot and the sun obscured. He reads the signs; mortal danger to him and his tribe.

. . .

The younger? Let us say it: he is reduced in scope, and of two minds, and knows little peace in the world. In the short run, time smiles upon him, the gods (his brother is right, this one serves strange gods, in spite of all his protestations)—they pour out their gifts: prosperity, armies, political hegemony, colonies.

But time is a long run as well, and favor turns to a frown; he has "gained the whole world," and suffered all but irreparable loss.

. . .

A dilemma. The Jesus whom he purportedly serves is—a Jew. Scripture makes it plain. He opens his testament, and it is as though a hand leapt from the page and grasped him in a vise. *Tolle et lege.* Take and read.

But he cannot read, or he reads wrong. The centuries, the prosperity, the armies, the political hegemony, the colonies— these are lethal benefits indeed, inhibitions against biblical literacy. They cast a film over his eyes. What is he to make of "Love your enemies"? what of the words spoken on the mount of beatitudes, the silence from Calvary? What to make of Jesus? Alas, this believer has taken up the sword; its blade lies across his vision, dazzling, blinding.

. . .

And today? A kind of uneasy truce. It is fraught with danger, and not only for the two combatants. There are third parties to this perennial quarrel! People who cross lines, cross borders, interfere, enact claims, walk into "spheres of influence."

. . .

Their contretemps has taken a secular form. (The sword, the secular form.) Each has taken an empire to his bosom; my beloved, my god.

But their quarrel is by no means resolved through this arrogant move, which their Bible has forbidden again and again. The dispute in fact grows more virulent than ever, selfish, violent, contemptuous of those once known as God's own, the Anawim.

The two have also grown strangely alike; physical resemblance is echoed in a common outlook on the world. Each of them breathes in unison the bracing air of "the nations." There is a heady sense of arrival, of standing on an equal dynastic footing. Each is now a kind of colossus bestriding the world—one foot planted in a temple, the other in a palace.

Each is also highly skilled in religious talk, invocation, memory, symbol. Each claims a testament, each has enlisted an army. Each claims a double credential: Bible in one hand, sword in the other. Inevitably, each persecutes the prophets in his midst, an old story. (We are, after all, in the epoch of Kings, Jeremiah and Isaiah and their oracles of judgment are declared by common consent irrelevant.)

Each brother has at command moreover a "religious" establishment, a temple ritual, whose main office, if one can so put things, is to grind out emblems of assurance, to fashion idols, blessings, prophecies of deliverance and prospering. Such "religious leaders" and their works have been scorchingly derided in the books of prophets; but this is of no point and arouses no trouble of spirit.

.   .   .

A most peculiar epoch, our own.

For obvious reasons, it is not advantageous that the two, in their peculiar secular epiphanies, destroy one another. The elder in any case, in comparison with the younger, is a lesser titan. And the younger has cleansed his limbs and weapons, for a time, of their evidence of carnage. He spouts ecumenism like a Roman fountain. His present mood is this: he longs with respect to his brother, to leave as legacy a less maculate history.

But this resolve comes and goes, dark mood and brightsome. And the situation meantime could hardly be said to improve. That troublesome matter of the third parties haunts them both; old hatreds, unresolved angers, murderous jealousies, these circulate and poison the air. If the younger brother is resolved to suspend hostilities for a time (his current mask shows a phiz both respectable and democratic), if he has ceremoniously hung up his sword at some shrine, has ceased hounding the elder about the earth, this must be understood as no change of heart—except for the worse.

.   .   .

Let us speak of a tactical adjustment. To this younger warrior something momentous and satisfactory has occurred. He has come on other victims in the world. They act as a relief to his merciless impulse; they may be thought of as a species of judas goats, substitute sacrifices.

.   .   .

And the elder? Unreflective, blind, he mimes his brother. Between the two meantime, an unsteady truce holds. Alas, it brings small comfort to the world.

The mirror game continues, played out in the dark.

For either to see in the mirror the truth, the blood, the clone, the mockery and mime, the contempt, the sedulous aping, each would require a measure of light; let us say at least a glimmer of twilight.

But they are in the dark; it might be said they thicken the dark. And the game goes on.

The mirror is bloodied; the blood is not theirs. Third parties. The blood is Palestinian, Iraqi, Kuwaiti, Salvadoran, Nicaraguan, Panamanian, Grenadian, Vietnamese, Laotian, Cambodian. In our lifetime. And more to flow.

.   .   .

The book of *Acts* remains open, unfinished, waiting in a sense; a sense both hopeful and horrific. It lurks there like a preternatural third eye, waiting. Or like a scribe's hand, quill ready, eye alert. What acts are to follow the acts of apostles?

Let us set them down; better, let us enact them, repeat them, dwell on them, improvise, invoke them, stand with them. Acts of Dorothy Day, of Archbishop Romero, of Thomas Merton, of the murdered Jesuits, of that vast unnamed "cloud of witnesses" who live and labor and die in fidelity to the word. For whom the word made supreme and sole sense, in a senseless time.

. . .

The original book lives two lives; the lives chiefly of Peter and Paul, and their leonine beginnings and bequeathings.

Then the book lives on in other lives; in the sense of absolute relevance (that much abused word) the book after all being God's word about the ideal human, as humans summon to their travail again and again, the "boldness" of the Spirit.

Wickedness, goodness, then and now. The great dead and the evil dead and ourselves, the shambles, the glory we make of our lives. Crime and innocence, retribution and malfeasance—acts of that time and this. This time contradicting and suppressing and denying the tradition, trampling it under in a rampage of greed and violence; or withstanding, standing with the ancient summons. Even unto the shedding of blood, the blood freely given.

We will never have done with it: the open book, both judgment and blessing.

. . .

As Luke takes leave of Paul, in mid-sentence so to speak, the curious bondage of the apostle continues: "under the law" he "lodged privately, with a soldier in charge." It is a parable of Christian life, and Paul will make much of it in his letter to the Roman Christians.

With what difficulty he and we, ever so gradually come to know our enslavement to the law, and its contradictions; how we are led into existence on a close or slack leash—but always, at the far end of things, an iron hand "has taken us in charge." Under that charge, that leash (always just short of release), we come on whatever freedom we claim.

Say it is not to the advantage of the law that we be dealt with, for whatever reason, in capital fashion. Or it is; and we are so dealt with. This curious and crepuscular light in which we dwell, somewhere between twilight and dawn; a "meantime" granted us perhaps; and then swift as a noose the dark comes down. Or the regnant sun, and a new day is up.

.   .   .

It is our story; unsatisfactory to be sure, unfinished as Paul's as he moves about Rome under that gimlet eye.

"He stayed at Rome two full years at his own expense, with a welcome for all who came to him." The essential work goes on. Luke reduces it to bare bones. "He proclaimed the realm of God and taught the facts about the Lord Jesus Christ quite openly, without hindrance."

And leave it at that....

APPENDIX

The Acts of the Apostles

ACTS OF THE APOSTLES

1 IN the first part of my work, Theophilus, I gave an account of all that Jesus did and taught from the beginning ² until the day when he was taken up to heaven, after giving instructions through the Holy Spirit to the apostles whom he had chosen. ³ To these men he showed himself after his death and gave ample proof that he was alive: he was seen by them over a period of forty days and spoke to them about the kingdom of God. ⁴ While he was in their company he directed them not to leave Jerusalem. 'You must wait', he said, 'for the gift promised by the Father, of which I told you; ⁵ John, as you know, baptized with water, but within the next few days you will be baptized with the Holy Spirit.'

⁶ When they were all together, they asked him, 'Lord, is this the time at which you are to restore sovereignty to Israel?' ⁷ He answered, 'It is not for you to know about dates or times which the Father has set within his own control. ⁸ But you will receive power when the Holy Spirit comes upon you; and you will bear witness for me in Jerusalem, and throughout all Judaea and Samaria, and even in the farthest corners of the earth.'

⁹ After he had said this, he was lifted up before their very eyes, and a cloud took him from their sight. ¹⁰ They were gazing intently into the sky as he went, and all at once there stood beside them two men robed in white, ¹¹ who said, 'Men of Galilee, why stand there looking up into the sky? This Jesus who has been taken from you up to heaven will come in the same way as you have seen him go.'

The church in Jerusalem

¹² THEY then returned to Jerusalem from the hill called Olivet, which is near the city, no farther than a sabbath day's journey. ¹³ On their arrival they went to the upstairs room where they were lodging: Peter and John and James and Andrew, Philip and Thomas, Bartholomew and Matthew, James son of Alphaeus, Simon the Zealot, and Judas son of James. ¹⁴ All these with one accord were constantly at prayer, together with a group of women, and Mary the mother of Jesus, and his brothers.

¹⁵ It was during this time that Peter stood up before the assembled brotherhood, about one hundred and twenty in all, and said: ¹⁶ 'My friends, the prophecy in scripture, which the Holy Spirit uttered concerning Judas through the mouth of David, was bound to come true; Judas acted as guide to those who arrested Jesus— ¹⁷ he was one of our number and had his place in this ministry.' ¹⁸ (After buying a plot of land with the price of his villainy, this man fell headlong and burst open so that all his entrails spilled out; ¹⁹ everyone in Jerusalem came to hear of this, and in their own language they named the plot Akeldama, which means 'Blood Acre'.) ²⁰ 'The words I have in mind', Peter continued, 'are in the book of Psalms: "Let his homestead fall desolate; let there be none to inhabit it." And again, "Let his charge be given to another." ²¹ Therefore one of those who bore us company all the while the Lord Jesus was going about among us, ²² from his baptism by John until the day when he was taken up from us—one of those must now join us as a witness to his resurrection.'

²³ Two names were put forward: Joseph, who was known as Barsabbas and bore the added name of Justus, and Matthias. ²⁴ Then they prayed and said, 'You know the hearts of everyone, Lord; declare which of these two you have chosen ²⁵ to receive this office of ministry and apostleship which Judas abandoned to go where he belonged.' ²⁶ They drew lots, and the lot fell to Matthias; so he was elected to be an apostle with the other eleven.

2 THE day of Pentecost had come, and they were all together in one place. ² Suddenly there came from the sky what sounded like a strong, driving wind, a noise which filled the whole house where they were sitting. ³ And there appeared to them flames like tongues of fire distributed among them and coming to rest on each one. ⁴ They were all filled with the Holy

Spirit and began to talk in other tongues, as the Spirit gave them power of utterance.

⁵ Now there were staying in Jerusalem devout Jews drawn from every nation under heaven. ⁶ At this sound a crowd of them gathered, and were bewildered because each one heard his own language spoken; ⁷ they were amazed and in astonishment exclaimed, 'Surely these people who are speaking are all Galileans! ⁸ How is it that each of us can hear them in his own native language? ⁹ Parthians, Medes, Elamites; inhabitants of Mesopotamia, of Judaea and Cappadocia, of Pontus and Asia, ¹⁰ of Phrygia and Pamphylia, of Egypt and the districts of Libya around Cyrene; visitors from Rome, both Jews and proselytes; ¹¹ Cretans and Arabs—all of us hear them telling in our own tongues the great things God has done.' ¹² They were all amazed and perplexed, saying to one another, 'What can this mean?' ¹³ Others said contemptuously, 'They have been drinking!'

¹⁴ But Peter stood up with the eleven, and in a loud voice addressed the crowd: 'Fellow-Jews, and all who live in Jerusalem, listen and take note of what I say. ¹⁵ These people are not drunk, as you suppose; it is only nine in the morning! ¹⁶ No, this is what the prophet Joel spoke of: ¹⁷ "In the last days, says God, I will pour out my Spirit on all mankind; and your sons and daughters shall prophesy; your young men shall see visions, and your old men shall dream dreams. ¹⁸ Yes, on my servants and my handmaids I will pour out my Spirit in those days, and they shall prophesy. ¹⁹ I will show portents in the sky above, and signs on the earth below—blood and fire and a pall of smoke. ²⁰ The sun shall be turned to darkness, and the moon to blood, before that great, resplendent day, the day of the Lord, shall come. ²¹ Everyone who calls on the name of the Lord on that day shall be saved."

²² 'Men of Israel, hear me: I am speaking of Jesus of Nazareth, singled out by God and made known to you through miracles, portents, and signs, which God worked among you through him, as you well know. ²³ By the deliberate will and plan of God he was given into your power,

and you killed him, using heathen men to crucify him. ²⁴ But God raised him to life again, setting him free from the pangs of death, because it could not be that death should keep him in its grip.

²⁵ 'For David says of him:

I foresaw that the Lord would be
 with me for ever,
with him at my right hand I cannot
 be shaken;
²⁶ therefore my heart is glad
 and my tongue rejoices;
 moreover, my flesh shall dwell in
 hope,
²⁷ for you will not abandon me to
 death,
 nor let your faithful servant suffer
 corruption.
²⁸ You have shown me the paths of life;
 your presence will fill me with joy.

²⁹ 'My friends, nobody can deny that the patriarch David died and was buried; we have his tomb here to this very day. ³⁰ It is clear therefore that he spoke as a prophet who knew that God had sworn to him that one of his own direct descendants should sit on his throne; ³¹ and when he said he was not abandoned to death, and his flesh never saw corruption, he spoke with foreknowledge of the resurrection of the Messiah. ³² Now Jesus has been raised by God, and of this we are all witnesses. ³³ Exalted at God's right hand he received from the Father the promised Holy Spirit, and all that you now see and hear flows from him. ³⁴ For it was not David who went up to heaven; his own words are: "The Lord said to my Lord, 'Sit at my right hand ³⁵ until I make your enemies your footstool.'" ³⁶ Let all Israel then accept as certain that God has made this same Jesus, whom you crucified, both Lord and Messiah.'

³⁷ When they heard this they were cut to the heart, and said to Peter and the other apostles, 'Friends, what are we to do?' ³⁸ 'Repent', said Peter, 'and be baptized, every one of you, in the name of Jesus the Messiah; then your sins will be forgiven and you will receive the gift of the Holy Spirit. ³⁹ The promise is to you and to your children and to all who are far away, to everyone whom the Lord our God may call.'

2:33 **at:** *or* by.

⁴⁰ He pressed his case with many other arguments and pleaded with them: 'Save yourselves from this crooked age.' ⁴¹ Those who accepted what he said were baptized, and some three thousand were added to the number of believers that day. ⁴² They met constantly to hear the apostles teach and to share the common life, to break bread, and to pray. ⁴³ A sense of awe was felt by everyone, and many portents and signs were brought about through the apostles. ⁴⁴ All the believers agreed to hold everything in common: ⁴⁵ they began to sell their property and possessions and distribute to everyone according to his need. ⁴⁶ One and all they kept up their daily attendance at the temple, and, breaking bread in their homes, they shared their meals with unaffected joy, ⁴⁷ as they praised God and enjoyed the favour of the whole people. And day by day the Lord added new converts to their number.

3 ONE day at three in the afternoon, the hour of prayer, Peter and John were on their way up to the temple. ² Now a man who had been a cripple from birth used to be carried there and laid every day by the temple gate called Beautiful to beg from people as they went in. ³ When he saw Peter and John on their way into the temple, he asked for alms. ⁴ They both fixed their eyes on him, and Peter said, 'Look at us.' ⁵ Expecting a gift from them, the man was all attention. ⁶ Peter said, 'I have no silver or gold; but what I have I give you: in the name of Jesus Christ of Nazareth, get up and walk.' ⁷ Then, grasping him by the right hand he helped him up; and at once his feet and ankles grew strong; ⁸ he sprang to his feet, and started to walk. He entered the temple with them, leaping and praising God as he went. ⁹ Everyone saw him walking and praising God, ¹⁰ and when they recognized him as the man who used to sit begging at Beautiful Gate they were filled with wonder and amazement at what had happened to him. ¹¹ While he still clung to Peter and John all the people came running in astonishment towards them in Solomon's Portico, as it is called. ¹² Peter saw them coming and met them with these words: 'Men of

Israel, why be surprised at this? Why stare at us as if we had made this man walk by some power or godliness of our own? ¹³⁻¹⁴ The God of Abraham, Isaac, and Jacob, the God of our fathers, has given the highest honour to his servant Jesus, whom you handed over for trial and disowned in Pilate's court—disowned the holy and righteous one when Pilate had decided to release him. You asked for the reprieve of a murderer, ¹⁵ and killed the Prince of life. But God raised him from the dead; of that we are witnesses. ¹⁶ The name of Jesus, by awakening faith, has given strength to this man whom you see and know, and this faith has made him completely well as you can all see.

¹⁷ 'Now, my friends, I know quite well that you acted in ignorance, as did your rulers; ¹⁸ but this is how God fulfilled what he had foretold through all the prophets: that his Messiah would suffer. ¹⁹ Repent, therefore, and turn to God, so that your sins may be wiped out. Then the Lord may grant you a time of recovery ²⁰ and send the Messiah appointed for you, that is, Jesus. ²¹ He must be received into heaven until the time comes for the universal restoration of which God has spoken through his holy prophets from the beginning. ²² Moses said, "The Lord God will raise up for you a prophet like me from among yourselves. Listen to everything he says to you, ²³ for anyone who refuses to listen to that prophet must be cut off from the people." ²⁴ From Samuel onwards, every prophet who spoke predicted this present time.

²⁵ 'You are the heirs of the prophets, and of that covenant which God made with your fathers when he said to Abraham, "And in your offspring all the families on earth shall find blessing." ²⁶ When God raised up his servant, he sent him to you first, to bring you blessing by turning every one of you from your wicked ways.'

4 They were still addressing the people when the chief priests, together with the controller of the temple and the Sadducees, broke in on them, ² annoyed because they were proclaiming the resurrection from the dead by teaching the people about Jesus. ³ They were arrested

3:22 **a prophet like me**: *or* a prophet as he raised up me.   4:1 **the chief priests**: *some witnesses omit* chief.

and, as it was already evening, put in prison for the night. ⁴ But many of those who had heard the message became believers, bringing the number of men to about five thousand.

⁵ Next day the Jewish rulers, elders, and scribes met in Jerusalem. ⁶ There were present Annas the high priest, Caiaphas, John, Alexander, and all who were of the high-priestly family. ⁷ They brought the apostles before the court and began to interrogate them. 'By what power', they asked, 'or by what name have such men as you done this?' ⁸ Then Peter, filled with the Holy Spirit, answered, 'Rulers of the people and elders, ⁹ if it is about help given to a sick man that we are being questioned today, and the means by which he was cured, ¹⁰ this is our answer to all of you and to all the people of Israel: it was by the name of Jesus Christ of Nazareth, whom you crucified, and whom God raised from the dead; through him this man stands here before you fit and well. ¹¹ This Jesus is the stone, rejected by you the builders, which has become the corner-stone. ¹² There is no salvation through anyone else; in all the world no other name has been granted to mankind by which we can be saved.'

¹³ Observing that Peter and John were uneducated laymen, they were astonished at their boldness and took note that they had been companions of Jesus; ¹⁴ but with the man who had been cured standing in full view beside them, they had nothing to say in reply. ¹⁵ So they ordered them to leave the court, and then conferred among themselves. ¹⁶ 'What are we to do with these men?' they said. 'It is common knowledge in Jerusalem that a notable miracle has come about through them; and we cannot deny it. ¹⁷ But to stop this from spreading farther among the people, we had better caution them never again to speak to anyone in this name.' ¹⁸ They then called them in and ordered them to refrain from all public speaking and teaching in the name of Jesus.

¹⁹ But Peter and John replied: 'Is it right in the eyes of God for us to obey you rather than him? Judge for yourselves. ²⁰ We cannot possibly give up speaking about what we have seen and heard.'

²¹ With a repeated caution the court discharged them. They could not see how they were to punish them, because the people were all giving glory to God for what had happened. ²² The man upon whom this miracle of healing had been performed was over forty years old.

²³ As soon as they were discharged the apostles went back to their friends and told them everything that the chief priests and elders had said. ²⁴ When they heard it, they raised their voices with one accord and called upon God.

'Sovereign Lord, Maker of heaven and earth and sea and of everything in them, ²⁵ you said by the Holy Spirit, through the mouth of David your servant,

Why did the Gentiles rage
and the peoples hatch their futile
  plots?
²⁶ The kings of the earth took their
  stand
and the rulers made common cause
against the Lord and against his
  Messiah.

²⁷ 'They did indeed make common cause in this very city against your holy servant Jesus whom you anointed as Messiah. Herod and Pontius Pilate conspired with the Gentiles and with the peoples of Israel ²⁸ to do all the things which, under your hand and by your decree, were foreordained. ²⁹ And now, O Lord, mark their threats, and enable those who serve you to speak your word with all boldness. ³⁰ Stretch out your hand to heal and cause signs and portents to be done through the name of your holy servant Jesus.'

³¹ When they had ended their prayer, the building where they were assembled rocked, and all were filled with the Holy Spirit and spoke God's word with boldness.

³² THE whole company of believers was united in heart and soul. Not one of them claimed any of his possessions as his own; everything was held in common. ³³ With great power the apostles bore witness to the resurrection of the Lord Jesus, and all were held in high esteem. ³⁴ There was never a needy person among them, because those who had property in land or houses would sell it, bring the proceeds of

---

4:6 John: *some witnesses read* Jonathan.   4:33 all ... esteem: *or* grace was strongly at work in them all.

the sale, [35] and lay them at the feet of the apostles, to be distributed to any who were in need. [36] For instance Joseph, surnamed by the apostles Barnabas (which means 'Son of Encouragement'), a Levite and by birth a Cypriot, [37] sold an estate which he owned; he brought the money and laid it at the apostles' feet. 5 But a man called Ananias sold a property, [2] and with the connivance of his wife Sapphira kept back some of the proceeds, and brought part only to lay at the apostles' feet. [3] Peter said, 'Ananias, how was it that Satan so possessed your mind that you lied to the Holy Spirit by keeping back part of the price of the land? [4] While it remained unsold, did it not remain yours? Even after it was turned into money, was it not still at your own disposal? What made you think of doing this? You have lied not to men but to God.' [5] When Ananias heard these words he dropped dead; and all who heard were awestruck. [6] The younger men rose and covered his body, then carried him out and buried him.

[7] About three hours passed, and his wife came in, unaware of what had happened. [8] Peter asked her, 'Tell me, were you paid such and such a price for the land?' 'Yes,' she replied, 'that was the price.' [9] Peter said, 'Why did the two of you conspire to put the Spirit of the Lord to the test? Those who buried your husband are there at the door, and they will carry you away.' [10] At once she dropped dead at his feet. When the young men came in, they found her dead; and they carried her out and buried her beside her husband.

[11] Great awe fell on the whole church and on all who heard of this. [12] Many signs and wonders were done among the people by the apostles. All the believers used to meet by common consent in Solomon's Portico; [13] no one from outside their number ventured to join them, yet people in general spoke highly of them. [14] An ever-increasing number of men and women who believed in the Lord were added to their ranks. [15] As a result the sick were carried out into the streets and laid there on beds and stretchers, so that at least Peter's shadow might fall on one or another as he passed by; [16] and the people from the towns round Jerusalem flocked in, bringing those who were ill or harassed by unclean spirits, and all were cured.

[17] Then the high priest and his colleagues, the Sadducean party, were goaded by jealousy [18] to arrest the apostles and put them in official custody. [19] But during the night, an angel of the Lord opened the prison doors, led them out, and said, [20] 'Go, stand in the temple and tell the people all about this new life.' [21] Accordingly they entered the temple at daybreak and went on with their teaching.

When the high priest arrived with his colleagues they summoned the Sanhedrin, the full Council of the Israelite nation, and sent to the jail for the prisoners. [22] The officers who went to the prison failed to find them there, so they returned and reported, [23] 'We found the jail securely locked at every point, with the warders at their posts by the doors, but on opening them we found no one inside.' [24] When they heard this, the controller of the temple and the chief priests were at a loss to know what could have become of them, [25] until someone came and reported: 'The men you put in prison are standing in the temple teaching the people.' [26] Then the controller went off with the officers and fetched them, but without use of force, for fear of being stoned by the people.

[27] When they had been brought in and made to stand before the Council, the high priest began his examination. [28] 'We gave you explicit orders', he said, 'to stop teaching in that name; and what has happened? You have filled Jerusalem with your teaching, and you are trying to hold us responsible for that man's death.' [29] Peter replied for the apostles: 'We must obey God rather than men. [30] The God of our fathers raised up Jesus; after you had put him to death by hanging him on a gibbet, [31] God exalted him at his right hand as leader and saviour, to grant Israel repentance and forgiveness of sins. [32] And we are witnesses to all this, as is the Holy Spirit who is given by God to those obedient to him.'

[33] This touched them on the raw, and they wanted to put them to death. [34] But a member of the Council rose to his feet, a Pharisee called Gamaliel, a teacher of the

5:31 **at his right hand**: *or* with his right hand.

law held in high regard by all the people. He had the men put outside for a while, [35] and then said, 'Men of Israel, be very careful in deciding what to do with these men. [36] Some time ago Theudas came forward, making claims for himself, and a number of our people, about four hundred, joined him. But he was killed and his whole movement was destroyed and came to nothing. [37] After him came Judas the Galilean at the time of the census; he induced some people to revolt under his leadership, but he too perished and his whole movement was broken up. [38] Now, my advice to you is this: keep clear of these men; let them alone. For if what is being planned and done is human in origin, it will collapse; [39] but if it is from God, you will never be able to stamp it out, and you risk finding yourselves at war with God.'

[40] Convinced by this, they sent for the apostles and had them flogged; then they ordered them to give up speaking in the name of Jesus, and discharged them. [41] The apostles went out from the Council rejoicing that they had been found worthy to suffer humiliation for the sake of the name. [42] And every day they went steadily on with their teaching in the temple and in private houses, telling the good news of Jesus the Messiah.

The church moves outwards

6 DURING this period, when disciples were growing in number, a grievance arose on the part of those who spoke Greek, against those who spoke the language of the Jews; they complained that their widows were being overlooked in the daily distribution. [2] The Twelve called the whole company of disciples together and said, 'It would not be fitting for us to neglect the word of God in order to assist in the distribution. [3] Therefore, friends, pick seven men of good repute from your number, men full of the Spirit and of wisdom, and we will appoint them for this duty; [4] then we can devote ourselves to prayer and to the ministry of the word.' [5] This proposal proved acceptable to the whole company. They elected Stephen, a man full of faith and of the Holy Spirit, along with Philip, Prochorus, Nicanor, Timon, Parmenas, and Nicolas

of Antioch, who had been a convert to Judaism, [6] and presented them to the apostles, who prayed and laid their hands on them.

[7] The word of God spread more and more widely; the number of disciples in Jerusalem was increasing rapidly, and very many of the priests adhered to the faith.

[8] Stephen, full of grace and power, began to do great wonders and signs among the people. [9] Some members of the synagogue called the Synagogue of Freedmen, comprising Cyrenians and Alexandrians and people from Cilicia and Asia, came forward and argued with Stephen, [10] but could not hold their own against the inspired wisdom with which he spoke. [11] They then put up men to allege that they had heard him make blasphemous statements against Moses and against God. [12] They stirred up the people and the elders and scribes, set upon him and seized him, and brought him before the Council. [13] They produced false witnesses who said, 'This fellow is for ever saying things against this holy place and against the law. [14] For we have heard him say this Jesus of Nazareth will destroy this place and alter the customs handed down to us by Moses.' [15] All who were sitting in the Council fixed their eyes on him, and his face seemed to them like the face of an angel.

7 Then the high priest asked him, 'Is this true?' [2] He replied, 'My brothers, fathers of this nation, listen to me. The God of glory appeared to Abraham our ancestor while he was in Mesopotamia, before he had settled in Harran, [3] and said: "Leave your country and your kinsfolk, and come away to a land that I will show you." [4] Thereupon he left the land of the Chaldaeans and settled in Harran. From there, after his father's death, God led him to migrate to this land where you now live. [5] He gave him no foothold in it, nothing to call his own, but promised to give it as a possession for ever to him and to his descendants after him, though he was then childless. [6] This is what God said: "Abraham's descendants shall live as aliens in a foreign land, held in slavery and oppression for four hundred years. [7] And I will pass judgement", he said, "on

6:1 **those who spoke Greek**: *lit.* the Hellenists.   **those who spoke the language of the Jews**: *lit.* the Hebrews.

the nation whose slaves they are; and after that they shall escape and worship me in this place." [8] God gave Abraham the covenant of circumcision, and so, when his son Isaac was born, he circumcised him on the eighth day; and Isaac was the father of Jacob, and Jacob of the twelve patriarchs.

[9] 'The patriarchs out of jealousy sold Joseph into slavery in Egypt, but God was with him [10] and rescued him from all his troubles. He gave him wisdom which so commended him to Pharaoh king of Egypt that he appointed him governor of Egypt and of the whole royal household.

[11] 'When famine struck all Egypt and Canaan, causing great distress, and our ancestors could find nothing to eat, [12] Jacob heard that there was food in Egypt and sent our fathers there. This was their first visit. [13] On the second visit Joseph made himself known to his brothers, and his ancestry was disclosed to Pharaoh. [14] Joseph sent for his father Jacob and the whole family, seventy-five persons in all; [15] and Jacob went down into Egypt. There he and our fathers ended their days. [16] Their remains were later removed to Shechem and buried in the tomb for which Abraham paid a sum of money to the sons of Hamor at Shechem.

[17] 'Now as the time approached for God to fulfil the promise he had made to Abraham, our people in Egypt grew and increased in numbers. [18] At length another king, who knew nothing of Joseph, ascended the throne of Egypt. [19] He employed cunning to harm our race, and forced our ancestors to expose their children so that they should not survive. [20] It was at this time that Moses was born. He was a fine child, and pleasing to God. For three months he was nursed in his father's house; [21] then when he was exposed, Pharaoh's daughter adopted him and brought him up as her own son. [22] So Moses was trained in all the wisdom of the Egyptians, a powerful speaker and a man of action.

[23] 'He was approaching the age of forty, when it occurred to him to visit his fellow-countrymen the Israelites. [24] Seeing one of them being ill-treated, he went to his aid, and avenged the victim by striking down the Egyptian. [25] He thought his countrymen would understand that God was offering them deliverance through him, but they did not understand. [26] The next day he came upon two of them fighting, and tried to persuade them to make up their quarrel. "Men, you are brothers!" he said. "Why are you ill-treating one another?" [27] But the man who was at fault pushed him away. "Who made you ruler and judge over us?" he said. [28] "Are you going to kill me as you killed the Egyptian yesterday?" [29] At this Moses fled the country and settled in Midianite territory. There two sons were born to him.

[30] 'After forty years had passed, an angel appeared to him in the flame of a burning bush in the desert near Mount Sinai. [31] Moses was amazed at the sight, and as he approached to look more closely, the voice of the Lord came to him: [32] "I am the God of your fathers, the God of Abraham, Isaac, and Jacob." Moses was terrified and did not dare to look. [33] Then the Lord said to him, "Take off your sandals; the place where you are standing is holy ground. [34] I have indeed seen how my people are oppressed in Egypt and have heard their groans; and I have come down to rescue them. Come now, I will send you to Egypt."

[35] 'This Moses, whom they had rejected with the words, "Who made you ruler and judge?"—this very man was commissioned as ruler and liberator by God himself, speaking through the angel who appeared to him in the bush. [36] It was Moses who led them out, doing signs and wonders in Egypt, at the Red Sea, and for forty years in the desert. [37] It was he who said to the Israelites, "God will raise up for you from among yourselves a prophet like me." [38] It was he again who, in the assembly in the desert, kept company with the angel, who spoke to him on Mount Sinai, and with our forefathers, and received the living utterances of God to pass on to us.

[39] 'Our forefathers would not accept his leadership but thrust him aside. They wished themselves back in Egypt, [40] and said to Aaron, "Make us gods to go before us. As for this fellow Moses, who brought us out of Egypt, we do not know what has become of him." [41] That was when they

---

7:37 **like me:** *or* as he raised up me.

made the bull-calf and offered sacrifice to the idol, and held festivities in honour of what their hands had made. ⁴²So God turned away from them and gave them over to the worship of the host of heaven, as it stands written in the book of the prophets: "Did you bring me victims and offerings those forty years in the desert, you people of Israel? ⁴³No, you carried aloft the shrine of Moloch and the star of the god Rephan, the images which you had made for your adoration. I will banish you beyond Babylon."

⁴⁴'Our forefathers had the Tent of the Testimony in the desert, as God commanded when he told Moses to make it after the pattern which he had seen. ⁴⁵In the next generation, our fathers under Joshua brought it with them when they dispossessed the nations whom God drove out before them, and so it was until the time of David. ⁴⁶David found favour with God and begged leave to provide a dwelling-place for the God of Jacob; ⁴⁷but it was Solomon who built him a house. ⁴⁸However, the Most High does not live in houses made by men; as the prophet says: ⁴⁹"Heaven is my throne and earth my footstool. What kind of house will you build for me, says the Lord; where shall my resting-place be? ⁵⁰Are not all these things of my own making?"

⁵¹'How stubborn you are, heathen still at heart and deaf to the truth! You always resist the Holy Spirit. You are just like your fathers! ⁵²Was there ever a prophet your fathers did not persecute? They killed those who foretold the coming of the righteous one, and now you have betrayed him and murdered him. ⁵³You received the law given by God's angels and yet you have not kept it.'

⁵⁴This touched them on the raw, and they ground their teeth with fury. ⁵⁵But Stephen, filled with the Holy Spirit, and gazing intently up to heaven, saw the glory of God, and Jesus standing at God's right hand. ⁵⁶'Look!' he said. 'I see the heavens opened and the Son of Man standing at the right hand of God.' ⁵⁷At this they gave a great shout, and stopped their ears; they made a concerted rush at him, ⁵⁸threw him out of the city, and set about stoning him. The witnesses laid their coats at the feet of a young man named Saul. ⁵⁹As they stoned him Stephen called out, 'Lord Jesus, receive my spirit.' ⁶⁰He fell on his knees and cried aloud, 'Lord, do not hold this sin against them,' and with that he died. ¹Saul was among those who approved of his execution.

The church in Judaea and Samaria

THAT day was the beginning of a time of violent persecution for the church in Jerusalem; and all except the apostles were scattered over the country districts of Judaea and Samaria. ²Stephen was given burial by devout men, who made a great lamentation for him. ³Saul, meanwhile, was harrying the church; he entered house after house, seizing men and women and sending them to prison.

⁴As for those who had been scattered, they went through the country preaching the word. ⁵Philip came down to a city in Samaria and began proclaiming the Messiah there. ⁶As the crowds heard Philip and saw the signs he performed, everyone paid close attention to what he had to say. ⁷In many cases of possession the unclean spirits came out with a loud cry, and many paralysed and crippled folk were cured; ⁸and there was great rejoicing in that city.

⁹A man named Simon had been in the city for some time and had captivated the Samaritans with his magical arts, making large claims for himself. ¹⁰Everybody, high and low, listened intently to him. 'This man', they said, 'is that power of God which is called "The Great Power".' ¹¹They listened because they had for so long been captivated by his magic. ¹²But when they came to believe Philip, with his good news about the kingdom of God and the name of Jesus Christ, men and women alike were baptized. ¹³Even Simon himself believed, and after his baptism was constantly in Philip's company. He was captivated when he saw the powerful signs and miracles that were taking place.

¹⁴When the apostles in Jerusalem heard that Samaria had accepted the word of God, they sent off Peter and John, ¹⁵who went down there and prayed for the converts, asking that they might receive the Holy Spirit. ¹⁶Until then the Spirit had not come upon any of them;

7:46 *for ... Jacob: some witnesses read* for the house of Jacob.

they had been baptized into the name of the Lord Jesus, that and nothing more. [17] So Peter and John laid their hands on them, and they received the Holy Spirit. [18] When Simon observed that the Spirit was bestowed through the laying on of the apostles' hands, he offered them money [19] and said, 'Give me too the same power, so that anyone I lay my hands on will receive the Holy Spirit.' [20] Peter replied, 'You thought God's gift was for sale? Your money can go with you to damnation! [21] You have neither part nor share in this, for you are corrupt in the eyes of God. [22] Repent of this wickedness of yours and pray the Lord to forgive you for harbouring such a thought. [23] I see that bitter gall and the chains of sin will be your fate.' [24] Simon said to them, 'Pray to the Lord for me, and ask that none of the things you have spoken of may befall me.'

[25] After giving their testimony and speaking the word of the Lord, they took the road back to Jerusalem, bringing the good news to many Samaritan villages on the way.

[26] Then the angel of the Lord said to Philip, 'Start out and go south to the road that leads down from Jerusalem to Gaza.' (This is the desert road.) [27] He set out and was on his way when he caught sight of an Ethiopian. This man was a eunuch, a high official of the Kandake, or queen, of Ethiopia, in charge of all her treasure; had been to Jerusalem on a pilgrimage [28] and was now returning home, sitting in his carriage and reading aloud from the prophet Isaiah. [29] The Spirit said to Philip, 'Go and meet the carriage.' [30] When Philip ran up he heard him reading from the prophet Isaiah and asked, 'Do you understand what you are reading?' [31] He said, 'How can I without someone to guide me?' and invited Philip to get in and sit beside him.

[32] The passage he was reading was this: 'He was led like a sheep to the slaughter; like a lamb that is dumb before the shearer, he does not open his mouth. [33] He has been humiliated and has no redress. Who will be able to speak of his posterity? For he is cut off from the world of the living.'

[34] 'Please tell me', said the eunuch to Philip, 'who it is that the prophet is speaking about here: himself or someone else?' [35] Then Philip began and, starting from this passage, he told him the good news of Jesus. [36] As they were going along the road, they came to some water. 'Look,' said the eunuch, 'here is water: what is to prevent my being baptized?' [38] and he ordered the carriage to stop. Then they both went down into the water, Philip and the eunuch, and he baptized him. [39] When they came up from the water the Spirit snatched Philip away; the eunuch did not see him again, but went on his way rejoicing. [40] Philip appeared at Azotus, and toured the country, preaching in all the towns till he reached Caesarea.

9 SAUL, still breathing murderous threats against the Lord's disciples, went to the high priest [2] and applied for letters to the synagogues at Damascus authorizing him to arrest any followers of the new way whom he found, men or women, and bring them to Jerusalem. [3] While he was still on the road and nearing Damascus, suddenly a light from the sky flashed all around him. [4] He fell to the ground and heard a voice saying, 'Saul, Saul, why are you persecuting me?' [5] 'Tell me, Lord,' he said, 'who you are.' The voice answered, 'I am Jesus, whom you are persecuting. [6] But now get up and go into the city, and you will be told what you have to do.' [7] Meanwhile the men who were travelling with him stood speechless; they heard the voice but could see no one. [8] Saul got up from the ground, but when he opened his eyes he could not see; they led him by the hand and brought him into Damascus. [9] He was blind for three days, and took no food or drink.

[10] There was in Damascus a disciple named Ananias. He had a vision in which he heard the Lord say: 'Ananias!' 'Here I am, Lord,' he answered. [11] The Lord said to him, 'Go to Straight Street, to the house of Judas, and ask for a man from Tarsus named Saul. You will find him at prayer; [12] he has had a vision of a man named Ananias coming in and laying hands on him to restore his sight.' [13] Ananias

---

8:36 **baptized**: *some witnesses add* [37] Philip said, 'If you wholeheartedly believe, it is permitted.' He replied, 'I believe that Jesus Christ is the Son of God.'

answered, 'Lord, I have often heard about this man and all the harm he has done your people in Jerusalem. [14] Now he is here with authority from the chief priests to arrest all who invoke your name.' [15] But the Lord replied, 'You must go, for this man is my chosen instrument to bring my name before the nations and their kings, and before the people of Israel. [16] I myself will show him all that he must go through for my name's sake.'

[17] So Ananias went and, on entering the house, laid his hands on him and said, 'Saul, my brother, the Lord Jesus, who appeared to you on your way here, has sent me to you so that you may recover your sight and be filled with the Holy Spirit.' [18] Immediately it was as if scales had fallen from his eyes, and he regained his sight. He got up and was baptized, [19] and when he had eaten his strength returned.

He stayed some time with the disciples in Damascus. [20] Without delay he proclaimed Jesus publicly in the synagogues, declaring him to be the Son of God. [21] All who heard were astounded. 'Is not this the man', they said, 'who was in Jerusalem hunting down those who invoke this name? Did he not come here for the sole purpose of arresting them and taking them before the chief priests?' [22] But Saul went from strength to strength, and confounded the Jews of Damascus with his cogent proofs that Jesus was the Messiah.

[23] When some time had passed, the Jews hatched a plot against his life; [24] but their plans became known to Saul. They kept watch on the city gates day and night so that they might murder him; [25] but one night some disciples took him and, lowering him in a basket, let him down over the wall.

[26] On reaching Jerusalem he tried to join the disciples, but they were all afraid of him, because they did not believe that he really was a disciple. [27] Barnabas, however, took him and introduced him to the apostles; he described to them how on his journey Saul had seen the Lord and heard his voice, and how at Damascus he had spoken out boldly in the name of Jesus. [28] Saul now stayed with them, moving about freely in Jerusalem. [29] He spoke out boldly and openly in the name of the Lord, talking and debating with the Greek-speaking Jews. But they planned to murder him, [30] and when the brethren discovered this they escorted him down to Caesarea and sent him away to Tarsus.

[31] MEANWHILE the church, throughout Judaea, Galilee, and Samaria, was left in peace to build up its strength, and to live in the fear of the Lord. Encouraged by the Holy Spirit, it grew in numbers.

[32] In the course of a tour Peter was making throughout the region he went down to visit God's people at Lydda. [33] There he found a man named Aeneas who had been bedridden with paralysis for eight years. [34] Peter said to him, 'Aeneas, Jesus Christ cures you; get up and make your bed!' and immediately he stood up. [35] All who lived in Lydda and Sharon saw him; and they turned to the Lord.

[36] In Joppa there was a disciple named Tabitha (in Greek, Dorcas, meaning 'Gazelle'), who filled her days with acts of kindness and charity. [37] At that time she fell ill and died; and they washed her body and laid it in a room upstairs. [38] As Lydda was near Joppa, the disciples, who had heard that Peter was there, sent two men to him with the urgent request, 'Please come over to us without delay.' [39] At once Peter went off with them. When he arrived he was taken up to the room, and all the widows came and stood round him in tears, showing him the shirts and coats that Dorcas used to make while she was with them. [40] Peter sent them all outside, and knelt down and prayed; then, turning towards the body, he said, 'Tabitha, get up.' She opened her eyes, saw Peter, and sat up. [41] He gave her his hand and helped her to her feet. Then he called together the members of the church and the widows and showed her to them alive. [42] News of it spread all over Joppa, and many came to believe in the Lord. [43] Peter stayed on in Joppa for some time at the house of a tanner named Simon.

10 At Caesarea there was a man named Cornelius, a centurion in the Italian Cohort, as it was called. [2] He was a devout man, and he and his whole family joined in the worship of God; he gave generously to help the Jewish

9:29 **Greek-speaking Jews**: *lit.* Hellenists.

people, and was regular in his prayers to God. ³One day about three in the afternoon he had a vision in which he clearly saw an angel of God come into his room and say, 'Cornelius!' ⁴Cornelius stared at him in terror. 'What is it, my lord?' he asked. The angel said, 'Your prayers and acts of charity have gone up to heaven to speak for you before God. ⁵Now send to Joppa for a man named Simon, also called Peter: ⁶he is lodging with another Simon, a tanner, whose house is by the sea.' ⁷When the angel who spoke to him had gone, he summoned two of his servants and a military orderly who was a religious man, ⁸told them the whole story, and ordered them to Joppa.

⁹Next day about noon, while they were still on their way and approaching the city, Peter went up on the roof to pray. ¹⁰He grew hungry and wanted something to eat, but while they were getting it ready, he fell into a trance. ¹¹He saw heaven opened, and something coming down that looked like a great sheet of sailcloth; it was slung by the four corners and was being lowered to the earth, ¹²and in it he saw creatures of every kind, four-footed beasts, reptiles, and birds. ¹³There came a voice which said to him, 'Get up, Peter, kill and eat.' ¹⁴But Peter answered, 'No, Lord! I have never eaten anything profane or unclean.' ¹⁵The voice came again, a second time: 'It is not for you to call profane what God counts clean.' ¹⁶This happened three times, and then the thing was taken up into heaven.

¹⁷While Peter was still puzzling over the meaning of the vision he had seen, the messengers from Cornelius had been asking the way to Simon's house, and now arrived at the entrance. ¹⁸They called out and asked if Simon Peter was lodging there. ¹⁹Peter was thinking over the vision, when the Spirit said to him, 'Some men are here looking for you; ²⁰get up and go downstairs. You may go with them without any misgiving, for it was I who sent them.' ²¹Peter came down to the men and said, 'You are looking for me? Here I am. What brings you here?' ²²'We are from the centurion Cornelius,' they replied, 'a good and religious man, acknowledged as such by the whole Jewish nation. He was directed by a holy angel to send for you to his house and hear what you have to say.' ²³So Peter asked them in and gave them a night's lodging.

Next day he set out with them, accompanied by some members of the congregation at Joppa, ²⁴and on the following day arrived at Caesarea. Cornelius was expecting them and had called together his relatives and close friends. ²⁵When Peter arrived, Cornelius came to meet him, and bowed to the ground in deep reverence. ²⁶But Peter raised him to his feet and said, 'Stand up; I am only a man like you.' ²⁷Still talking with him he went in and found a large gathering. ²⁸He said to them, 'I need not tell you that a Jew is forbidden by his religion to visit or associate with anyone of another race. Yet God has shown me clearly that I must not call anyone profane or unclean; ²⁹that is why I came here without demur when you sent for me. May I ask what was your reason for doing so?'

³⁰Cornelius said, 'Three days ago, just about this time, I was in the house here saying the afternoon prayers, when suddenly a man in shining robes stood before me. ³¹He said: "Cornelius, your prayer has been heard and your acts of charity have spoken for you before God. ³²Send to Simon Peter at Joppa, and ask him to come; he is lodging in the house of Simon the tanner, by the sea." ³³I sent to you there and then, and you have been good enough to come. So now we are all met here before God, to listen to everything that the Lord has instructed you to say.'

³⁴Peter began: 'I now understand how true it is that God has no favourites, ³⁵but that in every nation those who are god-fearing and do what is right are acceptable to him. ³⁶He sent his word to the Israelites and gave the good news of peace through Jesus Christ, who is Lord of all. ³⁷I need not tell you what has happened lately all over the land of the Jews, starting from Galilee after the baptism proclaimed by John. ³⁸You know how God anointed Jesus of Nazareth with the Holy Spirit and with power. Because God was with him he went about doing good and healing all who were oppressed by the devil. ³⁹And we can bear witness to all that he did in the Jewish countryside and in Jerusalem. They put him to death, hanging him on a gibbet; ⁴⁰but God raised him to life on the third day, and allowed him to be clearly seen, ⁴¹not by

the whole people, but by witnesses whom God had chosen in advance—by us, who ate and drank with him after he rose from the dead. ⁴² He commanded us to proclaim him to the people, and affirm that he is the one designated by God as judge of the living and the dead. ⁴³ It is to him that all the prophets testify, declaring that everyone who trusts in him receives forgiveness of sins through his name.'

⁴⁴ Peter was still speaking when the Holy Spirit came upon all who were listening to the message. ⁴⁵ The believers who had come with Peter, men of Jewish birth, were amazed that the gift of the Holy Spirit should have been poured out even on Gentiles, ⁴⁶ for they could hear them speaking in tongues of ecstasy and acclaiming the greatness of God. Then Peter spoke: ⁴⁷ 'Is anyone prepared to withhold the water of baptism from these persons, who have received the Holy Spirit just as we did?' ⁴⁸ Then he ordered them to be baptized in the name of Jesus Christ. After that they asked him to stay on with them for a time.

11 News came to the apostles and the members of the church in Judaea that Gentiles too had accepted the word of God; ² and when Peter came up to Jerusalem those who were of Jewish birth took issue with him. ³ 'You have been visiting men who are uncircumcised,' they said, 'and sitting at table with them!' ⁴ Peter began by laying before them the facts as they had happened.

⁵ 'I was at prayer in the city of Joppa,' he said, 'and while in a trance I had a vision: I saw something coming down that looked like a great sheet of sailcloth, slung by the four corners and lowered from heaven till it reached me. ⁶ I looked intently to make out what was in it and I saw four-footed beasts, wild animals, reptiles, and birds. ⁷ Then I heard a voice saying to me, "Get up, Peter, kill and eat." ⁸ But I said, "No, Lord! Nothing profane or unclean has ever entered my mouth." ⁹ A voice from heaven came a second time: "It is not for you to call profane what God counts clean." ¹⁰ This happened three times, and then they were all drawn up again into heaven. ¹¹ At that very moment three men who had been

sent to me from Caesarea arrived at the house where I was staying; ¹² and the Spirit told me to go with them. My six companions here came with me and we went into the man's house. ¹³ He told us how he had seen an angel standing in his house who said, "Send to Joppa for Simon Peter. ¹⁴ He will speak words that will bring salvation to you and all your household." ¹⁵ Hardly had I begun speaking, when the Holy Spirit came upon them, just as upon us at the beginning, ¹⁶ and I recalled what the Lord had said: "John baptized with water, but you will be baptized with the Holy Spirit." ¹⁷ God gave them no less a gift than he gave us when we came to believe in the Lord Jesus Christ. How could I stand in God's way?'

¹⁸ When they heard this their doubts were silenced, and they gave praise to God. 'This means', they said, 'that God has granted life-giving repentance to the Gentiles also.'

¹⁹ MEANWHILE those who had been scattered after the persecution that arose over Stephen made their way to Phoenicia, Cyprus, and Antioch, bringing the message to Jews only and to no others. ²⁰ But there were some natives of Cyprus and Cyrene among them, and these, when they arrived at Antioch, began to speak to Gentiles as well, telling them the good news of the Lord Jesus. ²¹ The power of the Lord was with them, and a great many became believers and turned to the Lord.

²² The news reached the ears of the church in Jerusalem; and they sent Barnabas to Antioch. ²³ When he arrived and saw the divine grace at work, he rejoiced and encouraged them all to hold fast to the Lord with resolute hearts, ²⁴ for he was a good man, full of the Holy Spirit and of faith. And large numbers were won over to the Lord.

²⁵ He then went off to Tarsus to look for Saul; ²⁶ and when he had found him, he brought him to Antioch. For a whole year the two of them lived in fellowship with the church there, and gave instruction to large numbers. It was in Antioch that the disciples first got the name of Christians.

²⁷ During this period some prophets came down from Jerusalem to Antioch,

11:11 **I was:** *some witnesses read* we were.   11:12 **with them:** *some witnesses add* making no distinctions; *others add* without any misgiving, *as in 10:20.*

[28] and one of them, Agabus by name, was inspired to stand up and predict a severe and world-wide famine, which in fact occurred in the reign of Claudius. [29] So the disciples agreed to make a contribution, each according to his means, for the relief of their fellow-Christians in Judaea. [30] This they did, and sent it off to the elders, entrusting it to Barnabas and Saul.

12 It was about this time that King Herod launched an attack on certain members of the church. [2] He beheaded James, the brother of John, [3] and, when he saw that the Jews approved, proceeded to arrest Peter also. This happened during the festival of Unleavened Bread. [4] Having secured him, he put him in prison under a military guard, four squads of four men each, meaning to produce him in public after Passover. [5] So, while Peter was held in prison, the church kept praying fervently to God for him. [6] On the very night before Herod had planned to produce him, Peter was asleep between two soldiers, secured by two chains, while outside the doors sentries kept guard over the prison. [7] All at once an angel of the Lord stood there, and the cell was ablaze with light. He tapped Peter on the shoulder to wake him. 'Quick! Get up!' he said, and the chains fell away from Peter's wrists. [8] The angel said, 'Do up your belt and put on your sandals.' He did so. 'Now wrap your cloak round you and follow me.' [9] Peter followed him out, with no idea that the angel's intervention was real: he thought it was just a vision. [10] They passed the first guard-post, then the second, and reached the iron gate leading out into the city. This opened for them of its own accord; they came out and had walked the length of one street when suddenly the angel left him. [11] Then Peter came to himself. 'Now I know it is true,' he said: 'the Lord has sent his angel and rescued me from Herod's clutches and from all that the Jewish people were expecting.' [12] Once he had realized this, he made for the house of Mary, the mother of John Mark, where a large company was at prayer. [13] He knocked at the outer door and a maidservant called Rhoda came to answer it. [14] She recognized Peter's voice and was so overjoyed that instead of opening the door she ran in and announced that Peter was standing outside. [15] 'You are crazy,' they told her; but she insisted that it was so. Then they said, 'It must be his angel.'

[16] Peter went on knocking, and when they opened the door and saw him, they were astounded. [17] He motioned to them with his hand to keep quiet, and described to them how the Lord had brought him out of prison. 'Tell James and the members of the church,' he said. Then he left the house and went off elsewhere.

[18] When morning came, there was consternation among the soldiers: what could have become of Peter? [19] Herod made careful search, but failed to find him, so he interrogated the guards and ordered their execution.

Afterwards Herod left Judaea to reside for a while at Caesarea. [20] He had for some time been very angry with the people of Tyre and Sidon, who now by common agreement presented themselves at his court. There they won over Blastus the royal chamberlain, and sued for peace, because their country drew its supplies from the king's territory. [21] On an appointed day Herod, attired in his royal robes and seated on the rostrum, addressed the populace; [22] they responded, 'It is a god speaking, not a man!' [23] Instantly an angel of the Lord struck him down, because he had usurped the honour due to God; he was eaten up with worms and so died.

[24] Meanwhile the word of God continued to grow and spread; [25] and Barnabas and Saul, their task fulfilled, returned from Jerusalem, taking John Mark with them.

Paul's work among the Gentiles

13 THERE were in the church at Antioch certain prophets and teachers: Barnabas, Simeon called Niger, Lucius of Cyrene, Manaen, a close friend of Prince Herod, and Saul. [2] While they were offering worship to the Lord and fasting, the Holy Spirit said, 'Set Barnabas and Saul apart for me, to do the work to which I have called them.' [3] Then, after further fasting and prayer, they laid their hands on them and sent them on their way.

12:25 from Jerusalem: *some witnesses read* to Jerusalem.

⁴ These two, sent out on their mission by the Holy Spirit, came down to Seleucia, and from there sailed to Cyprus. ⁵ Arriving at Salamis, they declared the word of God in the Jewish synagogues; they had John with them as their assistant. ⁶ They went through the whole island as far as Paphos, and there they came upon a sorcerer, a Jew who posed as a prophet, Barjesus by name. ⁷ He was in the retinue of the governor, Sergius Paulus, a learned man, who had sent for Barnabas and Saul and wanted to hear the word of God. ⁸ This Elymas the sorcerer (so his name may be translated) opposed them, trying to turn the governor away from the faith. ⁹ But Saul, also known as Paul, filled with the Holy Spirit, fixed his eyes on him ¹⁰ and said, 'You are a swindler, an out-and-out fraud! You son of the devil and enemy of all goodness, will you never stop perverting the straight ways of the Lord? ¹¹ Look now, the hand of the Lord strikes: you shall be blind, and for a time you shall not see the light of the sun.' At once mist and darkness came over his eyes, and he groped about for someone to lead him by the hand. ¹² When the governor saw what had happened he became a believer, deeply impressed by what he learnt about the Lord.

¹³ Sailing from Paphos, Paul and his companions went to Perga in Pamphylia; John, however, left them and returned to Jerusalem. ¹⁴ From Perga they continued their journey as far as Pisidian Antioch. On the sabbath they went to synagogue and took their seats; ¹⁵ and after the readings from the law and the prophets, the officials of the synagogue sent this message to them: 'Friends, if you have anything to say to the people by way of exhortation, let us hear it.' ¹⁶ Paul stood up, raised his hand for silence, and began.

'Listen, men of Israel and you others who worship God! ¹⁷ The God of this people, Israel, chose our forefathers. When they were still living as aliens in Egypt, he made them into a great people and, with arm outstretched, brought them out of that country. ¹⁸ For some forty years he bore with their conduct in the desert. ¹⁹ Then in the Canaanite country, after overthrowing seven nations, whose lands he gave them to be their heritage ²⁰ for some four hundred and fifty years, he appointed judges for them until the time of the prophet Samuel.

²¹ 'It was then that they asked for a king, and God gave them Saul son of Kish, a man of the tribe of Benjamin. He reigned for forty years ²² before God removed him and appointed David as their king, with this commendation: "I have found David the son of Jesse to be a man after my own heart; he will carry out all my purposes." ²³ This is the man from whose descendants God, as he promised, has brought Israel a saviour, Jesus. ²⁴ John had made ready for his coming by proclaiming a baptism in token of repentance to the whole people of Israel; ²⁵ and, nearing the end of his earthly course, John said, "I am not the one you think I am. No, after me comes one whose sandals I am not worthy to unfasten."

²⁶ 'My brothers, who come of Abraham's stock, and others among you who worship God, we are the people to whom this message of salvation has been sent. ²⁷ The people of Jerusalem and their rulers did not recognize Jesus, or understand the words of the prophets which are read sabbath by sabbath; indeed, they fulfilled them by condemning him. ²⁸ Though they failed to find grounds for the sentence of death, they asked Pilate to have him executed. ²⁹ When they had carried out all that the scriptures said about him, they took him down from the gibbet and laid him in a tomb. ³⁰ But God raised him from the dead; ³¹ and over a period of many days he appeared to those who had come up with him from Galilee to Jerusalem, and they are now his witnesses before our people.

³² 'We are here to give you the good news that God, who made the promise to the fathers, ³³ has fulfilled it for the children by raising Jesus from the dead, as indeed it stands written in the second Psalm: "You are my son; this day I have begotten you." ³⁴ Again, that he raised him from the dead, never to be subjected to corruption, he declares in these words: "I will give you the blessings promised to David, holy and sure." ³⁵ This is borne out by another passage: "You will not let

---

13:18 he ... conduct: *some witnesses read* he sustained them.   13:33 for the children: *some witnesses read* for our children; *others read* for us their children.

your faithful servant suffer corruption."
[36] As for David, when he had served the purpose of God in his own generation, he died and was gathered to his fathers, and suffered corruption; [37] but the one whom God raised up did not suffer corruption. [38] You must understand, my brothers, it is through him that forgiveness of sins is now being proclaimed to you. [39] It is through him that everyone who has faith is acquitted of everything for which there was no acquittal under the law of Moses. [40] Beware, then, lest you bring down upon yourselves the doom proclaimed by the prophets: [41] "See this, you scoffers, marvel, and begone; for I am doing a deed in your days, a deed which you will never believe when you are told of it.'"

[42] As they were leaving the synagogue they were asked to come again and speak on these subjects next sabbath; [43] and after the congregation had dispersed, many Jews and gentile worshippers went with Paul and Barnabas, who spoke to them and urged them to hold fast to the grace of God.

[44] On the following sabbath almost the whole city gathered to hear the word of God. [45] When the Jews saw the crowds, they were filled with jealous resentment, and contradicted what Paul had said with violent abuse. [46] But Paul and Barnabas were outspoken in their reply. 'It was necessary', they said, 'that the word of God should be declared to you first. But since you reject it and judge yourselves unworthy of eternal life, we now turn to the Gentiles. [47] For these are our instructions from the Lord: "I have appointed you to be a light for the Gentiles, and a means of salvation to earth's farthest bounds."' [48] When the Gentiles heard this, they were overjoyed and thankfully acclaimed the word of the Lord, and those who were marked out for eternal life became believers. [49] Thus the word of the Lord spread throughout the region. [50] But the Jews stirred up feeling among those worshippers who were women of standing, and among the leading men of the city; a campaign of persecution was started against Paul and Barnabas, and they were expelled from the district. [51] They shook the dust off their feet in protest against them and went to Iconium. [52] And the disciples were filled with joy and with the Holy Spirit.

14 At Iconium they went together into the Jewish synagogue and spoke to such purpose that Jews and Greeks in large numbers became believers. [2] But the unconverted Jews stirred up the Gentiles and poisoned their minds against the Christians. [3] So Paul and Barnabas stayed on for some time, and spoke boldly and openly in reliance on the Lord, who confirmed the message of his grace by enabling them to work signs and miracles. [4] The populace was divided, some siding with the Jews, others with the apostles. [5] A move was made by Gentiles and Jews together, with the connivance of the city authorities, to maltreat them and stone them, [6] and when they became aware of this, they made their escape to the Lycaonian cities of Lystra and Derbe and the surrounding country. [7] There they continued to spread the good news.

[8] At Lystra a cripple, lame from birth, who had never walked in his life, [9] sat listening to Paul as he spoke. Paul fixed his eyes on him and, seeing that he had the faith to be cured, [10] said in a loud voice, 'Stand up straight on your feet'; and he sprang up and began to walk. [11] When the crowds saw what Paul had done, they shouted, in their native Lycaonian, 'The gods have come down to us in human form!' [12] They called Barnabas Zeus, and Paul they called Hermes, because he was the spokesman. [13] The priest of Zeus, whose temple was just outside the city, brought oxen and garlands to the gates, and he and the people were about to offer sacrifice. [14] But when the apostles Barnabas and Paul heard of it, they tore their clothes and rushed into the crowd shouting, [15] 'Men, why are you doing this? We are human beings, just like you. The good news we bring tells you to turn from these follies to the living God, who made heaven and earth and sea and everything in them. [16] In past ages he has allowed all nations to go their own way; [17] and yet he has not left you without some clue to his nature, in the benefits he bestows: he sends you rain from heaven and the crops in their seasons, and gives you food in plenty and keeps you in good heart.' [18] Even with these words they barely managed to prevent the crowd from offering sacrifice to them.

[19] Then Jews from Antioch and Iconium

came on the scene and won over the crowds. They stoned Paul, and dragged him out of the city, thinking him dead. [20] The disciples formed a ring round him, and he got to his feet and went into the city. Next day he left with Barnabas for Derbe.

[21] After bringing the good news to that town and gaining many converts, they returned to Lystra, then to Iconium, and then to Antioch, [22] strengthening the disciples and encouraging them to be true to the faith. They warned them that to enter the kingdom of God we must undergo many hardships. [23] They also appointed for them elders in each congregation, and with prayer and fasting committed them to the Lord in whom they had put their trust.

[24] They passed through Pisidia and came into Pamphylia. [25] When they had delivered the message at Perga, they went down to Attalia, [26] and from there sailed to Antioch, where they had originally been commended to the grace of God for the task which they had now completed. [27] On arrival there, they called the congregation together and reported all that God had accomplished through them, and how he had thrown open the gates of faith to the Gentiles. [28] And they stayed for some time with the disciples there.

15 SOME people who had come down from Judaea began to teach the brotherhood that those who were not circumcised in accordance with Mosaic practice could not be saved. [2] That brought them into fierce dissension and controversy with Paul and Barnabas, and it was arranged that these two and some others from Antioch should go up to Jerusalem to see the apostles and elders about this question.

[3] They were sent on their way by the church, and travelled through Phoenicia and Samaria, telling the full story of the conversion of the Gentiles, and causing great rejoicing among all the Christians. [4] When they reached Jerusalem they were welcomed by the church and the apostles and elders, and they reported all that God had accomplished through them. [5] But some of the Pharisaic party

who had become believers came forward and declared, 'Those Gentiles must be circumcised and told to keep the law of Moses.'

[6] The apostles and elders met to look into this matter, [7] and, after a long debate, Peter rose to address them. 'My friends,' he said, 'in the early days, as you yourselves know, God made his choice among you: from my lips the Gentiles were to hear and believe the message of the gospel. [8] And God, who can read human hearts, showed his approval by giving the Holy Spirit to them as he did to us. [9] He made no difference between them and us; for he purified their hearts by faith. [10] Then why do you now try God's patience by laying on the shoulders of these converts a yoke which neither we nor our forefathers were able to bear? [11] For our belief is that we are saved in the same way as they are: by the grace of the Lord Jesus.'

[12] At that the whole company fell silent and listened to Barnabas and Paul as they described all the signs and portents that God had worked among the Gentiles through them.

[13] When they had finished speaking, James summed up: 'My friends,' he said, 'listen to me. [14] Simon has described how it first happened that God, in his providence, chose from among the Gentiles a people to bear his name. [15] This agrees with the words of the prophets: as scripture has it,

[16] Thereafter I will return and
    rebuild the fallen house of David;
  I will rebuild its ruins and set it up
    again,
[17] that the rest of mankind may seek
    the Lord,
  all the Gentiles whom I have claimed
    for my own.
  Thus says the Lord, who is doing this
[18] as he made known long ago.

[19] 'In my judgement, therefore, we should impose no irksome restrictions on those of the Gentiles who are turning to God; [20] instead we should instruct them by letter to abstain from things polluted by contact with idols, from fornication, from anything that has been strangled,

15:14 Simon: Gk Simeon.   15:20 from fornication ... blood: *some witnesses omit* from fornication; *others omit* from anything that has been strangled; *some add* (*after* blood) and to refrain from doing to others what they would not like done to themselves.

and from blood. ²¹ Moses, after all, has never lacked spokesmen in every town for generations past; he is read in the synagogues sabbath by sabbath.'

²² Then, with the agreement of the whole church, the apostles and elders resolved to choose representatives and send them to Antioch with Paul and Barnabas. They chose two leading men in the community, Judas Barsabbas and Silas, ²³ and gave them this letter to deliver:

From the apostles and elders to our brothers of gentile origin in Antioch, Syria, and Cilicia. Greetings!
²⁴ We have heard that some of our number, without any instructions from us, have disturbed you with their talk and unsettled your minds. ²⁵ In consequence, we have resolved unanimously to send to you our chosen representatives with our well-beloved Barnabas and Paul, ²⁶ who have given up their lives to the cause of our Lord Jesus Christ; ²⁷ so we are sending Judas and Silas, who will, by word of mouth, confirm what is written in this letter. ²⁸ It is the decision of the Holy Spirit, and our decision, to lay no further burden upon you beyond these essentials: ²⁹ you are to abstain from meat that has been offered to idols, from blood, from anything that has been strangled, and from fornication. If you keep yourselves free from these things you will be doing well. Farewell.

³⁰ So they took their leave and travelled down to Antioch, where they called the congregation together and delivered the letter. ³¹ When it was read, all rejoiced at the encouragement it brought, ³² and Judas and Silas, who were themselves prophets, said much to encourage and strengthen the members. ³³ After spending some time there, they took their leave with the good wishes of the brethren, to return to those who had sent them. ³⁵ But Paul and Barnabas stayed on at Antioch, where, along with many others, they taught and preached the word of the Lord.

³⁶ AFTER a while Paul said to Barnabas, 'Let us go back and see how our brothers are getting on in the various towns where we proclaimed the word of the Lord.' ³⁷ Barnabas wanted to take John Mark with them; ³⁸ but Paul insisted that the man who had deserted them in Pamphylia and had not gone on to share in their work was not the man to take with them now. ³⁹ The dispute was so sharp that they parted company. Barnabas took Mark with him and sailed for Cyprus. ⁴⁰ Paul chose Silas and started on his journey, commended by the brothers to the grace of the Lord. ⁴¹ He travelled through Syria and Cilicia bringing new strength to the churches.

16 He went on to Derbe and then to Lystra, where he found a disciple named Timothy, the son of a Jewish Christian mother and a gentile father, ² well spoken of by the Christians at Lystra and Iconium. ³ Paul wanted to take him with him when he left, so he had him circumcised out of consideration for the Jews who lived in those parts, for they all knew that his father was a Gentile. ⁴ As they made their way from town to town they handed on the decisions taken by the apostles and elders in Jerusalem and enjoined their observance. ⁵ So, day by day, the churches grew stronger in faith and increased in numbers.

⁶ They travelled through the Phrygian and Galatian region, prevented by the Holy Spirit from delivering the message in the province of Asia. ⁷ When they approached the Mysian border they tried to enter Bithynia, but, as the Spirit of Jesus would not allow them, ⁸ they passed through Mysia and reached the coast at Troas. ⁹ During the night a vision came to Paul: a Macedonian stood there appealing to him, 'Cross over to Macedonia and help us.' ¹⁰ As soon as he had seen this vision, we set about getting a passage to Macedonia, convinced that God had called us to take the good news there.

¹¹ We sailed from Troas and made a straight run to Samothrace, the next day to Neapolis, ¹² and from there to Philippi, a leading city in that district of Macedonia and a Roman colony. Here we stayed for

15:29 **from anything ... fornication**: *some witnesses omit* from anything that has been strangled; *some omit* and from fornication; *and some witnesses add* and refrain from doing to others what you would not like done to yourselves. 15:33 **sent them**: *some witnesses add* ³⁴ But Silas decided to remain there. 16:6 **through ... region**: *or* through Phrygia and the Galatian region.

some days, [13] and on the sabbath we went outside the city gate by the riverside, where we thought there would be a place of prayer; we sat down and talked to the women who had gathered there. [14] One of those listening was called Lydia, a dealer in purple fabric, who came from the city of Thyatira; she was a worshipper of God, and the Lord opened her heart to respond to what Paul said. [15] She was baptized, and her household with her, and then she urged us, 'Now that you have accepted me as a believer in the Lord, come and stay at my house.' And she insisted on our going.

[16] Once, on our way to the place of prayer, we met a slave-girl who was possessed by a spirit of divination and brought large profits to her owners by telling fortunes. [17] She followed Paul and the rest of us, shouting, 'These men are servants of the Most High God, and are declaring to you a way of salvation.' [18] She did this day after day, until, in exasperation, Paul rounded on the spirit. 'I command you in the name of Jesus Christ to come out of her,' he said, and it came out instantly.

[19] When the girl's owners saw that their hope of profit had gone, they seized Paul and Silas and dragged them to the city authorities in the main square; [20] bringing them before the magistrates, they alleged, 'These men are causing a disturbance in our city; they are Jews, [21] and they are advocating practices which it is illegal for us Romans to adopt and follow.' [22] The mob joined in the attack; and the magistrates had the prisoners stripped and gave orders for them to be flogged. [23] After a severe beating they were flung into prison and the jailer was ordered to keep them under close guard. [24] In view of these orders, he put them into the inner prison and secured their feet in the stocks.

[25] About midnight Paul and Silas, at their prayers, were singing praises to God, and the other prisoners were listening, [26] when suddenly there was such a violent earthquake that the foundations of the jail were shaken; the doors burst open and all the prisoners found their fetters unfastened. [27] The jailer woke up to see the prison doors wide open and, assuming that the prisoners had escaped, drew his sword intending to kill himself. [28] But Paul shouted, 'Do yourself no harm; we are all here.' [29] The jailer called for lights, rushed in, and threw himself down before Paul and Silas, trembling with fear. [30] He then escorted them out and said, 'Sirs, what must I do to be saved?' [31] They answered, 'Put your trust in the Lord Jesus, and you will be saved, you and your household,' [32] and they imparted the word of the Lord to him and to everyone in his house. [33] At that late hour of the night the jailer took them and washed their wounds, and there and then he and his whole family were baptized. [34] He brought them up into his house, set out a meal, and rejoiced with his whole household in his new-found faith in God.

[35] When daylight came, the magistrates sent their officers with the order, 'Release those men.' [36] The jailer reported these instructions to Paul: 'The magistrates have sent an order for your release. Now you are free to go in peace.' [37] But Paul said to the officers: 'We are Roman citizens! They gave us a public flogging and threw us into prison without trial. Are they now going to smuggle us out by stealth? No indeed! Let them come in person and escort us out.' [38] The officers reported his words to the magistrates. Alarmed to hear that they were Roman citizens, [39] they came and apologized to them, and then escorted them out and requested them to go away from the city. [40] On leaving the prison, they went to Lydia's house, where they met their fellow-Christians and spoke words of encouragement to them, and then they took their departure.

17 THEY now travelled by way of Amphipolis and Apollonia and came to Thessalonica, where there was a Jewish synagogue. [2] Following his usual practice Paul went to their meetings; and for the next three sabbaths he argued with them, quoting texts of scripture [3] which he expounded and applied to show that the Messiah had to suffer and rise from the dead. 'And this Jesus', he said, 'whom I am proclaiming to you is the Messiah.' [4] Some of them were convinced and joined Paul and Silas, as did a

16:13 **where ... prayer:** *some witnesses read* where there was a recognized place of prayer.

great number of godfearing Gentiles and a good many influential women.

⁵ The Jews in their jealousy recruited some ruffians from the dregs of society to gather a mob. They put the city in an uproar, and made for Jason's house with the intention of bringing Paul and Silas before the town assembly. ⁶ Failing to find them, they dragged Jason himself and some members of the congregation before the magistrates, shouting, 'The men who have made trouble the whole world over have now come here, ⁷ and Jason has harboured them. All of them flout the emperor's laws, and assert there is a rival king, Jesus.' ⁸ These words alarmed the mob and the magistrates also, ⁹ who took security from Jason and the others before letting them go.

¹⁰ As soon as darkness fell, the members of the congregation sent Paul and Silas off to Beroea; and, on arrival, they made their way to the synagogue. ¹¹ The Jews here were more fair-minded than those at Thessalonica: they received the message with great eagerness, studying the scriptures every day to see whether it was true. ¹² Many of them therefore became believers, and so did a fair number of Gentiles, women of standing as well as men. ¹³ But when the Thessalonian Jews learnt that the word of God had now been proclaimed by Paul in Beroea, they followed him there to stir up trouble and rouse the rabble. ¹⁴ At once the members of the congregation sent Paul down to the coast, while Silas and Timothy both stayed behind. ¹⁵ Paul's escort brought him as far as Athens, and came away with instructions for Silas and Timothy to rejoin him with all speed.

¹⁶ While Paul was waiting for them at Athens, he was outraged to see the city so full of idols. ¹⁷ He argued in the synagogue with the Jews and gentile worshippers, and also in the city square every day with casual passers-by. ¹⁸ Moreover, some of the Epicurean and Stoic philosophers joined issue with him. Some said, 'What can this charlatan be trying to say?' and others, 'He would appear to be a propagandist for foreign deities'—this because he was preaching about Jesus and the Resurrection. ¹⁹ They brought him to the Council of the Areopagus and asked, 'May we know what this new doctrine is that you propound? ²⁰ You are introducing ideas that sound strange to us, and we should like to know what they mean.' ²¹ Now, all the Athenians and the resident foreigners had time for nothing except talking or hearing about the latest novelty.

²² Paul stood up before the Council of the Areopagus and began: 'Men of Athens, I see that in everything that concerns religion you are uncommonly scrupulous. ²³ As I was going round looking at the objects of your worship, I noticed among other things an altar bearing the inscription "To an Unknown God". What you worship but do not know—this is what I now proclaim.

²⁴ 'The God who created the world and everything in it, and who is Lord of heaven and earth, does not live in shrines made by human hands. ²⁵ It is not because he lacks anything that he accepts service at our hands, for he is himself the universal giver of life and breath—indeed of everything. ²⁶ He created from one stock every nation of men to inhabit the whole earth's surface. He determined their eras in history and the limits of their territory. ²⁷ They were to seek God in the hope that, groping after him, they might find him; though indeed he is not far from each one of us, ²⁸ for in him we live and move, in him we exist; as some of your own poets have said, "We are also his offspring." ²⁹ Being God's offspring, then, we ought not to suppose that the deity is like an image in gold or silver or stone, shaped by human craftsmanship and design. ³⁰ God has overlooked the age of ignorance; but now he commands men and women everywhere to repent, ³¹ because he has fixed the day on which he will have the world judged, and justly judged, by a man whom he has designated; of this he has given assurance to all by raising him from the dead.'

³² When they heard about the raising of the dead, some scoffed; others said, 'We will hear you on this subject some other time.' ³³ So Paul left the assembly. ³⁴ Some men joined him and became believers, including Dionysius, a member of the

17:19 **to . . . Areopagus:** *or* to Mars' Hill.   17:22 **before . . . Areopagus:** *or* in the middle of Mars' Hill.
17:26 **determined . . . history:** *or* fixed the ordered seasons.

Council of the Areopagus; and also a woman named Damaris, with others besides.

18 After this he left Athens and went to Corinth. ² There he met a Jew named Aquila, a native of Pontus, and his wife Priscilla; they had recently arrived from Italy because Claudius had issued an edict that all Jews should leave Rome. Paul approached them ³ and, because he was of the same trade, he made his home with them; they were tentmakers and Paul worked with them. ⁴ He also held discussions in the synagogue sabbath by sabbath, trying to convince both Jews and Gentiles.

⁵ Then Silas and Timothy came down from Macedonia, and Paul devoted himself entirely to preaching, maintaining before the Jews that the Messiah is Jesus. ⁶ When, however, they opposed him and resorted to abuse, he shook out the folds of his cloak and declared, 'Your blood be on your own heads! My conscience is clear! From now on I shall go to the Gentiles.' ⁷ With that he left, and went to the house of a worshipper of God named Titius Justus, who lived next door to the synagogue. ⁸ Crispus, the president of the synagogue, became a believer in the Lord, as did all his household; and a number of Corinthians who heard him believed and were baptized. ⁹ One night in a vision the Lord said to Paul, 'Have no fear: go on with your preaching and do not be silenced. ¹⁰ I am with you, and no attack shall harm you, for I have many in this city who are my people.' ¹¹ So he settled there for eighteen months, teaching the word of God among them.

¹² But when Gallio was proconsul of Achaia, the Jews made a concerted attack on Paul and brought him before the court. ¹³ 'This man', they said, 'is inducing people to worship God in ways that are against the law.' ¹⁴ Paul was just about to speak when Gallio declared, 'If it had been a question of crime or grave misdemeanour, I should, of course, have given you Jews a patient hearing, ¹⁵ but if it is some bickering about words and names and your Jewish law, you may settle it yourselves. I do not intend to be a judge of these matters.' ¹⁶ And he dismissed them from the court. ¹⁷ Then they all attacked Sosthenes, the president of the synagogue, and beat him up in full view of the tribunal. But all this left Gallio quite unconcerned.

¹⁸ Paul stayed on at Corinth for some time, and then took leave of the congregation. Accompanied by Priscilla and Aquila, he sailed for Syria, having had his hair cut off at Cenchreae in fulfilment of a vow. ¹⁹ They put in at Ephesus, where he parted from his companions; he himself went into the synagogue and held a discussion with the Jews. ²⁰ He was asked to stay longer, but he declined ²¹ and set sail from Ephesus, promising, as he took leave of them, 'I shall come back to you if it is God's will.' ²² On landing at Caesarea, he went up and greeted the church; and then went down to Antioch. ²³ After some time there he set out again on a journey through the Galatian country and then through Phrygia, bringing new strength to all the disciples.

²⁴ THERE arrived at Ephesus a Jew named Apollos, an Alexandrian by birth, an eloquent man, powerful in his use of scriptures. ²⁵ He had been instructed in the way of the Lord and was full of spiritual fervour; and in his discourses he taught accurately the facts about Jesus, though the only baptism he knew was John's. ²⁶ He now began to speak boldly in the synagogue, where Priscilla and Aquila heard him; they took him in hand and expounded the way to him in greater detail. ²⁷ Finding that he wanted to go across to Achaia, the congregation gave him their support, and wrote to the disciples there to make him welcome. From the time of his arrival, he was very helpful to those who had by God's grace become believers, ²⁸ for he strenuously confuted the Jews, demonstrating publicly from the scriptures that the Messiah is Jesus.

19 While Apollos was at Corinth, Paul travelled through the inland regions till he came to Ephesus, where he found a number of disciples. ² When he asked them, 'Did you receive the Holy Spirit when you became believers?' they replied, 'No, we were not even told that there is a Holy Spirit.' ³ He asked, 'Then what baptism were you given?' 'John's

18:24 *an eloquent man*: *or* a learned man.   18:26 *the way*: *some witnesses read* the way of God.

baptism,' they answered. [4] Paul said, 'The baptism that John gave was a baptism in token of repentance, and he told the people to put their trust in one who was to come after him, that is, in Jesus.' [5] On hearing this they were baptized into the name of the Lord Jesus; [6] and when Paul had laid his hands on them, the Holy Spirit came upon them and they spoke in tongues of ecstasy and prophesied. [7] There were about a dozen men in all.

[8] During the next three months he attended the synagogue and with persuasive argument spoke boldly about the kingdom of God. [9] When some proved obdurate and would not believe, speaking evil of the new way before the congregation, he withdrew from them, taking the disciples with him, and continued to hold discussions daily in the lecture hall of Tyrannus. [10] This went on for two years, with the result that the whole population of the province of Asia, both Jews and Gentiles, heard the word of the Lord. [11] God worked extraordinary miracles through Paul: [12] when handkerchiefs and scarves which had been in contact with his skin were carried to the sick, they were cured of their diseases, and the evil spirits came out of them.

[13] Some itinerant Jewish exorcists tried their hand at using the name of the Lord Jesus on those possessed by evil spirits; they would say, 'I adjure you by Jesus whom Paul proclaims.' [14] There were seven sons of Sceva, a Jewish chief priest, who were doing this, [15] when the evil spirit responded, 'Jesus I recognize, Paul I know, but who are you?' [16] The man with the evil spirit flew at them, overpowered them all, and handled them with such violence that they ran out of the house battered and naked. [17] Everybody in Ephesus, Jew and Gentile alike, got to know of it, and all were awestruck, while the name of the Lord Jesus gained in honour. [18] Moreover many of those who had become believers came and openly confessed that they had been using magical spells. [19] A good many of those who formerly practised magic collected their books and burnt them publicly, and when the total value was reckoned up it came to fifty thousand pieces of silver. [20] In such ways the word of the Lord showed its power, spreading more and more widely and effectively.

[21] When matters had reached this stage, Paul made up his mind to visit Macedonia and Achaia and then go on to Jerusalem. 'After I have been there,' he said, 'I must see Rome also.' [22] He sent two of his assistants, Timothy and Erastus, to Macedonia, while he himself stayed some time longer in the province of Asia.

[23] It was about this time that the Christian movement gave rise to a serious disturbance. [24] There was a man named Demetrius, a silversmith who made silver shrines of Artemis, and provided considerable employment for the craftsmen. [25] He called a meeting of them and of the workers in allied trades, and addressed them: 'As you men know, our prosperity depends on this industry. [26] But this fellow Paul, as you can see and hear for yourselves, has perverted crowds of people with his propaganda, not only at Ephesus but also in practically the whole of the province of Asia; he tells them that gods made by human hands are not gods at all. [27] There is danger for us here; it is not only that our line of business will be discredited, but also that the sanctuary of the great goddess Artemis will cease to command respect; and then it will not be long before she who is worshipped by all Asia and the civilized world is brought down from her divine pre-eminence.'

[28] On hearing this, they were enraged, and began to shout, 'Great is Artemis of the Ephesians!' [29] The whole city was in an uproar; they made a concerted rush into the theatre, hustling along with them Paul's travelling companions, the Macedonians Gaius and Aristarchus. [30] Paul wanted to appear before the assembly but the other Christians would not let him. [31] Even some of the dignitaries of the province, who were friendly towards him, sent a message urging him not to venture into the theatre. [32] Meanwhile some were shouting one thing, some another, for the assembly was in an uproar and most of them did not know what they had all come for. [33] Some of the crowd explained the trouble to Alexander, whom the Jews had pushed to the front, and he, motioning for silence, attempted to make a defence before the assembly. [34] But when they recognized that he was a Jew, one shout arose from them all: 'Great is Artemis of the Ephesians!' and they kept it up for about two hours.

³⁵ The town clerk, however, quietened the crowd. 'Citizens of Ephesus,' he said, 'all the world knows that our city of Ephesus is temple warden of the great Artemis and of that image of her which fell from heaven. ³⁶ Since these facts are beyond dispute, your proper course is to keep calm and do nothing rash. ³⁷ These men whom you have brought here as offenders have committed no sacrilege and uttered no blasphemy against our goddess. ³⁸ If, therefore, Demetrius and his craftsmen have a case against anyone, there are assizes and there are proconsuls; let the parties bring their charges and countercharges. ³⁹ But if it is a larger question you are raising, it will be dealt with in the statutory assembly. ⁴⁰ We certainly run the risk of being charged with riot for this day's work. There is no justification for it, and it would be impossible for us to give any explanation of this turmoil.' ⁴¹ With that he dismissed the assembly.

20 WHEN the disturbance was over, Paul sent for the disciples and, after encouraging them, said goodbye and set out on his journey to Macedonia. ² He travelled through that region, constantly giving encouragement to the Christians, and finally reached Greece. ³ When he had spent three months there and was on the point of embarking for Syria, a plot was laid against him by the Jews, so he decided to return by way of Macedonia. ⁴ He was accompanied by Sopater son of Pyrrhus from Beroea, Aristarchus and Secundus from Thessalonica, Gaius of Derbe, and Timothy, and from Asia Tychicus and Trophimus. ⁵ These went ahead and waited for us at Troas; ⁶ we ourselves sailed from Philippi after the Passover season, and five days later rejoined them at Troas, where we spent a week.

⁷ On the Saturday night, when we gathered for the breaking of bread, Paul, who was to leave next day, addressed the congregation and went on speaking until midnight. ⁸ Now there were many lamps in the upstairs room where we were assembled, ⁹ and a young man named Eutychus, who was sitting on the window-ledge, grew more and more drowsy as Paul went on talking, until, completely overcome by sleep, he fell from the third storey to the ground, and was picked up dead. ¹⁰ Paul went down, threw himself upon him, and clasped him in his arms. 'Do not distress yourselves,' he said to them; 'he is alive.' ¹¹ He then went upstairs, broke bread and ate, and after much conversation, which lasted until dawn, he departed. ¹² And they took the boy home, greatly relieved that he was alive.

¹³ We went on ahead to the ship and embarked for Assos, where we were to take Paul aboard; this was the arrangement he had made, since he was going to travel by road. ¹⁴ When he met us at Assos, we took him aboard and proceeded to Mitylene. ¹⁵ We sailed from there and next day arrived off Chios. On the second day we made Samos, and the following day we reached Miletus. ¹⁶ Paul had decided to bypass Ephesus and so avoid having to spend time in the province of Asia; he was eager to be in Jerusalem on the day of Pentecost, if that were possible. ¹⁷ He did, however, send from Miletus to Ephesus and summon the elders of the church. ¹⁸ When they joined him, he spoke to them as follows.

'You know how, from the day that I first set foot in the province of Asia, I spent my whole time with you, ¹⁹ serving the Lord in all humility amid the sorrows and trials that came upon me through the intrigues of the Jews. ²⁰ You know that I kept back nothing that was for your good: I delivered the message to you, and taught you, in public and in your homes; ²¹ with Jews and Gentiles alike I insisted on repentance before God and faith in our Lord Jesus. ²² Now, as you see, I am constrained by the Spirit to go to Jerusalem. I do not know what will befall me there, ²³ except that in city after city the Holy Spirit assures me that imprisonment and hardships await me. ²⁴ For myself, I set no store by life; all I want is to finish the race, and complete the task which the Lord Jesus assigned to me, that of bearing my testimony to the gospel of God's grace.

²⁵ 'One thing more: I have gone about among you proclaiming the kingdom, but now I know that none of you will ever see my face again. ²⁶ That being so, I here and

20: 6 **after ... season**: *lit.* after the days of Unleavened Bread.

now declare that no one's fate can be laid at my door; I have kept back nothing; [27] I have disclosed to you the whole purpose of God. [28] Keep guard over yourselves and over all the flock of which the Holy Spirit has given you charge, as shepherds of the church of the Lord, which he won for himself by his own blood. [29] I know that when I am gone, savage wolves will come in among you and will not spare the flock. [30] Even from your own number men will arise who will distort the truth in order to get the disciples to break away and follow them. [31] So be on the alert; remember how with tears I never ceased to warn each one of you night and day for three years.

[32] 'And now I commend you to God and to the word of his grace, which has power to build you up and give you your heritage among all those whom God has made his own. [33] I have not wanted anyone's money or clothes for myself; [34] you all know that these hands of mine earned enough for the needs of myself and my companions. [35] All along I showed you that it is our duty to help the weak in this way, by hard work, and that we should keep in mind the words of the Lord Jesus, who himself said, "Happiness lies more in giving than in receiving."'

[36] As he finished speaking, he knelt down with them all and prayed. [37] There were loud cries of sorrow from them all, as they folded Paul in their arms and kissed him; [38] what distressed them most was his saying that they would never see his face again. Then they escorted him to the ship.

21 We tore ourselves away from them and, putting to sea, made a straight run and came to Cos; next day to Rhodes, and thence to Patara. [2] There we found a ship bound for Phoenicia, so we went aboard and sailed in her. [3] We came in sight of Cyprus and, leaving it to port, we continued our voyage to Syria and put in at Tyre, where the ship was to unload her cargo. [4] We sought out the disciples and stayed there a week. Warned by the Spirit, they urged Paul to abandon his visit to Jerusalem. [5] But when our time ashore was ended, we left and continued our journey; and they and their wives and children all escorted us out of the city.

We knelt down on the beach and prayed, [6] and then bade each other goodbye; we went on board, and they returned home.

[7] We made the passage from Tyre and reached Ptolemais, where we greeted the brotherhood and spent a day with them. [8] Next day we left and came to Caesarea, where we went to the home of Philip the evangelist, who was one of the Seven, and stayed with him. [9] He had four unmarried daughters, who possessed the gift of prophecy. [10] When we had been there several days, a prophet named Agabus arrived from Judaea. [11] He came to us, took Paul's belt, bound his own feet and hands with it, and said, 'These are the words of the Holy Spirit: Thus will the Jews in Jerusalem bind the man to whom this belt belongs, and hand him over to the Gentiles.' [12] When we heard this, we and the local people begged and implored Paul to abandon his visit to Jerusalem. [13] Then Paul gave his answer: 'Why all these tears? Why are you trying to weaken my resolution? I am ready, not merely to be bound, but even to die at Jerusalem for the name of the Lord Jesus.' [14] So, as he would not be dissuaded, we gave up and said, 'The Lord's will be done.'

[15] At the end of our stay we packed our baggage and took the road up to Jerusalem. [16] Some of the disciples from Caesarea came along with us, to direct us to a Cypriot named Mnason, a Christian from the early days, with whom we were to spend the night. [17] On our arrival at Jerusalem, the congregation welcomed us gladly.

[18] Next day Paul paid a visit to James; we accompanied him, and all the elders were present. [19] After greeting them, he described in detail all that God had done among the Gentiles by means of his ministry. [20] When they heard this, gave praise to God. Then they said to Paul: 'You observe, brother, how many thousands of converts we have among the Jews, all of them staunch upholders of the law. [21] Now they have been given certain information about you: it is said that you teach all the Jews in the gentile world to turn their backs on Moses, and tell them not to circumcise their children or follow our way of life. [22] What is to be done,

---

20:28 **of the Lord ... blood:** *some witnesses read* of God, which he won for himself by the blood of his Own.

then? They are sure to hear that you have arrived. ²³ Our proposal is this: we have four men here who are under a vow; ²⁴ take them with you and go through the ritual of purification together, and pay their expenses, so that they may have their heads shaved; then everyone will know that there is nothing in the reports they have heard about you, but that you are yourself a practising Jew and observe the law. ²⁵ As for the gentile converts, we sent them our decision that they should abstain from meat that has been offered to idols, from blood, from anything that has been strangled, and from fornication.' ²⁶ So Paul took the men, and next day, after going through the ritual of purification with them, he went into the temple to give notice of the date when the period of purification would end and the offering be made for each of them.

Paul's work in Jerusalem

²⁷ BUT just before the seven days were up, the Jews from the province of Asia saw him in the temple. They stirred up all the crowd and seized him, ²⁸ shouting, 'Help us, men of Israel! This is the fellow who attacks our people, our law, and this sanctuary, and spreads his teaching the whole world over. What is more, he has brought Gentiles into the temple and profaned this holy place.' ²⁹ They had previously seen Trophimus the Ephesian with him in the city, and assumed that Paul had brought him into the temple.

³⁰ The whole city was in a turmoil, and people came running from all directions. They seized Paul and dragged him out of the temple, and at once the doors were shut. ³¹ They were bent on killing him, but word came to the officer commanding the cohort that all Jerusalem was in an uproar. ³² He immediately took a force of soldiers with their centurions and came down at the double to deal with the riot. When the crowd saw the commandant and his troops, they stopped beating Paul. ³³ As soon as the commandant could reach Paul, he arrested him and ordered him to be shackled with two chains; he enquired who he was and what he had been doing. ³⁴ Some in the crowd shouted one thing, some another, and as the commandant could not get at the truth

because of the hubbub, he ordered him to be taken to the barracks. ³⁵ When Paul reached the steps, he found himself carried up by the soldiers because of the violence of the mob; ³⁶ for the whole crowd was at their heels yelling, 'Kill him!'

³⁷ Just before he was taken into the barracks Paul said to the commandant, 'May I have a word with you?' The commandant said, 'So you speak Greek? ³⁸ Then you are not the Egyptian who started a revolt some time ago and led a force of four thousand terrorists out into the desert?' ³⁹ Paul replied, 'I am a Jew from Tarsus in Cilicia, a citizen of no mean city. May I have your permission to speak to the people?' ⁴⁰ When this was given, Paul stood on the steps and raised his hand to call for the attention of the people. As soon as quiet was restored, he addressed them in the Jewish language:

22 'Brothers and fathers, give me a hearing while I put my case to you.' ² When they heard him speaking to them in their own language, they listened more quietly. ³ 'I am a true-born Jew,' he began, 'a native of Tarsus in Cilicia. I was brought up in this city, and as a pupil of Gamaliel I was thoroughly trained in every point of our ancestral law. I have always been ardent in God's service, as you all are today. ⁴ And so I persecuted this movement to the death, arresting its followers, men and women alike, and committing them to prison, ⁵ as the high priest and the whole Council of Elders can testify. It was they who gave me letters to our fellow-Jews at Damascus, and I was on my way to make arrests there also and bring the prisoners to Jerusalem for punishment. ⁶ What happened to me on my journey was this: when I was nearing Damascus, about midday, a great light suddenly flashed from the sky all around me. ⁷ I fell to the ground, and heard a voice saying: "Saul, Saul, why do you persecute me?" ⁸ I answered, "Tell me, Lord, who you are." "I am Jesus of Nazareth, whom you are persecuting," he said. ⁹ My companions saw the light, but did not hear the voice that spoke to me. ¹⁰ "What shall I do, Lord?" I asked, and he replied, "Get up, and go on to Damascus; there you will be told all that

21:25 **from anything ... strangled:** *some witnesses omit.*

you are appointed to do." ¹¹ As I had been blinded by the brilliance of that light, my companions led me by the hand, and so I came to Damascus.

¹² 'There a man called Ananias, a devout observer of the law and well spoken of by all the Jews who lived there, ¹³ came and stood beside me, and said, "Saul, my brother, receive your sight again!" Instantly I recovered my sight and saw him. ¹⁴ He went on: "The God of our fathers appointed you to know his will and to see the Righteous One and to hear him speak, ¹⁵ because you are to be his witness to tell the world what you have seen and heard. ¹⁶ Do not delay. Be baptized at once and wash away your sins, calling on his name."

¹⁷ 'After my return to Jerusalem, as I was praying in the temple I fell into a trance ¹⁸ and saw him there, speaking to me. "Make haste", he said, "and leave Jerusalem quickly, for they will not accept your testimony about me." ¹⁹ "But surely, Lord," I answered, "they know that I imprisoned those who believe in you and flogged them in every synagogue; ²⁰ when the blood of Stephen your witness was shed I stood by, approving, and I looked after the clothes of those who killed him." ²¹ He said to me, "Go, for I mean to send you far away to the Gentiles."'

²² Up to this point the crowd had given him a hearing; but now they began to shout, 'Down with the scoundrel! He is not fit to be alive!' ²³ And as they were yelling and waving their cloaks and flinging dust in the air, ²⁴ the commandant ordered him to be brought into the barracks, and gave instructions that he should be examined under the lash, to find out what reason there was for such an outcry against him. ²⁵ But when they tied him up for the flogging, Paul said to the centurion who was standing there, 'Does the law allow you to flog a Roman citizen, and an unconvicted one at that?' ²⁶ When the centurion heard this, he went and reported to the commandant: 'What are you about? This man is a Roman citizen.' ²⁷ The commandant came to Paul and asked, 'Tell me, are you a Roman citizen?' 'Yes,' said he. ²⁸ The commandant rejoined, 'Citizenship cost me a large sum of money.' Paul said, 'It was mine by birth.' ²⁹ Then those who were about to examine him promptly withdrew; and the commandant himself was alarmed when he realized that Paul was a Roman citizen and that he had put him in irons.

Paul's trials

³⁰ THE following day, wishing to be quite sure what charge the Jews were bringing against Paul, he released him and ordered the chief priests and the entire Council to assemble. He then brought Paul down to stand before them.

23 With his eyes steadily fixed on the Council, Paul said, 'My brothers, all my life to this day I have lived with a perfectly clear conscience before God.' ² At this the high priest Ananias ordered his attendants to strike him on the mouth. ³ Paul retorted, 'God will strike you, you whitewashed wall! You sit there to judge me in accordance with the law; then, in defiance of the law, you order me to be struck!' ⁴ The attendants said, 'Would you insult God's high priest?' ⁵ 'Brothers,' said Paul, 'I had no idea he was high priest; scripture, I know, says: "You shall not abuse the ruler of your people."'

⁶ Well aware that one section of them were Sadducees and the other Pharisees, Paul called out in the Council, 'My brothers, I am a Pharisee, a Pharisee born and bred; and the issue in this trial is our hope of the resurrection of the dead.' ⁷ At these words the Pharisees and Sadducees fell out among themselves, and the assembly was divided. ⁸ (The Sadducees deny that there is any resurrection or angel or spirit, but the Pharisees believe in all three.) ⁹ A great uproar ensued; and some of the scribes belonging to the Pharisaic party openly took sides and declared, 'We find no fault with this man; perhaps an angel or spirit has spoken to him.' ¹⁰ In the mounting dissension, the commandant was afraid that Paul would be torn to pieces, so he ordered the troops to go down, pull him out of the crowd, and bring him into the barracks.

¹¹ The following night the Lord appeared to him and said, 'Keep up your courage! You have affirmed the truth about me in Jerusalem, and you must do the same in Rome.'

¹² When day broke, the Jews banded together and took an oath not to eat or drink until they had killed Paul. ¹³ There were more than forty in the conspiracy;

14 they went to the chief priests and elders and said, 'We have bound ourselves by a solemn oath not to taste food until we have killed Paul. 15 It is now up to you and the rest of the Council to apply to the commandant to have him brought down to you on the pretext of a closer investigation of his case; we have arranged to make away with him before he reaches you.'

16 The son of Paul's sister, however, learnt of the plot and, going to the barracks, obtained entry, and reported it to Paul, 17 who called one of the centurions and said, 'Take this young man to the commandant; he has something to report.' 18 The centurion brought him to the commandant and explained, 'The prisoner Paul sent for me and asked me to bring this young man to you; he has something to tell you.' 19 The commandant took him by the arm, drew him aside, and asked him, 'What is it you have to report?' 20 He replied, 'The Jews have agreed on a plan: they will request you to bring Paul down to the Council tomorrow on the pretext of obtaining more precise information about him. 21 Do not listen to them; for a party more than forty strong are lying in wait for him, and they have sworn not to eat or drink until they have done away with him. They are now ready, waiting only for your consent.' 22 The commandant dismissed the young man, with orders not to let anyone know that he had given him this information.

23 He then summoned two of his centurions and gave them these orders: 'Have two hundred infantry ready to proceed to Caesarea, together with seventy cavalrymen and two hundred light-armed troops; parade them three hours after sunset, 24 and provide mounts for Paul so that he may be conducted under safe escort to Felix the governor.' 25 And he wrote a letter to this effect:

26 From Claudius Lysias to His Excellency the Governor Felix. Greeting.

27 This man was seized by the Jews and was on the point of being murdered when I intervened with the troops, and, on discovering that he was a Roman citizen, I removed him to safety. 28 As I wished to ascertain the ground of their charge against him, I brought him down to their Council. 29 I found that their case had to do with controversial matters of their law, but there was no charge against him which merited death or imprisonment. 30 Information, however, has now been brought to my notice of an attempt to be made on the man's life, so I am sending him to you without delay, and have instructed his accusers to state their case against him before you.

31 Acting on their orders, the infantry took custody of Paul and brought him by night to Antipatris. 32 Next day they returned to their barracks, leaving the cavalry to escort him the rest of the way. 33 When the cavalry reached Caesarea, they delivered the letter to the governor, and handed Paul over to him. 34 He read the letter, and asked him what province he was from; and learning that he was from Cilicia 35 he said, 'I will hear your case when your accusers arrive.' He ordered him to be held in custody at his headquarters in Herod's palace.

24 FIVE days later the high priest Ananias came down, accompanied by some of the elders and an advocate named Tertullus, to lay before the governor their charge against Paul. 2-3 When the prisoner was called, Tertullus opened the case.

'Your excellency,' he said to Felix, 'we owe it to you that we enjoy unbroken peace, and it is due to your provident care that, in all kinds of ways and in all sorts of places, improvements are being made for the good of this nation. We appreciate this, and are most grateful to you. 4 And now, not to take up too much of your time, I crave your indulgence for a brief statement of our case. 5 We have found this man to be a pest, a fomenter of discord among the Jews all over the world, a ringleader of the sect of the Nazarenes. 6 He made an attempt to profane the temple and we arrested him. 8 If you examine him yourself you can ascertain the truth of all the charges we bring against him.' 9 The Jews supported the

24:6 **arrested him:** *some witnesses add* It was our intention to try him under our law; 7 but Lysias the commandant intervened and forcibly removed him out of our hands, (8) ordering his accusers to come before you.

charge, alleging that the facts were as he stated.

[10] The governor then motioned to Paul to speak, and he replied as follows: 'Knowing as I do that for many years you have administered justice to this nation, I make my defence with confidence. [11] As you can ascertain for yourself, it is not more than twelve days since I went up to Jerusalem on a pilgrimage. [12] They did not find me in the temple arguing with anyone or collecting a crowd, or in the synagogues or anywhere else in the city; [13] and they cannot make good the charges they now bring against me. [14] But this much I will admit: I am a follower of the new way (the "sect" they speak of), and it is in that manner that I worship the God of our fathers; for I believe all that is written in the law and the prophets, [15] and in reliance on God I hold the hope, which my accusers too accept, that there is to be a resurrection of good and wicked alike. [16] Accordingly I, no less than they, train myself to keep at all times a clear conscience before God and man.

[17] 'After an absence of several years I came to bring charitable gifts to my nation and to offer sacrifices. [18] I was ritually purified and engaged in this service when they found me in the temple; I had no crowd with me, and there was no disturbance. But some Jews from the province of Asia were there, [19] and if they had any charge against me, it is they who ought to have been in court to state it. [20] Failing that, it is for these persons here present to say what crime they discovered when I was brought before the Council, [21] apart from this one declaration which I made as I stood there: "The issue in my trial before you today is the resurrection of the dead."'

[22] Then Felix, who was well informed about the new way, adjourned the hearing. 'I will decide your case when Lysias the commanding officer comes down,' he said. [23] He gave orders to the centurion to keep Paul under open arrest and not to prevent any of his friends from making themselves useful to him.

[24] Some days later Felix came with his wife Drusilla, who was a Jewess, and sent for Paul. He let him talk to him about faith in Christ Jesus, [25] but when the discourse turned to questions of morals, self-control, and the coming judgement, Felix became alarmed and exclaimed, 'Enough for now! When I find it convenient I will send for you again.' [26] He also had hopes of a bribe from Paul, so he sent for him frequently and talked with him. [27] When two years had passed, Felix was succeeded by Porcius Festus. Wishing to curry favour with the Jews, Felix left Paul in custody.

25 THREE days after taking up his appointment, Festus went up from Caesarea to Jerusalem, [2] where the chief priests and the Jewish leaders laid before him their charge against Paul. [3] They urged Festus to support them in their case and have Paul sent to Jerusalem, for they were plotting to kill him on the way. [4] Festus, however, replied, 'Paul is in safe custody at Caesarea, and I shall be leaving Jerusalem shortly myself; [5] so let your leading men come down with me, and if the man is at fault in any way, let them prosecute him.'

[6] After spending eight or ten days at most in Jerusalem, he went down to Caesarea, and next day he took his seat in court and ordered Paul to be brought before him. [7] When he appeared, the Jews who had come down from Jerusalem stood round bringing many grave charges, which they were unable to prove. [8] Paul protested: 'I have committed no offence against the Jewish law, or against the temple, or against the emperor.' [9] Festus, anxious to ingratiate himself with the Jews, turned to Paul and asked, 'Are you willing to go up to Jerusalem and stand trial on these charges before me there?' [10] But Paul said, 'I am now standing before the emperor's tribunal; that is where I ought to be tried. I have committed no offence against the Jews, as you very well know. [11] If I am guilty of any capital crime, I do not ask to escape the death penalty; if, however, there is no substance in the charges which these men bring against me, it is not open to anyone to hand me over to them. I appeal to Caesar!' [12] Then Festus, after conferring with his advisers, replied, 'You have appealed to Caesar: to Caesar you shall go!'

[13] Some days later King Agrippa and Bernice arrived at Caesarea on a courtesy visit to Festus. [14] They spent some time there, and during their stay Festus raised

Paul's case with the king. 'There is a man here', he said, 'left in custody by Felix; [15] and when I was in Jerusalem the chief priests and elders of the Jews brought a charge against him, demanding his condemnation. [16] I replied that it was not Roman practice to hand a man over before he had been confronted with his accusers and given an opportunity of answering the charge. [17] So when they had come here with me I lost no time, but took my seat in court the very next day and ordered the man to be brought before me. [18] When his accusers rose to speak, they brought none of the charges I was expecting; [19] they merely had certain points of disagreement with him about their religion, and about someone called Jesus, a dead man whom Paul alleged to be alive. [20] Finding myself out of my depth in such discussions, I asked if he was willing to go to Jerusalem and stand trial there on these issues. [21] But Paul appealed to be remanded in custody for his imperial majesty's decision, and I ordered him to be detained until I could send him to the emperor.' [22] Agrippa said to Festus, 'I should rather like to hear the man myself.' 'You shall hear him tomorrow,' he answered.

[23] Next day Agrippa and Bernice came in full state and entered the audience-chamber accompanied by high-ranking officers and prominent citizens; and on the orders of Festus, Paul was brought in. [24] Then Festus said, 'King Agrippa, and all you who are in attendance, you see this man: the whole body of the Jews approached me both in Jerusalem and here, loudly insisting that he had no right to remain alive. [25] It was clear to me, however, that he had committed no capital crime, and when he himself appealed to his imperial majesty, I decided to send him. [26] As I have nothing definite about him to put in writing for our sovereign, I have brought him before you all and particularly before you, King Agrippa, so that as a result of this preliminary enquiry I may have something to report. [27] There is no sense, it seems to me, in sending on a prisoner without indicating the charges against him.'

26 Agrippa said to Paul: 'You have our permission to give an account of yourself.' Then Paul stretched out his hand and began his defence.

[2] 'I consider myself fortunate, King Agrippa, that it is before you I am to make my defence today on all the charges brought against me by the Jews, [3] particularly as you are expert in all our Jewish customs and controversies. I beg you therefore to give me a patient hearing.

[4] 'My life from my youth up, a life spent from the first among my nation and in Jerusalem, is familiar to all Jews. [5] Indeed they have known me long enough to testify, if they would, that I belonged to the strictest group in our religion: I was a Pharisee. [6] It is the hope based on the promise God made to our forefathers that has led to my being on trial today. [7] Our twelve tribes worship with intense devotion night and day in the hope of seeing the fulfilment of that promise; and for this very hope I am accused, your majesty, and accused by Jews. [8] Why should Jews find it incredible that God should raise the dead?

[9] 'I myself once thought it my duty to work actively against the name of Jesus of Nazareth; [10] and I did so in Jerusalem. By authority obtained from the chief priests, I sent many of God's people to prison, and when they were condemned to death, my vote was cast against them. [11] In all the synagogues I tried by repeated punishment to make them commit blasphemy; indeed my fury rose to such a pitch that I extended my persecution to foreign cities.

[12] 'On one such occasion I was travelling to Damascus with authority and commission from the chief priests; [13] and as I was on my way, your majesty, at midday I saw a light from the sky, more brilliant than the sun, shining all around me and my companions. [14] We all fell to the ground, and I heard a voice saying to me in the Jewish language, "Saul, Saul, why do you persecute me? It hurts to kick like this against the goad." [15] I said, "Tell me, Lord, who you are," and the Lord replied, "I am Jesus, whom you are persecuting. [16] But now, get to your feet. I have appeared to you for a purpose: to appoint you my servant and witness, to tell what you have seen and what you shall yet see of me. [17] I will rescue you from your own people and from the Gentiles to whom I am sending you. [18] You are to open their eyes and to turn them from darkness to light, from the dominion of Satan to God, so that they

may obtain forgiveness of sins and a place among those whom God has made his own through faith in me."

¹⁹ 'So, King Agrippa, I did not disobey the heavenly vision. ²⁰ I preached first to the inhabitants of Damascus, and then to Jerusalem and all the country of Judaea, and to the Gentiles, calling on them to repent and turn to God, and to prove their repentance by their deeds. ²¹ That is why the Jews seized me in the temple and tried to do away with me. ²² But I have had God's help to this very day, and here I stand bearing witness to the great and to the lowly. I assert nothing beyond what was foretold by the prophets and by Moses: ²³ that the Messiah would suffer and that, as the first to rise from the dead, he would announce the dawn both to the Jewish people and to the Gentiles.'

²⁴ While Paul was thus making his defence, Festus shouted at the top of his voice, 'Paul, you are raving; too much study is driving you mad.' ²⁵ 'I am not mad, your excellency,' said Paul; 'what I am asserting is sober truth. ²⁶ The king is well versed in these matters, and I can speak freely to him. I do not believe that he can be unaware of any of these facts, for this has been no hole-and-corner business. ²⁷ King Agrippa, do you believe the prophets? I know you do.' ²⁸ Agrippa said to Paul, 'With a little more of your persuasion you will make a Christian of me.' ²⁹ 'Little or much,' said Paul, 'I wish to God that not only you, but all those who are listening to me today, might become what I am—apart from these chains!'

³⁰ With that the king rose, and with him the governor, Bernice, and the rest of the company, ³¹ and after they had withdrawn they talked it over. 'This man', they agreed, 'is doing nothing that deserves death or imprisonment.' ³² Agrippa said to Festus, 'The fellow could have been discharged, if he had not appealed to the emperor.'

Paul's journey to Rome

27 WHEN it was decided that we should sail for Italy, Paul and some other prisoners were handed over to a centurion named Julius, of the Augustan Cohort. ² We embarked in a ship of Adramyttium, bound for ports in the province of Asia, and put out to sea. Aristarchus, a Macedonian from Thessalonica, came with us. ³ Next day we landed at Sidon, and Julius very considerately allowed Paul to go to his friends to be cared for. ⁴ Leaving Sidon we sailed under the lee of Cyprus because of the head winds, ⁵ then across the open sea off the coast of Cilicia and Pamphylia, and so reached Myra in Lycia.

⁶ There the centurion found an Alexandrian vessel bound for Italy and put us on board. ⁷ For a good many days we made little headway, and we were hard put to it to reach Cnidus. Then, as the wind continued against us, off Salmone we began to sail under the lee of Crete, ⁸ and, hugging the coast, struggled on to a place called Fair Havens, not far from the town of Lasea.

⁹ By now much time had been lost, and with the Fast already over, it was dangerous to go on with the voyage. So Paul gave them this warning: ¹⁰ 'I can see, gentlemen, that this voyage will be disastrous; it will mean heavy loss, not only of ship and cargo but also of life.' ¹¹ But the centurion paid more attention to the captain and to the owner of the ship than to what Paul said; ¹² and as the harbour was unsuitable for wintering, the majority were in favour of putting to sea, hoping, if they could get so far, to winter at Phoenix, a Cretan harbour facing south-west and north-west. ¹³ When a southerly breeze sprang up, they thought that their purpose was as good as achieved, and, weighing anchor, they sailed along the coast of Crete hugging the land. ¹⁴ But before very long a violent wind, the Northeaster as they call it, swept down from the landward side. ¹⁵ It caught the ship and, as it was impossible to keep head to wind, we had to give way and run before it. ¹⁶ As we passed under the lee of a small island called Cauda, we managed with a struggle to get the ship's boat under control. ¹⁷ When they had hoisted it on board, they made use of tackle to brace the ship. Then, afraid of running on to the sandbanks of Syrtis, they put out a sea-anchor and let her drift. ¹⁸ Next day, as we were making very heavy weather, they began to lighten the

27:17 put ... sea-anchor: or lowered the mainsail.

319

ship; [19] and on the third day they jettisoned the ship's gear with their own hands. [20] For days on end there was no sign of either sun or stars, the storm was raging unabated, and our last hopes of coming through alive began to fade.

[21] When they had gone for a long time without food, Paul stood up among them and said, 'You should have taken my advice, gentlemen, not to put out from Crete: then you would have avoided this damage and loss. [22] But now I urge you not to lose heart; not a single life will be lost, only the ship. [23] Last night there stood by me an angel of the God whose I am and whom I worship. [24] "Do not be afraid, Paul," he said; "it is ordained that you shall appear before Caesar; and, be assured, God has granted you the lives of all who are sailing with you." [25] So take heart, men! I trust God: it will turn out as I have been told; [26] we are to be cast ashore on an island.'

[27] The fourteenth night came and we were still drifting in the Adriatic Sea. At midnight the sailors felt that land was getting nearer, [28] so they took a sounding and found twenty fathoms. Sounding again after a short interval they found fifteen fathoms; [29] then, fearing that we might be cast ashore on a rugged coast, they let go four anchors from the stern and prayed for daylight to come. [30] The sailors tried to abandon ship; they had already lowered the ship's boat, pretending they were going to lay out anchors from the bows, [31] when Paul said to the centurion and the soldiers, 'Unless these men stay on board you cannot reach safety.' [32] At that the soldiers cut the ropes of the boat and let it drop away.

[33] Shortly before daybreak Paul urged them all to take some food. 'For the last fourteen days', he said, 'you have lived in suspense and gone hungry; you have eaten nothing. [34] So have something to eat, I beg you; your lives depend on it. Remember, not a hair of your heads will be lost.' [35] With these words, he took bread, gave thanks to God in front of them all, broke it, and began eating. [36] Then they plucked up courage, and began to take food themselves. [37] All told there were on board two hundred and seventy-six of us. [38] After they had eaten as much as they wanted, they lightened the ship by dumping the grain into the sea.

[39] When day broke, they did not recognize the land, but they sighted a bay with a sandy beach, on which they decided, if possible, to run ashore. [40] So they slipped the anchors and let them go; at the same time they loosened the lashings of the steering-paddles, set the foresail to the wind, and let her drive to the beach. [41] But they found themselves caught between cross-currents and ran the ship aground, so that the bow stuck fast and remained immovable, while the stern was being pounded to pieces by the breakers. [42] The soldiers thought they had better kill the prisoners for fear that any should swim away and escape; [43] but the centurion was determined to bring Paul safely through, and prevented them from carrying out their plan. He gave orders that those who could swim should jump overboard first and get to land; [44] the rest were to follow, some on planks, some on parts of the ship. And thus it was that all came safely to land.

28 Once we had made our way to safety, we identified the island as Malta. [2] The natives treated us with uncommon kindness: because it had started to rain and was cold they lit a bonfire and made us all welcome. [3] Paul had got together an armful of sticks and put them on the fire, when a viper, driven out by the heat, fastened on his hand. [4] The natives, seeing the snake hanging on to his hand, said to one another, 'The man must be a murderer; he may have escaped from the sea, but divine justice would not let him live.' [5] Paul, however, shook off the snake into the fire and was none the worse. [6] They still expected him to swell up or suddenly drop down dead, but after waiting a long time without seeing anything out of the way happen to him, they changed their minds and said, 'He is a god.'

[7] In that neighbourhood there were lands belonging to the chief magistrate of the island, whose name was Publius. He took us in and entertained us hospitably for three days. [8] It so happened that this man's father was in bed suffering from recurrent bouts of fever and dysentery. Paul visited him and, after prayer, laid his hands on him and healed him; [9] whereupon the other sick people on the island came and were cured. [10] They honoured us with many marks of respect, and when

we were leaving they put on board the supplies we needed. ¹¹ Three months had passed when we put to sea in a ship which had wintered in the island; she was the *Castor and Pollux* of Alexandria. ¹² We landed at Syracuse and spent three days there; ¹³ then we sailed up the coast and arrived at Rhegium. Next day a south wind sprang up and we reached Puteoli in two days. ¹⁴ There we found fellow-Christians and were invited to stay a week with them. And so to Rome. ¹⁵ The Christians there had had news of us and came out to meet us as far as Appii Forum and the Three Taverns, and when Paul saw them, he gave thanks to God and took courage.

¹⁶ WHEN we entered Rome Paul was allowed to lodge privately, with a soldier in charge of him. ¹⁷ Three days later he called together the local Jewish leaders, and when they were assembled, he said to them: 'My brothers, I never did anything against our people or against the customs of our forefathers; yet I was arrested in Jerusalem and handed over to the Romans. ¹⁸ They examined me and would have liked to release me because there was no capital charge against me; ¹⁹ but the Jews objected, and I had no option but to appeal to Caesar; not that I had any accusation to bring against my own people. ²⁰ This is why I have asked to see and talk to you; it is for loyalty to the hope of Israel that I am in these chains.' ²¹ They replied, 'We have had no communication about you from Judaea, nor has any countryman of ours arrived with any report or gossip to your discredit. ²² We should like to hear from you what your views are; all we know about this sect is that no one has a good word to say for it.'

²³ So they fixed a day, and came in large numbers to his lodging. From dawn to dusk he put his case to them; he spoke urgently of the kingdom of God and sought to convince them about Jesus by appealing to the law of Moses and the prophets. ²⁴ Some were won over by his arguments; others remained unconvinced. ²⁵ Without reaching any agreement among themselves they began to disperse, but not before Paul had spoken this final word: 'How well the Holy Spirit spoke to your fathers through the prophet Isaiah ²⁶ when he said, "Go to this people and say: You may listen and listen, but you will never understand; you may look and look, but you will never see. ²⁷ For this people's mind has become dull; they have stopped their ears and closed their eyes. Otherwise, their eyes might see, their ears hear, and their mind understand, and then they might turn again, and I would heal them." ²⁸ Therefore take note that this salvation of God has been sent to the Gentiles; the Gentiles will listen.'

³⁰ He stayed there two full years at his own expense, with a welcome for all who came to him; ³¹ he proclaimed the kingdom of God and taught the facts about the Lord Jesus Christ quite openly and without hindrance.

28:28 **listen**: *some witnesses add* ²⁹ After he had spoken, the Jews went away, arguing vigorously among themselves.